Amazing Grace

Amazing Grace

A HISTORY OF
INDIANA METHODISM
1801–2001

E. Carver McGriff

PROVIDENCE HOUSE PUBLISHERS
Franklin, Tennessee

Printed in the United States of America

0 5   0 4   0 3   0 2   0 1   1   2   3   4   5

Library of Congress Catalog Card Number: 2001087928

ISBN: 1-57736-221-7
ISBN: 1-57736-243-8 (pbk.)

Cover design by Gary Bozeman

Photos on cover not appearing in book are courtesy of Indiana Area UMC Communications

Photos and captions in book selected and written by Lynne DeMichele

PROVIDENCE HOUSE PUBLISHERS
238 Seaboard Lane Franklin, Tennessee 37067
800-321-5692
www.providencehouse.com

TO ALL THE OTHER FAITHFUL PEOPLE
AND CONGREGATIONS
WHOSE STORIES BELONG HERE.

Contents

Bishop Woodie W. White.

Foreword

Wher it came to my attention that, in 2001, Indiana United Methodism would be celebrating its bicentennial (1801–2001), I thought this might be an appropriate opportunity to retrieve the stories that comprise the Indiana Area of the United Methodist Church and to compile a brief history that would be both informative and inspiring.

Every congregation and each Annual Conference, however successful, became so by building on a foundation that preceded them. Even so-called "new church" starts do not spring up from nothing. They arise out of a history and structure that not only birthed them, but perceived and conceived them. We are all indebted to the past, a past not without its flaws, but a past whose strength has made possible the present. Our past is important.

Hence, *Amazing Grace: The History of Indiana Methodism 1801-2001*. Dr. Carver McGriff has produced a work that tells the stories of Methodism in Indiana as experienced in what is now the Indiana Area of the United Methodist Church.

It is not intended to be a "history" of Methodism in the classical sense, merely by concentrating on facts, events and the distant past, but a sharing of stories, memories, and experiences of those who have lived the stories or who passed them on to others. It is a glimpse into the past, distant and near. It is a "living" history!

Amazing Grace will provide those new to United Methodism in Indiana an introduction to its past as well as, hopefully, a better understanding of its present as they help to shape its future. For the many who will have experienced some of its history, it will be an opportunity for reflection and reminiscing. For all who read it, I hope they will be inspired by the witness of countless in this Hoosier Land.

One looks to the past and history not to glorify it, but to learn from and be inspired by it. That is my hope for all who read this volume. To be inspired and informed by those forebears who seemed to do so much in their day and make such a difference in the lives of people and the structures of society.

God has blessed the people of the Indiana Area with gifts and resources unimagined by the people called Methodists, who pioneered and made possible what is enjoyed and too often taken for granted today. The more than thirteen hundred congregations, three universities, facilities for the aging as well as youth, hospitals, community centers and ministries all represent the witness, courage and generosity of Hoosier Methodists.

May those who read this story of an ordinary people made extraordinary by their faith in God be inspired to be for the future what these Hoosier Methodists were for the past.

Woodie W. White, Bishop
The Indiana Area
The United Methodist Church
January, 2001

Preface

When Lynne DeMichele, Indiana Area Director of Communications and editor of the *Hoosier United Methodist News,* asked me to write a history of the United Methodist Church in Indiana covering two hundred years, I was honored, intrigued, and ready to try. After all, I thought, my experience in the church is varied enough. Five years as an active layman at First Methodist Church, Bloomington, where two pastors—Merrill McFall and Ben Garrison—were close friends. And then those two, along with the Hound of Heaven, sent me off to Garrett Seminary. After a year as a regular attender at First Church, Evanston, I spent two years in a memorable learning experience serving Waynetown Church and, an outpoint, Wesley Church in the Northwest Conference. It was there that I—a city boy—learned something about harvesting corn and how beautiful a new sow can be.

Following graduation, I served five years in a working-class neighborhood at Asbury Church, Indianapolis, as founding pastor. Then came a long pastorate at St. Luke's on Indianapolis's far north side, followed, since retirement, by many a visit around the church world while based with Allen Rumble at Zionsville Church. So, I thought, I can do this.

Yeah, right! Then it dawned on me that there are something like thirteen hundred Methodist churches in Indiana—rural, inner-city, small community, urban, suburban, and neighborhood—and a good many more pastors than that. Add to that all those who led the way through the past, and I belatedly understood: there are thousands of wonderful stories about pastors and lay men and women, and grand histories of each of those churches. Then there are the universities, the camps, the hospitals, the splendid mission programs; the debates about theology, Civil Rights, Vietnam, homosexuality, the Good News movement, and women in ministry, and there are all our bishops with their varied gifts and personalities, and the movement of the church into the suburbs, and . . . you get the point. All of it can't be told—not in detail, not in a few hundred pages. What was I to do?

Thanks to many helpful colleague pastors and laypeople, I have undertaken to find those events and stories which can serve as examples of our Wonderful Story. I have tried to discern what will serve to inform the reader of the romance, the adventure of our past, and especially the results of our collective faith. I have tried to do honor to all my fellow pastors and all the fine lay men and women who have led the church by telling a few of their stories, any one of which might very well have been that of many of the faithful. I have access to all the conference journals, but you can read those. I'm not writing so some future researcher can uncover dates and places. Last year I read Tom Brokaw's fine treatment of the past, *The Greatest Generation*. In it he told many tales about the men and women who served in various armed forces during World War 2. I happened to have served in the army in a combat unit. But so did several million men and a few women. I realized that not all of our stories could be told. So I valued the fact that others reading Brokaw's book would have a pretty good idea what we all had done. So with this little book. I must plead with those of you who were part of this great movement called Methodism to bear with me as we look back upon the essence of the times in which we lived and allow some of our friends who journeyed with us to represent us all.

Acknowledgments

I wish to thank the following people who took time to visit with me as together we looked back across the years and forward to the future: William Schwein, Laura Walker, Woodie White, Allen Rumble, Linda McCoy, Kent Millard, Dick Hamilton, Leroy Hodapp, Robb Kell, Greg McGarvey, Jim Morin, Dean Stuckey, Jim Jones, Lynne DeMichele, Jerry Thomas, Linda Craig, Bob Gingery, Al Nunery, Grace Nunery, Carnell Scott, John Wolf, Ralph Steele, Marcus Blaising, Phil Amerson, Susan Ruach, Riley Case, Harold Leininger, David G. Owen, David Lawson, Charles Hutchinson, Charles Ballard, Don LaSuer, Virgil Bjork, Sheldon Dueker, Steve Burris, Jim Gentry, Warren Saunders, Wes Wilson, Kate Lehman Walker, and Charles Harrison.

A Preliminary Word to
New Methodists

For those who are new to Methodism, it is important to know that once each year a gathering is held, always in early summer. Called Annual Conference, it is attended by each clergyperson and by an equal number of lay members (each church chooses the same number of delegates as they have had clergy assigned.) The conference lasts several days and transacts the business of the church in a combination of small committee meetings and open assembly of all members. Worship services and many speeches are intermixed with reports by the various commissions and committees of the conference. Keep in mind that the word *conference* refers both to the gathering described and also to a geographical area, Indiana being divided into two conferences, North and South. The line across the middle of the state is located just above Indianapolis.

The gathering of the Annual Conference does several things. It affords members an opportunity to stay in touch with each other and to share in making decisions about various issues confronting the church. It assures that the laity are empowered to help oversee

South Indiana Annual Conference has been held at Indiana University since 1969. This is the 2000 session at the IU auditorium. Photo by Linda Hoopes.

the life of the church. It reminds everyone that we are part of a whole and that Jesus Christ has called us together for a common mission. It enables the bishop to address the clergy together. It usually presents a well-known speaker who reminds us of our mission. It also provides a venue where people can make speeches, some of which are insightful, some of which are, well, long. One superintendent, Reverend E. A. Clegg, offered a bit of doggerel back in 1950 to describe this characteristic of a conference:

> There are thorns on all the roses
> There is fuzz on all the peaches
> There was never a conference yet
> Without some lengthy speeches!

Nonetheless, Annual Conference is a very important part of the culture of the United Methodist Church, and it helps maintain the sense of solidarity so necessary to our denominational identity.

Each conference is divided into smaller geographical units called districts, and each of these is presided over by a minister who temporarily holds the title of district superintendent, usually for a period of six years, before returning to a church as a pastor once again. The entire area is presided over by a bishop who is elected for life, but who sometimes moves from one area to another under prescribed rules.

One question I have posed to several older clergy who have served in leadership roles through the years is how the two Indiana conferences differ in regard to their inherent cultures and how they view each other. Answers have varied. It is definitely true that the two differ. A good analogy is that of the graduates of Indiana University and Purdue University. Each school is better than the other, depending on whom one asks. People who have served in one conference tend to have a conviction that in all truth, setting aside any prejudice, "mine is the stronger one." On rare occasions, a minister is transferred from one conference to the other. That person often feels adrift for quite some time since most ministers develop a feeling of loyalty to their own conference. The quickest way for a bishop to encounter a morale problem for one conference is to transfer someone from the other one when a district or a large church is open. Morale is always an issue for clergy because, by the nature of the work, ministers often feel lonely. Retired Bishop Sheldon Dueker recently remarked that many clergy today are feeling isolated and alone. He also observed that the role of a bishop has been changing in the past several years.

Based on comments made by several leaders or former leaders of both conferences, it would seem that from up north, the South Conference is viewed as Indianapolis plus surrounding churches, which are mainly rural, very conservative, and remote from the most pressing issues facing society today. Outside of Indianapolis, farming or small communities form the particular cultures of most congregations. Scattered throughout, however, are pockets of sophistication in places like Greencastle, Evansville, and of course Bloomington with Indiana University. While the very largest churches in the Indiana area are in the south, particularly in Indianapolis, sizes quickly drop down to medium and small congregations. While the people of Indiana are basically conservative, pastors of the large Indianapolis churches are not seen as conservative, which leads many North Conference observers to think of themselves as being more conservative theologically than the South. Riley Case, longtime pastor of St. Luke's Church in Kokomo, points out the strong influence of Taylor University in Upland, a very conservative religious school. That influence is waning now, but many pastors and other church leaders were Taylor graduates, and the effect of this in the 1950s and '60s was noticeably conservative.

Looking north, South Indiana Conference people see a large number of good-sized congregations, though no extremely large ones. There are many more large, urban areas in the north than in the south. The Calumet area is viewed as only partially included in the North Conference, being closely associated with the larger Chicago area. It is more industrial and strongly Catholic, with many churches in the Calumet District having suffered declining attendance in recent years. Quite a number of small North

School of the Prophets 1967 at DePauw University, Greencastle. Photo courtesy of Indiana Area Communications.

Conference churches are staffed by seminary students because of the proximity of Garrett-Evangelical Theological Seminary, which prepares young men and women for ordination into the Methodist Church. It is one of the denomination's largest graduate schools. Purdue University at Lafayette is a counterpart to Indiana University in the south, though the cultures of the two schools differ markedly.

One problem the Indiana area currently faces is a lack of means by which pastors and leading laity can interchange with their counterparts from the other conference and perhaps make new friends in the process. The one venue where this was traditionally done was the School of the Prophets, an annual area-wide continuing education program for clergy. People could make or renew acquaintances with pastors of the other conference, exchange ideas about ministry, and generally build mutual rapport as workers in the vineyard. Unfortunately, times change. The people in the North Conference decided the benefits did not justify the cost, and the school was discontinued in the early 1990s. At present, apart from a few people in special appointments whose responsibilities take them farther afield, the typical pastor makes her or his friends close to home in his or her own conference. Thanks to the *Hoosier United Methodist News*, Methodists are still kept apprised of the goings-on in the other conference.

*Fond memories bring the light
Of other days around me;
The smiles, the tears . . .
—Thomas Moore*

Introduction

Healthy minded people try not to live in the past. Our fast racing future calls us, dashing, into new adventures, new excitement, new revealings by the god of new creation: the computer. Last year *Newsweek* magazine featured an article entitled "The Coming Technological Revolution." Those of us who thought we had just weathered such a revolution apparently ain't seen nuthin' yet. One survey proclaimed that in the year 2000 there were twice as many things to buy as in 1985. By the time my thirteen-year-old grandson is out of college, that could double again. Already we can browse through the mall, wander through our favorite book section of Barnes and Noble, examine the latest fashions by the Gap, sell a few shares of stock—and do all of that in a half hour on the Internet, without leaving home. And of course our churches are prime beneficiaries, what with PowerPoint®, video clips, homilies distributed via e-mail, and databases which have the added advantage of eliminating one part-time secretary; and of course the year's schedule, safely tucked away in a pocket on a PalmPilot®, is immediately accessible when the cell phone rings on the highway.

So what of the past? Is there anything from our history which can enlighten, which can ennoble, which can make the way which lies ahead more clear? What about those men who rode horses through snowstorms, slept in forests, and knew that half of them would die before their thirtieth birthdays, yet pressed on to bring the gospel word to small communities of pioneers? What of those faithful servants who brought the church through the westward movement, the divisive struggles of the Civil War, the Great Depression, through two World Wars, and countless other conflicts—people who established universities, and hospitals, and children's homes, the men and women who trained their children for honorable lives, who took their places in the growing new nation, all of them undergirded by the simple faith of the Methodist Church? Do their lives speak a needed word to our times?

What of those courageous laypeople and pastors who stepped forth to lead in the Civil Rights movement, who endured the struggles, the endless debates, the inner conflict as a new bright dawn broke within America? And what of those who remained faithful as a war they didn't understand threatened to corrupt our nation's way of life, those who stepped forth to endure rejection and sometimes vilification to stand by what they believed? And those who kept the faith when our campuses erupted in conflict and violence, and many of our children turned to sex and drugs, when long-treasured values wavered under the spiritual and intellectual assaults of minds cut loose from ancient verities—does their heroism call any of us home?

Oh yes, those days demanded strong hearts, ready faith: men, women, children, and the Methodist Church, often leading the way, sometimes wrong, often right, always determined. Of many opinions, yet of one faith, the people called Methodist have never faltered in facing and transcending changing times. The writer of Hebrews said that Jesus Christ "is the same yesterday, and today, and for ever." Each of us stands in a long train of those whom Christ has informed and strengthened and led. And all of us— those of yesterday, those who carry on, and those who yet await their calling—are bound together in that Spirit which, to those who have the eyes to discern, can be seen touching down again and again with wondrous splendor to lead us on our way.

Sinners? Yes! Each of us has sometimes foundered, said and done those things which burn us in memory. Forgiven? Yes! John Wesley, the founder of our church, writing in his *Character of a Methodist* said it for us: "Through Christ and Christ alone Methodists have received forgiveness for their sins." And his next words were these: "Methodists never forget this."

So, then our history matters. Our remembrance honors our past, but more importantly, points our future. John Eccles, Nobel laureate, wrote: "Without memory we are hollow persons, not only empty of a past but lacking a foundation upon which to build the future." Editorial writer Cal Thomas wrote: "A culture maintains its identity by passing on the sum of its values and experiences from one generation to the next . . . else the culture dies or survives only as a hollow shell." And so, as with high optimism we prepare for the future, we now turn to honor the past.

CHAPTER ONE

Do all the good you can,
By all the means you can,
In all the ways you can,
In all the places you can,
At all the times you can,
To all the people you can,
As long as ever you can.
—John Wesley's rule

The Story Begins: The Lord's Horseman

Try to imagine several hundred coal miners gathered outside the entrance to a mine on a cold, dreary dawn in Newcastle, England. The year is 1740. Facing a long and demanding day's work, these men have nonetheless come a half hour early to listen to the loud-voiced, spellbinding Anglican priest who rose at 4:00 A.M. and rode his horse to the mine to tell these waiting miners, most of whom would never have been willing to set foot in an Anglican church, about a loving God. But this man, this itinerant preacher, sends thrills through these hard-bitten men with his message of God's love and acceptance for anyone who wants to be saved. It is a startling new way to understand the Bible's word, offering hope to people who have always thought themselves unworthy of God's love.

But John Wesley's sermon this day has a sharp bite to it, too. Once God's grace is accepted, he warns, the new convert must cease certain kinds of conduct and must understand that dishonesty and dissipation of any kind can have dire consequences. They must, if they are wise, "flee the wrath to come." They must aspire to become

John Wesley.

better people. They must act in response to a divinely given spark in their hearts, moving their lives toward a piety which this preacher would call *sanctification*. Many of these men, learning now that wealth and social status play no part at all in God's assessment, hear this word of hope with its call to action and are moved to a new way of living. Many lives are changed on this cold, wonderful morning.

But not all in the crowd are moved. There are men who came to jeer. There are those who would make fun of this energetic young priest's demands. There are many who view this call to a holy life as a threat to their satisfying status quo. They are not about to give up their raucous lifestyles. So what if Wesley is jeopardizing his status within his own priesthood in order to tell them this saving word? So what if he is known to give away almost all of his money to help people in need? So what if he himself lives the very life to which he calls them and rises to an exhausting day's efforts seven days a week to bring his message of salvation to thousands of hardworking men and women who feel themselves unwelcome in the gold-encrusted, velvet clad churches of England? No! Many oppose John Wesley.

But thousands began joining small groups devoted to prayer, Bible reading, and mutual encouragement in the faith. John Wesley never intended to create a movement outside the Church of England. But his unorthodox, marvelously effective form of evangelism would set loose a force of such power as would win millions of people to Jesus Christ and would culminate in the founding of a new church. John Wesley's methods of preaching, calling people into small groups or classes, demanding a high-minded style of life, and encouraging generosity with one's money would soon win its adherents a title, not always meant as a compliment, of Methodists. This movement would spread like fire through dry grass. Gatherings like that of the coal miners would be repeated again and again in mines, in foundries, in town squares, and in open fields. This new grassroots, down-to-earth message would spread beyond England's borders into Europe, but mainly into the new world of America, where a leader assigned by Wesley, Francis Asbury, would oversee the proliferation of churches up and down the eastern seaboard of this new country.

Although the Methodist movement was never embraced by the Church of England, Methodist leaders in America still felt a certain loyalty to their mother church. They would retain many of the trappings of that church, including oversight by men called bishops. Many of the rubrics of the Anglican Church, now the Episcopal Church in America, would be copied and emulated. *The Book of Common Prayer* would be a basis for Methodist worship. While High Church forms of worship seemed largely meaningless to people raised outside the church, modified forms of worship with emphasis on preaching, Bible reading, singing, and free prayer, as well as bits of formal liturgy, would bear a dim similarity to the more formal worship of the Anglican Church. Methodists also gave a nod to their former parent by adding *Episcopal* to their name. Thus was born in America the Methodist Episcopal Church.

∾

It would be worth our time to take a brief look at this remarkable man, John Wesley. Born in 1703 as one of the many children

Charles Wesley.

of Samuel and Susannah Wesley, John especially bonded with his younger brother Charles, who would be John's close friend, confidant, and occasional critic throughout their long lives. Samuel Wesley was a nonconformist clergyman, rector of Epworth parish. John's faith received an early start when one day the Wesley parsonage was burned by rioters who disliked the elder Wesley and his nonconformist ways. The parsonage burned to the ground, and John, barely saved from a fiery death, thereafter referred to himself as "a brand plucked from the burning."

Both John and Charles attended Oxford University where they read voraciously, demonstrated outstanding scholarship, and committed themselves to the priesthood of the Church of England. John was ordained in 1728 upon his graduation and took his place as a devoted yet, as one biographer described him, slightly stuffy priest.

The Wesley's Oxford experience revealed deep qualities of kindness and generosity in both men, qualities which would eventually mature into exalted character traits destined to characterize the movement they would found. Though Charles would finally establish his home in Bristol and become a prolific writer of hymns, John would soon demonstrate a remarkably energetic commitment to Christian evangelism on a broad scale. Members of what they called the Holy Club, both men were tireless workers on behalf of the poor and underprivileged people of their community. Life was hard for nearly everyone in those days, and people in authority usually had very little patience with what they viewed as wrongdoing. There is a corner on Holywell Street in Oxford known today as the location where more than one student was hanged by the neck for misconduct. It was the era of debtor's prisons, orphanages, and workhouses. People who sought to alleviate human suffering were sadly in short supply. The eventual founding of such organizations as the Salvation Army and many other such humanitarian groups awaited the later maturation of churches with a zeal for social action. John and Charles Wesley had that zeal, which emanated from disciplined prayer, Bible study, and unembarrassed witnessing to their faith. However, as is true of college students of every age, they still had a lot to learn about life which could not be found in books.

In 1735 John went with General Oglethorpe to Georgia where he was appointed chaplain to the colonists and also where he announced that he had two objectives: to convert the Indians and to discover a deep, personal faith for himself. Charles tagged along as John's secretary. John's career in Georgia was distinguished by his total failure. His objectives to save his own soul and to convert the Indians were destined to be postponed in the former regard and to fail completely in the latter.

John immediately found himself at odds with Oglethorpe, a rather unbending, judgmental man in John's view. On one occasion, an angry Oglethorpe grumbled, "I never forgive." Wesley is reported to have replied, "Then, sir, I hope you never need to be forgiven." He discovered that the Indians had little interest in his demanding brand of Christianity. Perhaps as valuable as any of the lessons learned, John also discovered that he knew very little about women, by virtue of his love affair with one Sophey Hopkey. It seems Miss Hopkey felt a strong attraction to Mr. Wesley but an even stronger attraction to the idea of matrimony itself. When John procrastinated in asking the desired question, Miss Hopkey married a Mr. Williamson. John, miffed and presumably feeling rejected, promptly ruled that she was forthwith denied access to the Lord's Supper. John's lesson about women continued when Mrs. Williamson filed suit in a court of law in an effort to overturn this ill-advised bit of ecclesiastical arrogance. The suit remained unresolved for six months, at which point John Wesley—apparently realizing he was not cut out for mission work in Georgia—scurried back home to England where his brother had already wisely fled. John arrived home in 1738 a discouraged and defeated man of the cloth, now troubled by doubts about his calling. "All the time at Savannah I was thus beating the air," he wrote in his journal.

An encounter onboard his ship to America with a Moravian leader named August Spangenburg, whose calm courageous demeanor during a violent storm bore witness to that man's unshakable faith, had profoundly influenced John Wesley. He very much wanted such a faith. But John, now age thirty-six, had no such faith. He wrote in his journal "[I] who went to America to convert others, was never myself converted to God." And so began a period of spiritual struggle as John entered his own midnight of the soul. During this dark period, he seriously considered giving up his calling, as he knew his faith was failing. However, one day his friend Peter Boehler gave John some advice which many a preacher in later years would also find to be good counsel. Boehler said, "Preach faith till you have it; and then, because you have it, you will preach faith." This is what John Wesley began to do. Barely sustained, John Wesley once attended a worship service at St. Paul's Cathedral, followed by a stroll down Aldersgate Street ("very unwillingly"), where he happened upon a prayer service and heard a reading of Martin Luther's preface to the book of Romans. "My heart was strangely warmed," he later wrote.

For the first time, faith was something John Wesley not only hoped for, but could now feel. He remembered something Saint Paul had taught, which Martin Luther had learned: faith is not something you go out and find. It is a gift from God. When it pleases God to give that gift, it will be given. All a person can do is place oneself in the way of the means of grace. Attend worship. Receive Communion. Accept baptism. Read the Bible. Let God decide how and where true faith will be granted. Act out faith until you have it. Then you will act out faith because you have it.

Something providential happened. God was ready to use John Wesley at last. An evangelistic service was being held in the Bristol area by George Whitefield, a widely celebrated outdoor preacher. Whitefield wanted John to come to Bristol to preach at an important meeting; to preach, John was appalled to learn, in an open field. That would be anathema to an upstanding Anglican priest. For John, preaching was something to be done in the hallowed confines of a church. He must have prayed about this request for some time. It was a call to a totally unconventional means of winning people to Christ. But John Wesley also realized that if people refuse to attend a church and preaching is limited to the church, then masses of people would never hear the word. Paul himself said that faith comes by hearing the Word. So John Wesley made his decision. "I submitted to be more vile," he wrote, "and proclaimed in the highways the glad tidings of salvation." There, in a meadow at Baptist Mills in Kingswood, England, John Wesley began what would carry the spirit of the Great Awakening of New England throughout his own England, as John Wesley's soul burst forth from the darkness of doubt into the glorious sunlight of God's supreme gift, a faith bestowed. On April 2, 1739, the great Wesleyan revival which would change millions of lives began.

∼

John Wesley would continue his tireless ministry for some fifty years, from that day in April 1739, until his death on March 2, 1791. Just a short time before his death, he wrote in his journal: "I am now an old man, decayed from head to foot. My eyes are dim, my right hand shakes much; my mouth is hot and dry every morning; I have a lingering fever almost every day; my motion is weak and slow. However, blessed be God, I do not slack my labors. I can preach and write still." And so this remarkable man left a legacy for all the preachers who would follow in his train, a legacy of tireless commitment to the service of the Lord, unflagging zeal for the faith, and generosity both with material goods and with judgments of the struggling humanity whom he chose to serve. A short time later, this man who brought hope and spiritual liberation to his nation and to the new nation of America quietly had his expressed wish granted: "to rest only in the life beyond."

~

In truth, Wesley was an eccentric man, composed of many contradictions. He created what would become a democratic church, and yet he ruled his ministers with an iron fist. He appeared often intransigent when opposed, yet was perfectly capable of giving way. In his later years, his traveling companion was Joseph Bradford. One day he asked Bradford to mail some letters. Bradford replied that he would do so as soon as he preached a service. "No!" Wesley insisted. He wanted the letters mailed "*now*." Bradford refused, whereupon Wesley informed him that they must part ways. A short time later, Wesley again called on Bradford and asked if he recalled that they must now part ways. Bradford said he did. Wesley asked if Bradford was, in fact, ready to ask Wesley's pardon. Bradford, apparently every bit as stubborn as Wesley, replied that he was not. "Then I will yours, Joseph," Wesley said. Thus a friendship was saved, and evidence afforded that John Wesley, subject of much adulation as well as a great deal of criticism, admired people who had minds of their own.

Wesley was inclined toward High Church worship, yet decided on behalf of field preaching. He found great solace in *The Book of Common Prayer*, yet encouraged free prayer and open worship. He was a product of the Enlightenment, having a scholar's mind and placing importance on the ability of a normal person to reason his own way; yet he had many Calvinist leanings, convinced that God had total power to decide if and when a person was to receive a saving faith. Wesley believed that faith was a gift to be received, yet he believed that everyone had a bit of faith buried deep within the heart from birth, which he called *prevenient grace*. He urged that all true Christians must go on to perfection in this life, yet he knew full well that this was an ideal which no one could really attain. One could only strive for it. Elizabeth Browning would later catch the flavor of this in her line, "A man's reach should exceed his grasp, or what's a heaven for?" And so this complicated, remarkable man became the basis for a faith and a church which enriches the lives of so many of us today.

Perhaps it should be mentioned that at age forty-eight, John Wesley was married. The marriage was a miserable failure. One early biographer numbered Mrs. Wesley as one of the three worst wives in history, to which a later biographer added that John Wesley was very likely one of the worst husbands in history. In due course, they separated. She died at age seventy-one and John only heard of her death several days later. One present day observer remarked that if Mrs. Wesley had been a good and loving wife, there might never have been a Methodist church. As it was, John seems to have been up and out of the house at an early hour.

～

We have to wonder what preaching was like in the eighteenth and early–nineteenth centuries. Today we are so influenced by the media parading visual stories before us in which facial expressions and body language play a major role in communication, and we are so used to public address systems in our churches which allow subtlety of voice inflection and changes of vocal volume, we can hardly imagine someone preaching to four or five thousand people in an open field without a microphone. Jesus did it, of course. But so did John Wesley, George Whitefield, and many other well-known preachers of the time. The sheer vocal power required to preach effectively under those conditions seems astounding today. When we note that a few years ago one Indiana church of two hundred and fifty people found it necessary to install a public address system because their new preacher could not be heard in the back row, we have to acknowledge that, as an old saying goes, they were real men back in the old days. Throw in the

all-too-frequent interruptions by unwanted bystanders, and preaching
back then required people of exceptional courage and ability.

The audience was, of course, completely different from
today's congregations. Today we are so inundated with sensory
experiences, often to the point of sensory overload, that we can
only wonder what a revival service felt like to those folks who had
never heard a radio or seen a movie. Psychotherapist Paul
Tournier pointed out that unless a person learns to tune out much
of today's media assault, he or she can drown emotionally. By
comparison, the people of John Wesley's time (who may have on
rare occasions seen a stage play or read a newspaper) must have
been starved aesthetically. No doubt they found alternative
sources of enrichment. But a preaching service very likely met a
variety of their emotional needs, which are met—if not overwhelmed—in other ways for us.

We do know that much preaching was quite lively, or what
would later be referred to as "hellfire and brimstone" preaching.
The story is told of the time John Wesley was walking with his
friend Samuel Bradburn through Billingsgate Fish Market in
London. They came upon two women having a shouting match.
Bradburn, offended by the unseemly manner of speech of the two
ladies, muttered to Wesley, "Pray, let us go; I cannot stand it." To
which John Wesley replied, "Stay, Sammy, and learn how to
preach." This does not mean, however, that John Wesley was an
overly emotionalistic preacher. A friend of both Wesley and
Whitefield named John Hampson described Wesley's preaching
style as "the calm equal flow of a placid stream, gliding gently
within its banks, without the least ruffle or agitation upon its
surface." Hampson then compared this to Whitefield who "alter-
nately thundered and lightened upon his audience."

We know something of the content of those early sermons.
Were a preacher to use one of Wesley's written sermons in a church
today, it would seem too long, fraught with unfamiliar language,
lacking in illustrations, and heavy on the threat to anyone who
does not have a strong desire to "flee the wrath to come." But one
must remember the changes in culture and language from those
times to these. There is also evidence that Wesley strayed from his

Roadside Sermon, *an engraving depicting a circuit rider, from* The Illustrated History of Methodism, *published by the Methodist Book Concern in 1880.*

manuscripts. He told the story of asking a maid to read one of his sermons and report her reaction. This lady was only able to report back that she had difficulty understanding much of the language. This led Wesley to realize that if he was to reach the masses of people who, with very few exceptions, had little education, he must use simple, understandable language; this is a lesson that could benefit every preacher. It seems likely that his written sermons were designed for a different audience than were his spoken sermons, which means we can only partially recapture his preaching as it actually took place.

We know that Wesley was influenced by the preaching of Jonathan Edwards, the main force behind the Great Awakening in America's New England. One of Edwards's most famous sermons, "Sinners in the Hands of an Angry God," was preached at Enfield, Connecticut, in 1741. In that sermon, Edwards warned his listeners (or at least the nonbelievers among them) that they "deserve to be cast into Hell, so that divine justice never stands in the Way . . . Yea, Justice calls aloud for an infinite punishment." Addressed to a basically unlettered congregation, that kind of message no doubt received their undivided attention.

Peter Cartwright, an early circuit rider and Indiana preacher, who probably used both Wesley and Whitefield as models, reported of one of his services: "In about thirty minutes the power of God fell on the congregation in a manner seldom seen; the people fell in every direction, right and left, front and rear. It was supposed that not less than three hundred fell like dead men in mighty battle; and there was no need of calling mourners, for they were strewed all over the campground; loud wailing went up to heaven from sinners for mercy . . . our meeting lasted all night." We can only conclude from such reports that preaching contained a heavy emphasis on fear and a total lack of the dispassionate examination of the Scriptures which characterizes much preaching today. Another hint of change in sermonizing over the years is found in the title of a sermon preached by William McKendree in 1812 which is said to have been the persuading factor in McKendree's election as bishop a day or so later. His title was: "Is there no balm in Gilead? Is there no physician there? Why, then, is not the health of the daughter of my people recovered?" That would not fit very easily on a billboard today.

As Methodism spread to America, preaching centered more and more in small groups, often in homes or even in barns. It

probably assumed a more personal nature as these groups began
to proliferate. But the very large venue of the camp meeting, tent
revival service, or open-air community-wide gathering would
continue to be the main form of evangelism, and the spellbinding
preacher would rule the Christian day for quite some time.
Singing became a central part of Methodist worship. Singing in
most churches of the time was a rather dull affair, and there were
no official hymnals available. One writer described music in
England this way: "Psalms were drawled out in the congregation,
the tune set by a clerk whose sniveling voice often neutralized
such little effect as feeble metrical versions might have had." But
Charles Wesley helped put an end to that, as he turned out to be
a musician and a poet. He wrote many of the most familiar hymns
of the time. Some hymns like "Love Divine, All Loves Excelling"
and "Jesus, Lover of My Soul" are among today's most popular.
Others, while not necessarily classics, clearly expressed the
theology of the church. In his biography of the Wesleys, Umphrey
Lee reminds us of this ditty:

> O Jesus the rest
> Of spirit distressed,
> Receive a lost sinner that flies to thy breast.
> Long lost on a sea,
> Of trouble, I flee,
> To find an asylum, and pardon in Thee.

As Lee pointed out, some of these songs may not have been
great poetry, but they expressed the sentiments of the faith. Also,
most of the early Methodists were hardly literary critics. Many
hymns had words that were easily memorized, and the meter was
such that people often sang their hymns while going about their
day's activities. It was also popular then to use already familiar
tunes with new words written by the hymn writer. The reader may
get a feel for this, especially anyone who ever became acquainted
with the bar song "How Dry I Am" upon discovering that it is, in
fact, an old eighteenth-century hymn titled "O Happy Day." It has
been said that early Methodists learned their theology from their

hymns. The current hymnal of the United Methodist Church includes fifty-one hymns by Charles Wesley, as well as eight of his poems and six of his musical responses.

∾

There are several ideas inherent in early Wesleyan theology which we do well to keep in mind as we watch the ongoing story of Methodism unfold. These ideas evolve with time, of course. But they began with John Wesley and they remain his legacy to Methodism. Granted, the language has changed. We Indiana Methodists rarely hear words like *sanctification, justification, universality,* and *Christian perfection.* Not often are we warned to "flee the wrath to come" these days. Even *sin* was out for a long-time, though it has recently made a comeback. We have let words like *saved* and *salvation* become the property of our far more conservative friends. No matter. The truths these words describe are still true. And remember that for Wesley, theology was not a systematic statement of beliefs, but instead was experienced along the road of life. It was for him what Frederick Norwood, in his book *The Story of American Methodism,* called "a survival kit for pilgrims and refugees."

There are four ideas which are essential to keep in mind, for they underlie Methodism from the days of founder John Wesley to the present.

The first Wesleyan belief which underlies Methodism is the *universality of the church.* That is, everyone is welcome; the gospel is for all. No one has to qualify for membership by claiming to believe this or that. One needs only, to use Wesley's words, "desire to flee the wrath to come, and to be saved of their sins." It is true that our current membership vows inquire as to whether one accepts Jesus as Savior, believes in God and the Holy Spirit, and agrees to be supportive of the church. But these are basic questions, and even so, many a person joins the church with very little realistic idea what these vows truly mean. John Wesley did, at one time, require the issuing of tickets of member-ship so one might obtain admission to a small class meeting. But this was not to reject those who did not know Christ. It was to screen out the various troublemakers who often attended, or tried to, in order to engage in endless and unproductive debate. In fact, Wesley disdained doctrinal requirements. "If your heart is as my heart, give me your hand," he said. In describing a Methodist he wrote: "A Methodist is one who has the love of God shed abroad in his heart: that he who loveth God loves his Brother also. Loves not only God but loves his neighbor as himself, and does good unto all men, neighbors and strangers, friends and enemies."

Wesley believed that one could do little to obtain faith until God decided to grant faith as a gift. What one could do, however, was to present oneself where the means of grace might work. No doubt Wesley's own spiritual struggles provided the insight by which he arrived at this conviction. True, we may be accused of being wishy-washy by allowing a wide disparity of interpretation of the many implications of these basic beliefs. But we Methodists would argue that this is our strength. Put three or four Methodist preachers together today and ask a theological question, and it would not be surprising to get three or four somewhat differing opinions. But John Wesley was a product of the Enlightenment. He believed that God gave each of us a mind capable of reason, and we should use it.

Therein lies both the strength and the weakness of Methodism. We do agree on the basics: God created the world, Jesus was God's revelation of the divine will for us, the Bible is our only authority, God participates as what we call the Holy Spirit, God did call the church into being as the earthly embodiment of Christ's work on earth, and we are each to carry out Jesus' work on earth in service to others. But beyond those beliefs, if we allow that we each have the ability to make reasonable judgments in making sense out of these basic beliefs, we can't then very well allow anyone else the right to decide what my reasoning must lead me to believe.

For example, put four people in a room: a computer expert, a business executive, a poet, and a landscape painter. Two of them are male, two female. One is African-American, one Hispanic, one

Caucasian, and one Native American. Present the group with a theological question. They all may be "good Methodists," but you can bet your hat you will not get the same conclusions from each. Throw in family backgrounds: differing emotional, cultural, economic, and gender-based forces, and it is clear that in the absence of a highly authoritative hierarchical structure, people simply are not all going to interpret the Bible's teachings in the same way. In other words, John Wesley left the door open to religious freedom—and disagreement. And open it remains. Therefore, anyone is welcome to walk through.

This does need to be qualified. Until 1908, anyone wishing to join the Methodist Church in America was required to first become a probationer for six months. The *Discipline* stated that "It is manifestly our duty to fence in our society, and to preserve it from intruders; otherwise, we should soon become a desolate waste." This was not, however, an attempt to limit membership to a certain type of person. In the early days in America, there was great dissension among Christians regarding theology. Calvinists especially were inclined to battle for their own beliefs. We may think of today's fundamentalists who can be quite aggressive in pressing their own beliefs. It was fairly common for people to gain entrance to the early societies for the purpose of engaging in lengthy and, for the most part, useless theological debates. The probationary period was not designed to discourage any person who sincerely sought to be a Methodist from gaining full membership.

The second Wesleyan belief which underlies Methodism is that of *christian perfection*. This belief insists that each true Christian must so conduct his or her life as to finally become perfect. This, of course, is a troubling idea since honesty forces us to at least privately admit that we are a long way from perfect, some of us a very long way—even though we may be doing a fairly good job of practicing our faith at home and in the marketplace. As a matter of fact, the New Testament seems to require that we go to our graves with a healthy sense of our own sinfulness. Jesus himself, when called "good teacher," replied that "No one is good but God alone."

We need to understand what Wesley meant by the word *perfection*. Today we use that word to describe something or someone who is without flaw. That, of course, does not exist. But let's think of it, rather, as a goal or a life's mission. Many years ago, Bishop Richard Raines asked a group who were about to be ordained if they were willing to reply "Yes!" to the traditional question: "Are you going on to perfection in this life?" Wise beyond their years, so they thought, the group explained to Bishop Raines that this was impossible. No one can be perfect in this life. But Bishop Raines had the last word when he quietly replied: "If you're not going on to perfection, what are you going on to?"

Leslie Weatherhead provided a helpful analogy for understanding christian perfection. Suppose you have a set of tools: a screwdriver, a saw, a pair of pliers, and a hammer. And suppose you wish to drive a nail in a board. How would you do that with the tools at hand? The hammer would be the perfect tool. It might not be a perfect hammer—maybe it has a dent or two, a handle worn from much use. Its perfection lies in its appropriateness to the task. Likewise, as Christians we are to act out the life of Jesus as much as we are able. Peter Cartwright, the best known of the grand old circuit riders, wrote in the preface to his autobiography shortly before his death: "I ask for the forgiveness of the Methodist Episcopal Church, as one of her unworthy ministers, for any wrongs I may have done to her or to the world." But that man, like all of us are called to do, did the best he could with what he had to work with, given his life situation and whatever limitations may have hampered his life. As much as he could, he practiced his faith. That is christian perfection. In its application to our own time, it means that as Methodists, our lives are to be led selflessly, always aware of the trials faced by others, always willing to expend our resources to help others, always seeking to know what Jesus would have us do, and then doing that as faithfully as in us lies.

The third Wesleyan belief which underlies Methodism today is that of *the priesthood of all believers*. John Wesley, though at one time a thoroughgoing Anglican priest, later brushed aside much of the formalism of that church. He did not believe in apostolic succession, nor that the ordained clergy were somehow superior beings to the common lot of humanity. Instead he believed that lay as well as ordained people could serve the Lord and spread the faith. In fact, the early ministers had no ordination. The Methodist society was organized around small classes overseen by lay exhorters, preachers, leaders, and teachers. Once an individual professed a belief in God, acknowledged his own sinfulness, expressed a desire to avoid the wrath of God, and demonstrated gifts which would enable him to properly lead others in the faith, that person could thereupon undertake to become a minister. In fact, the first Methodist society in Indiana was founded by a preacher from Kentucky, Samuel Parker, who crossed the Ohio River into Clark County and convinced some farmers to allow him to establish a meeting house. This was in 1801 and was probably the very beginning of Methodism in Indiana. Incidentally, the use of the male pronoun above is accurate. While women are among the finest leaders of Methodism today, they had not yet been recognized as such in Wesley's time. It was crusty old Samuel Johnson who contended that "a woman preaching is like a dog walking on its hind legs; the wonder is not that he does it well but that he does it at all." That sentiment would, of course, be proven quite incorrect, but many, many years later.

All of this has important meaning for the church today. True, most Methodist churches have ordained ministers assigned to them. It is also true that the ordination system is somewhat confusing, even to many ordained people, as words like lay preacher, local deacon, local elder, traveling deacon, traveling elder, and diaconal ministers are thrown around. No matter, in a Methodist church laypeople provide a great deal of the inspired leadership which empowers a congregation. The work of ministry is to be done by the membership at large of any church. Ben Garrison used the analogy of a professor of surgery in a medical school who could train others to do surgery but obviously couldn't actually do all the surgeries. That is the preacher's job. So, the work of ministry is the responsibility of anyone who accepts membership in a Methodist church.

The fourth Wesleyan belief which underlies Methodism today is the call to *sacrificial giving.* All denominations emphasize generosity. But this was so particularly emphasized by John Wesley that it would come to characterize the Methodist Church throughout its years. John himself gave away most of his money, estimated by some at around two hundred thousand dollars. To illustrate how much money that was in eighteenth-century England, an advertisement from the early part of the twentieth century shows that enough gingham fabric to make a dress cost only nine cents at a dry goods store.

Charities founded and supported by the Methodist Church abound. Wesley's own rule was, "Gain all you can; save all you can; give all you can." In fact, Wesley's preaching created what today might be called a catch-22. His concept of Christian conduct led to good manners, cleanliness, and the quiet life, which had the effect of making people more successful in their work. This, in turn, began to lead to a more prosperous life which caused many people to aspire to the accumulation of wealth. As time went on, Wesley placed increasing emphasis on the importance of sacrificial giving for a truly Christian life.

In Indiana today, it is noteworthy that one of the nation's largest hospitals was founded by the Methodist Church, as well as were four fine private universities, DePauw, the University of Evansville, the University of Indianapolis, and Taylor University. Community centers such as Fletcher Place in Indianapolis and Broadway Christian Parish in South Bend have served many people as have a lengthy list of outreach ministries from local churches. There are Methodist homes for children and retirement homes for aging Methodists. But all of this and the splendid record of our churches across the state have been made possible by the generosity of countless individuals, because Methodists are committed to second-mile giving as a way of life. John Wesley was a practical man. He understood that generosity takes many forms. It involves acts of forgiveness, acts of kindness, turning the other cheek, and devoting time and energy to worthy causes. But it all works when people are generous with their money as well.

In Bunyan's priceless allegory *Pilgrim's Progress,* an old man presents the pilgrims with a riddle:

A man there was, though some did count him mad,
The more he cast away the more he had.

His answer to the confounded listeners was simple:

He that bestows his goods upon the poor,
Shall have as much again, and ten times more.

The Methodist Church Moves Westward

In America, many adventures lay ahead for Methodists. Francis Asbury came to lead this new movement on behalf of John Wesley. Asbury was, of course, an Englishman. But as one of his biographers Bishop William Fraser McDowell observed, by the end of his life Francis Asbury was an American with some English habits.

On December 24, 1784, Francis Asbury, in company with several companions including Dr. Thomas Coke, rode from Perry Hall in Baltimore to Lovely Lane Chapel where, beginning at 10:00 A.M., they would conduct the first General Conference of what was to become the Methodist Episcopal Church. One early writer described the setting this way: "The latter was a still rude structure, and Coke commended gratefully the kindness of the people in furnishing a large stove and backs to some of the seats for the comfort of the conference."

This gathering, which became known as the Christmas Conference, was the occasion on which Asbury and Coke were officially appointed superintendents of the new denomination, that

Francis Asbury.

title later amended to bishop. The title change took place several years following the conference and was written back into the records. It was also noted that while deep affection would always describe the American feelings toward John Wesley, his authority over the church would no longer exist. In response, Wesley would accept and understand this kindly separation and would warn the leaders that the title of bishop must never be used by one of its holders as a means of self-gratification or self-importance. Wesley's influence was of long duration, however, as the liturgy adopted by the conference was composed by Wesley.

Because John Wesley had opposed the American Revolution, all the ministers he had sent here, other than Francis Asbury, returned to England. This led to much suspicion of Methodist clergy, so much so that Asbury took early, though temporary, retirement. Many early Methodists were pacifists, which led to the widespread suspicion that their sentiments were more political than religious. However, as a result of the breakaway from England and the resultant severing of all but sentimental relations with Wesley, the Methodist Episcopal Church became a full-fledged reality. The very freedom for which Americans had fought now led to religious freedom in America, and the Methodists, with their emphasis on personal piety, Low Church worship, and ministry to the poor, imprisoned, and lost, began to attract a rapidly growing number of adherents. Even if John Wesley himself no longer determined the course of the Methodists in America, his beliefs and teachings would continue to define their faith.

⌒

The picture becomes a bit confusing. Two other denominations were also forming in early America which would play later roles in the Methodist Church we know today. One, the United Brethren, is generally associated with the name of Philip William Otterbein. While not precisely the founder of that church, Otterbein, as pastor of the German Evangelical Reformed Church was highly influential in its inception. One day in 1767, this evangelical preacher of wide acclaim attended a meeting in what to us seems a quite humble setting: a barn on a farm owned by Isaac Long. A Mennonite preacher named Martin Boehm was preaching to the small assembly. He delivered a sermon of such persuasive power that afterwards, Otterbein, overwhelmed with a sense of comradeship with this new friend, went to Boehm, extended his hand, and uttered the words which would be so treasured by later generations of United Brethren people: "We are brothers." These men shared values so similar to those of the Methodists that Otterbein later took part in the ordination of Francis Asbury as the first Methodist bishop in 1784.

Martin Boehm was greatly influenced by John Wesley's preaching and writings. He so rejected the very stringent doctrinal teachings of his own Mennonite tradition that he was eventually excommunicated by that group. Finally, after several meetings at which minutes were not recorded, a meeting was convened in the home of Peter Kemp on September 25, 1800, which was attended by fourteen German ministers, including Otterbein and Boehm. They did not intend to create a new denomination. However,

Philip William Otterbein.

moved by a desire to win people to Christ in very much the same way as the Methodists, yet wishing to retain their German roots, the result of the meeting was, in fact, the birthing of the United Brethren Church. It is not surprising that 168 years later they would merge with the Methodist Church. The final step in organization of this new denomination took place in 1815 at their first General Conference in a schoolhouse near Mount Pleasant, Pennsylvania.

~

Now we must look at another small group as Jacob Albright enters the picture. Of Lutheran stock, he was a sixteen-year-old drummer boy during the Revolution. Raised on a farm with a strict, ascetic home life, he assumed this personality in his approach to the Christian faith. He responded to the preaching of a Methodist preacher and a Reformed preacher, and he himself began a preaching ministry in eastern Pennsylvania and the

Shenandoah Valley. He formed several small groups devoted to Bible study, prayer, and a disciplined life. The main emphasis was on the Wesleyan idea of Christian perfection and the holy life. A conference was held in 1807, and Jacob Albright was elected bishop. In 1816 at the first General Conference, the Evangelical Association became a formal entity. While Wesley would influence the beliefs and teachings of this group, they retained use of the German language for several years. This obviously limited the number of converts to their group, and they slowly reverted to English. Drawn together by common German backgrounds and by mutual beliefs, this group finally merged with the United Brethren Church to become the Evangelical United Brethren Church, or the EUBs. We will see this group again much later.

~

And so the Methodist Episcopal Church began its movement west. Settlers were moving into Ohio, Kentucky, Tennessee, and the territory north of Kentucky which would become Indiana territory. Rich farmland beckoned. Families loaded their household goods in wagons, and despite the danger from weather, disease, and hostile Indians, they headed for this new land. Many others loaded their goods on flatboats and came west along the Ohio River.

A former circuit rider from the early days, William C. Smith, in a book published in 1867, gave us a picturesque description of the state of Indiana at the time of the arrival of the very earliest settlers. Describing the Indiana of about 1808, he wrote: "All middle and northern Indiana was a wild wilderness where the red man roamed over hills and valleys free, none to dispute his right save the wild beasts which sometimes contended with him for the mastery. . . ." Describing the conditions which awaited the newcomers, Smith reported,

> The first settlers of Indiana were subjected to hardships and toils to which the present inhabitants are entire strangers. They were shut up to their own resources for the means of living, and the necessities of life with all their ingenuity and

skill there were few . . . their cabins were built of unhewn logs
covered with clapboard, stick, and clay chimney . . . few of the
cabins of the first settlers had windows in them . . . a window
left an opening by which wild animals could enter, to the
dismay of the family. Wolves, bears, panthers, and wild cats
prowled around their dwellings in the darkness of the night.

Farther west, raising cattle would become the primary occupa-
tion. But in what would for awhile be known as the Western
Conference of the Methodist Episcopal Church, farming was the
predominant means of livelihood. This, of course, caused people to
band together in small settlements. Towns, tiny by today's
measure, came into existence, and along with the hardy, pious,
good-spirited people came the not surprising host of gamblers,
prostitutes, and outlaws. The pressing need for schools and
churches brought the Methodist Church in the form of circuit
riders. They were thoroughly dedicated men willing to give up any
kind of settled life for themselves in order to visit from one settlement to another, exhorting people in the faith, and setting up small
societies or classes. Once such a class was formed, a layman
steeped in the faith was appointed class leader. The circuit rider
would try to visit that community at least once each three months.
The conference convened by that man was the quarterly conference, a term still in use in the church.

The class meeting was the basic unit of early Methodism.
Ideal size was thought to be about a dozen people, though sizes
varied. It was believed that a feeling of community could best be
achieved in this way and that a feeling of closeness was the
desired hallmark of a Methodist Church. The class leader knew
each member by personality, background, and religious conviction. Each meeting was devoted to Bible reading, prayer, and to
bearing witness. Special emphasis was placed on a report by each
member as to his or her progress along the way to Christian
perfection. These class meetings characterized the Methodist
Church through the first half of the nineteenth century. This
would later reemerge in the small group movement of the latter
part of the twentieth century.

The emphasis on classes with the requirement that every true Methodist be a member of a class began to decline with the end of the circuit riding ministry, as pastors began to age and wish to settle down. The longevity of circuit riders was very limited and for every one like Peter Cartwright who lived to be eighty-seven years old, there must have been a dozen who died in their twenties and thirties. In any event, as populations grew, more and more preachers wished to settle or "locate," and this presented a somewhat different problem. Local lay leaders were accustomed to being in charge of their groups with only an occasional visit from a preacher. As preachers began to locate and thus be permanently present, the various lay leaders found themselves out of a job. Though they were volunteers, this was not always greeted with pleasure, especially since the lay leader was often better equipped for the job than the ordained preacher. This also meant a dimming of the vision of the priesthood of all believers and an increasing dependence on the clergy for leadership. Frederick Norwood in his book *The Story of American Methodism* wrote: "In short, without local preachers, exhorters, and class leaders, the circuit rider's work would have been impossible. The two forces, for better or worse, were destined to go together. The result was continual tension between authority and freedom, between centralization of leadership and democracy. It is of the very genius of Methodism. Without this tension it would not have fulfilled its destiny. The price was conflict."

Another of John Wesley's principles prevailed under Francis Asbury's leadership. Wesley felt that a preacher shouldn't remain very long in one location. Even as recently as 1960, a survey of the preachers of the North and Northwest Conferences in Indiana was conducted by one seminary which disclosed that the average tenure of a preacher was two years and a few months. In Asbury's time, he ordered that his preachers not get married, and even encouraged that they be paid poorly in order that they not be able to afford marriage. At one Annual Conference in Virginia, eighty-four men were in attendance. Asbury was delighted when a survey showed that only three of the men were married. One preacher named William Taylor reported in his memoirs that a preacher on trial, a state of apprenticeship, could not marry, nor could he marry for an additional four

years following ordination. Taylor recorded that if a preacher did
marry, he was appointed "to a very poor circuit where he and his
young wife could enjoy their honeymoon among the whippoorwills."

Alas, nature took its course. Hardy, virile, courageous young
men such as those who rode through the forests, slept many a
night under the stars, and faced dangers from which wise men
fled, were not long willing to live without the joys of a good
marriage. Once Francis Asbury had gone to a better life, ministers
began to marry, and as they did, many chose to settle down.
However, the concept of short pastorates and constant moves
would prevail almost to the present. Perhaps the advent of women
clergy which awaited the late–twentieth century signaled an end
to that concept.

∾

A wonderful insight into early religion is afforded by a report
from the autobiography of Peter Cartwright, perhaps the most
famous of all the early circuit riders. Cartwright, with "a counte-
nance like a mahogany knot," was raised in Kentucky, but served
a Methodist circuit in Indiana for a time. In his book, he described
what he reported as the first camp meeting, held at Cane Ridge in
northern Kentucky in about 1801. He wrote:

> many were moved to tears, and bitter and loud crying for
> mercy. The meeting was protracted for weeks. Ministers of all
> denominations flocked in from far and near. The meeting was
> kept up by night and day. Thousands heard of the mighty
> work, and came on foot and horseback, in carriages and
> wagons. It was supposed that there were in attendance at times
> during the meeting from twelve to twenty-five thousand
> people. Hundreds fell prostrate under the mighty power of
> God, as men slain in battle. Stands were erected in the woods
> from which preachers of different churches proclaimed repen-
> tance toward God and faith in our Lord Jesus Christ, and it
> was supposed, by eye and ear witnesses, that between one and
> two thousand souls were happily and powerfully converted to

God during that meeting. . . . The heavenly fire spread out in almost every direction. It was said, by truthful witnesses, that at times more than one thousand persons broke out into loud shouting all at once, and that the shouts could be heard for miles around. . . . From this camp meeting . . . the news spread through all the churches, and through all the land, and it excited great wonder and surprise; but it kindled a religious flame that spread all over Kentucky and through many other states.

Given the population size of that time, if the number of people attending that meeting was as Cartwright reports, we must assume that virtually every able-bodied person in the surrounding countryside with means of transportation must have made his or her way there. Incidentally, Cartwright also reported that much dissension resulted when preachers in attendance returned to their own churches. It prompted a division within the Presbyterian Church and reminds us that just because people become Christians does not mean they always get along together. John Wesley's hopes for Christian perfection were still a long way from fulfillment.

Cartwright gave us another insight into the working of early sermons by reporting a phenomenon called *the jerks*. He records that "a new exercise broke out among us called the jerks, which was overwhelming in its effect upon the bodies and minds of the people. No matter whether they were saints or sinners, they would be taken under a warm song or sermon, and seized with a convulsive jerking all over, which they could not by any possibility avoid, and the more they resisted the more they jerked." Referring to his more genteel congregants, Cartwright wrote: "To see those proud young gentlemen and young ladies, dressed in their silks, jewelry, and prunella from top to toe, take the jerks, would often excite my risibility. The first jerk or so, you would see their fine bonnets, caps, and combs fly; and so sudden would be the jerking of their heads that their long loose hair would crack almost as loud as a waggoner's whip."

He stated that he had seen as many as five hundred people laid flat on the floor from the jerks—people lying as though dead. Of course upon recovering, they were all converted to Jesus Christ. He told of a group of local thugs who came to disrupt his meeting one day. They were all drinking and making loud shouts in an effort to break up the service. So Cartwright began preaching at them, and the thugs also began to get the jerks. He reported that one of the meanest of them started to leave. But he had the jerks so bad that he fell to his knees. Determined not to be won, he tried to take a drink of whiskey. But his shaking hand knocked the bottle against a sapling and it shattered. Cartwright described what followed: "At length he fetched a very violent jerk, snapped his neck, fell, and soon expired, with his mouth full of cursing and bitterness." Cartwright further reported that he wasn't bothered any further by that gang of thugs. He also observed that "I always looked upon the jerks as a judgment sent from God . . ."

Another Cartwright story bears repeating. It seems two young men, accompanied by their young sisters, attended a service. When the preaching started, the young men got up and left while the two girls got the jerks before they could join their brothers. Soon word came to Cartwright that the two young men were waiting for him out near the horse lot and planned to horsewhip him for giving their sisters the jerks. It seems that prior to the beginning of the service, Cartwright, not feeling well, had been seen taking a drink from a vial of peppermint. He went to the horse lot and challenged the men about the horse whipping. They repeated their threats and referred to the vial of peppermint as evidence that Cartwright had used some devilish substance to cause the effect. In response, Cartwright drew the vial from his pocket and informed the two men that just as he had given the two girls the jerks, so he would do the same to them. He proceeded to take a sip of peppermint. Seeing this, the two men fled in terror.

It was Peter Cartwright who helped introduce Methodism to Indiana. It seems a large group of Shakers practiced their faith in an Indiana settlement called Busroe. The Methodists in that area were overseen by a fine gentleman called Brother Collins who was, however, an ineffective preacher. So the priests of the Shaker group had succeeded in winning a large portion of the immigrant population over to their own religion. At a loss, Brother Collins contacted the celebrated Peter Cartwright and asked him to come to Indiana from Kentucky and debate the Shakers. Those men, however, were well aware of Cartwright's verbal skills and refused to debate, contending that Cartwright was serving the Devil. He, in turn, pointed out to the congregations that if he were, indeed, serving the Devil, the Shaker priests had nothing to fear for surely God would side with them.

Reluctantly, a large number of people came to hear Cartwright. He promptly set forth a three-hour sermon, which effectively won forty-seven converts. In the following days, he visited house to house and, finally, succeeded in retrieving most of Brother Collins's departed members. By 1811, this circuit became the St. Vincennes circuit, attached to the Cumberland district, and Thomas Stilwell was appointed preacher in charge.

～

Peter Cartwright serves as a classic example of the early circuit riders. His autobiography is a splendid window into the lives of those men. They were strenuous by any standards. "Many nights, in early times, the itinerant had to camp out, without fire or food for man or beast," he wrote. They were men of fiery determination, ready for competition with all comers, not only in the preaching department, but in every form of life as well. When still in his late teens, Cartwright sought to join the Baptist Church but was turned away by preachers who didn't like his theology. He debated them in church one morning and was scolded by the preachers. When they discontinued the service, he announced to the departing people that he proposed to speak to them from a nearby log. He thereupon explained how superior he believed his Methodist faith to be in comparison with the Baptists, and many of the Baptist worshipers promptly joined a small congregation which Cartwright organized on the spot. This small group then became the nucleus of yet another Methodist congregation.

Cartwright did not have much patience with the rowdy element, who were not at all uncommon. On one occasion he was to preach at a camp meeting and word came to him that a group of older sons of some religious people from other churches planned to attack his sleeping tent mates following the evening's services. So Cartwright hunted up some old clothes and put an old hat on his head, and thus disguised, went out and mixed with what he called the rowdies. He learned where they had hidden their whiskey barrel. When they weren't watching, he stole the barrel. The rowdies, suspecting what he had done, demanded the return of the whiskey. He, of course, refused, and sneaking around some time later, overheard their plans to attack his camp. So, Cartwright went down to the nearby river and filled his pockets with stones. Sure enough, when it was very late and very dark, a crowd of the troublemakers approached the camp. Cartwright began pelting them with stones while yelling, "Here they are, here they are! Take them! Take them!" Caught by complete surprise and supposing themselves outnumbered and ambushed, the men turned and ran, and there was no further trouble at that camp meeting. Cartwright was at Vincennes in 1808 and was presiding elder of the Wabash District 1812–13.

The modern Methodist minister may be reminded of the fidelity to the itinerant system which underlies our system today by the story of one early Methodist circuit rider Reverend Samuel Parker. Parker is described by Charles Ferguson as "one of the most brilliant of the western preachers, from Illinois to Mississippi . . . sent to preside over the work of the Methodists in Illinois, Indiana, and Missouri." Parker had a splendid singing voice and was a popular preacher throughout the territory. Under his ministry, the number of Methodists in the Indiana area increased from 382 to more than 2000. At age thirty-nine, feeling that he was now well established in his ministry, he married and his wife soon became pregnant. But at the 1819 conference in Cincinnati, the bishops decided a great opportunity for the church existed in Mississippi, and Parker was the man to go. In fact, Parker was in failing health, the area to which he was being sent was a poor climate, and Parker's wife was about to deliver her baby. Nonetheless, he was ordered to go, and he did so without protest.

Illustration of "The Circuit Preacher" from Harper's Weekly, *Oct. 12, 1867. Photo courtesy of Indiana Historical Society.*

"An audible wave of sympathy swept the conference when the appointment was read out," wrote Ferguson. The baby died on the way. Parker arrived so ill, his health now having deteriorated, that he was unable to carry out his ministry. In effect, one of the great preachers of the time was lost to the church. However, as Ferguson reported, "The system remained intact."

~

While later generations of Methodist clergy would come to value a good theological education, the early circuit riders viewed anything beyond learning to read and write and perhaps "do ciphers" as unnecessary and, in fact, prone to breeding pride in ministers. Cartwright told of one encounter with a pompous religious educator who addressed Cartwright in Greek during a debate, knowing full well he would not have any idea what had just been said. In fact, Cartwright did not know. But he had learned a smattering of Dutch in his early years, and he proceeded to reply with a few Dutch words which the biblical scholar mistakenly took to be Hebrew. The man then announced that he had at last met an educated Methodist minister. Cartwright wrote: "I do not wish to undervalue education, but really, I have seen so many of these educated preachers who forcibly reminded me of lettuce growing under the shade of a peach tree, or like a gosling that had got the straddles by wading in the dew, that I turn away sick and faint."

He also expressed disdain for clergy who accepted positions other than that of circuit rider, observing that a minister serving on a denominational board or in some other office of the hierarchy was like a man riding his horse with the reins tied to a stump. This friendly antipathy between ministers serving local churches and those in denominational appointments of various kinds may very well characterize such relationships in all denominations to this very day. The negative attitude toward clergy education would persist for many years, but when it subsided and educational requirements for clergy were greatly increased, the resultant change in biblical interpretation and in systematic theology would be of earthquake proportions. This should not, however, leave us with the mistaken impression that these early preachers were a bunch of religious dummies. Education in the organized way which we are acquainted with simply was not available at that time. However, evidence reveals that many of these early preachers studied on their own, and their many journals show remarkable journalistic skill on the part of many writers.

Numerous records remain of the hardships faced by the early circuit riders. One example concerns William Burke who was scheduled to preach in a settlement near French Broad River. It seems Burke was informed that Indians had taken the warpath. The people had drawn together to construct a makeshift fort for protection. Fearful of attack, they declined to have him preach. Burke also had an appointment to preach in another settlement some distance away, but no one was willing to run the risk of escorting him. Undaunted, he set forth through heavy forest terrain, barely able to find his way. By good fortune, he finally found the settlement he sought. But those people also were fearful and unwilling to hold a meeting. Burke, who had been exposed to the constant danger of Indian attack, finally departed unscathed. On his next visit, he discovered that all residents of both settlements had been massacred.

Bishop Francis Asbury was a man of equal courage. Accompanied by several armed men, he rode for several days through Indian country in an area bounded by Kentucky, Tennessee, Ohio, and Indiana territory (though Indiana would not become a state for several years). Sleeping in the woods at night, Asbury had the men tie a rope around the camp at ankle level, leaving an opening through which they could run if necessary. His plan was that if Indians attacked, they would trip in the dark, and he and his men could escape. This group made their way safely, but demonstrated the undaunted courage of the early traveling ministers. Though no official record exists of the number of circuit riders killed by Indians, one book from that time reports that quite a few died that way and took that risk for granted as part of their calling.

Although contemporary history often assumes total antipathy between Indians and settlers, many preachers understood the "red man" and his plight. Reverend William C. Smith, writing in 1867 and having served as a circuit rider through the very early years, stated in their defense:

> To see what he believed to be his own taken from him by another not his own kindred, tongue, or people, made him feel that the wrong was too great to be submitted to—an outrage not to be borne without resistance and struggle; hence the bloody wars between the white and red man—the unnumbered massacres of men, women, and children . . . would white men, with all their boasted civilization have submitted to such a flagrant violation of what they considered their rights?

Another insight into the settings of the great majority of early Indiana churches or class meetings is provided by a book published in 1892 by an elderly pastor, John L. Smith, who described a worship setting from 1840:

> At one of these meetings held by Hull and Smith [apparently the author] at the house of John Life, on the north bank of the Mississinewa River, the divine power was so manifest that some of the most ungodly old trappers and hunters present were heard to say "we never saw anything like this before." Mr. Life's house was a log cabin 16x18 feet with a broad, open fireplace; puncheon floor; cat and clay chimney; clapboard roof held on by knees and weight poles. The one room of Mr. Life's cabin served as a church, sitting room, parlor, and bedroom. When the weather permitted, the cooking was done by a huge log fire outdoors, and at lunch time, the door-yard became the dining hall.

Smith also related the adventure of another preacher Thomas H. Files, who apparently drifted over from the Illinois Conference on some form of business when he was overtaken by the darkness of night. This was in the 1840s, and there were no inns available. So Files stopped at a farmhouse and identified himself as a Methodist preacher. The wife, surrounded by several children, said that her husband was away on business, but he was welcome to stay the night. Files offered to go on rather than cause any gossip, but the kind lady insisted he remain and use the guest room. When he had accepted the offer and settled down for a good night's sleep, he suddenly heard a loud scream. Leaping from bed, he stepped to the head of the stairs and realized a burglar had broken in and was demanding money. In a terrified voice, the woman told the intruder the money was upstairs. Files realized he must take some action. Looking about him, he saw a flint lock rifle leaning in the corner. He first thought to use it as a club when the man reached the top of the stairs. But he feared he might injure the man more seriously than he wished. So he decided to point the rifle and click the hammer threateningly, hoping the man would turn and run. This he did. However, to his surprise the rifle was loaded, and it fired, killing the interloper.

When some neighboring men arrived at the sound of the shot, they examined the burglar who had covered his face with lamp-black. When it was cleaned away, they discovered that the intruder was, in fact, the woman's husband's brother who lived nearby and knew that her husband had sold some stock the day before, collecting several hundred dollars. Reverend Files was held innocent of any misdoing.

Numerous stories remain of the adventures of those early circuit riders who, if we stop to think about it, played a major role in the civilizing of the early westward movement. There was not much in the way of law and order in those days. The native decency of the great majority of settlers was the primary reason for the healthy development of the Midwest region. Of course the Christian faith played an important part in that, and those early preachers encouraged the pietism of the early residents.

Another story concerns Reverend Ezra Manning, who is reputed to have arrived in a settlement in which the farm wives were up in arms because their husbands were spending too much time down at the Farmer's Dog saloon and not enough time in

worship. One day Reverend Manning paid a visit to the Farmer's
Dog. Striding into the saloon, he pulled a brace of pistols from his
belt and fired one into the ceiling. He then placed the other loaded
pistol on the bar and announced to the surprised denizens,
"Gentlemen, now that I have your attention, I'd like to tell you a
little bit about Jesus."

~

Indiana's Methodist history can probably be dated officially
from the day in 1801 when young Samuel Parker, mentioned
earlier, arrived in what is now Clarke County, Indiana. After
meeting with many of the farm population, he gathered them
together one day where they were joined by another preacher,
Edward Talbott, recently arrived from Kentucky. Neither man had
any formal credentials, but both had been converted by Methodist
preachers. Both had crossed the Ohio River and were now establishing what would be the first Methodist society in Indiana. We
who are preachers today with our car allowances, four-bedroom
homes, four-week vacations, and free tours of the Holy Land must
surely wonder at the power of the faith which led men like these
to set forth, carrying all their possessions on their saddles, not
knowing where they would sleep the next night, determined only
that at any cost, they would take the saving Word to a people
struggling to carve out a new community in a demanding new
world. Surely God was in that work.

This tiny new congregation would be the first of many such
small groups, nearly all composed of farmers and other settlers.
They read the Bible together, prayed together, and encouraged
each other in the Christian life. Little is known of Parker and
Talbott's society, but we must be impressed by the bravery and
sheer Christian zeal of men who, having no material support save
what might be supplied by the generosity of their new
constituents, undertook to bring the faith to these hardy people.
The account of Parker and Talbott is contained in a report to the
Annual Conference of the Indiana Conference of 1924. An
earlier publication, the *Illustrated History of Methodism*

Robertson Meeting House, also known as Old Bethel Church, was built by the first Methodist society in Indiana at the beginning of the nineteenth century.

published in 1880 dates the beginning in 1802 at a place called Gassoway, and it credits one Nathan Robertson with the formation of the first society. Somewhere between the two is probably the correct story. Tradition, however, accepts the date of 1801. It is also recorded that in 1802 a Methodist society was organized by Nathan Robertson near Charlestown, Clarke County, Indiana.

The Rev. William McKendree, presiding elder (which today would be a district superintendent), was destined to become a bishop of the then-Kentucky Conference. McKendree heard of this new, unofficial church, paid them a visit, preached sermons in the homes of families named Gazaway, Robertson, and Jacobs, and then returned to Louisville. A restored version of the original log church which stood on the Robertson property, built in 1807, can now be seen at Rivervale Methodist camp. Those of us used to worshiping in the fine church buildings which grace our cities today may be interested to learn what church was like in the beginning. Originally known as Old Bethel, the building was described by author Worth Trippy this way:

> A little church, twenty by thirty feet, built of hewed poplar logs, clapboard roof, and puncheon floor. Pews and pulpit were also made of puncheon boards. . . . It was first heated by a thick bed of coals brought into the church in iron kettles from a big bonfire in the nearby woods.

A short time later Reverend Benjamin Lakin showed up as the officially appointed pastor of what was then named the Salt River circuit. There doesn't seem to be any record of the fates of Parker and Talbott. One must assume they were properly rewarded for their initiative. In any event, this was the beginning of Indiana Methodism. Some time later, Peter Cartwright would replace Reverend Lakin. The author of the aforementioned book from 1880 wrote:

> In 1810 there were within the limits of Indiana only three circuits, four preachers and seven hundred and sixty members; but this was the beginning of a mighty host; and at present Indiana, with its four large conferences, its admirable churches, and its thriving literary institutions, may almost be claimed to be a Methodist state.

It may be interesting to note some statistics which indicate the growth of Methodism. Between 1800 and 1850, Methodists grew from 1.2 percent of the American population to 5.4 percent of a total population in 1850 of 23,192,000. This does not include the growing black Methodist groups, African Methodist Episcopal Church, and African Methodist Episcopal Zion. This growth did produce in Methodist leadership an emphasis on numbers which is still characteristic of Methodist record keeping. During the early–nineteenth century, Baptists were the closest competition numerically. The Presbyterians were the closest competition among the more educated populace, which was a small portion of the population as evidenced by the fact that as late as the year 1900 only 6 percent of Americans had graduated from high school and one in ten Americans couldn't read or write.

One of the perplexing problems facing frontier Indiana, indeed all of the frontier, was the prevalence of whiskey. Then as now, alcoholism was rampant. So one predictable emphasis of every circuit rider's sermonic repertoire was a rousing temperance sermon. One historian said that long before there was an organized temperance society, the Methodist Church was itself a de facto temperance society. Anyone joining a Methodist society was required to take the pledge. While one may wonder just how widely that pledge was observed by the early settlers, we know the early Methodist Church placed the temperance emphasis in the forefront of its call to the holy life. An early poet, George Young, bespoke this sentiment:

The word must be spoken that bids you depart—
Though the effort to speak it should shatter my heart—
Though in silence, with blighted affection, I pine,
Yet the lips that touch liquor must never touch mine.

Before turning to the next stage of Methodist development, the era leading up to and including the Civil War, it is worth recording one more tale of the circuit riders which indicates that while they were men of sterling character and piety, they were also canny gentlemen, wise in the ways of the world. This tale concerns one Reverend Lorenzo Dow, known as a somewhat eccentric gentleman. It seems Mr. Dow was spending the night in an inn. While the guests were at dinner, one late-arriving resident informed the innkeeper that his purse had been stolen and he wanted the thief to be caught. The innkeeper explained that he had no means by which to catch the thief. At this point, Mr. Dow stated that he believed he could do it. He asked that everyone leave the room, and that someone obtain a rooster from the barnyard. When the guests were readmitted to the dining room, Reverend Dow placed a large kettle over the rooster and informed the guests that he was going to blow out all the candles turning the room totally dark. He then asked that the residents pass by the kettle one by one and place their hands on it, at which point the rooster would crow when the guilty party's hand was on the kettle. He further insisted that this always worked. Accordingly, the people passed by the kettle-covered rooster one by one, each briefly placing a hand on the top of the overturned kettle. However, when all had passed by and there had been no sound from the rooster, it was assumed the ploy hadn't worked. But Reverend Dow calmly explained that he believed it had worked. The candles were lit, the guests were all asked to hold out their hands with which they had touched the kettle. All did so, and each hand was smeared with lampblack, all save one. "There," shouted Dow, "is your thief."

One early circuit rider William C. Smith paid tribute to the brave men who brought the gospel to the frontier. Writing in mid–nineteenth century, he wrote:

> Though the Methodist itinerant system had been violently opposed and ridiculed, it is that which just brought the gospel into Indiana. Though the itinerant Methodist preachers have been stigmatized as "itinerant circuit-riders" they were the men who first threaded the . . . newly blazed ways in search of the lost sheep of Israel. They were the men who swam rivers, slept in the woods alone at night, among wild beasts and savage men, in order to carry the glad tidings of salvation to the first settlers. Indiana is more indebted to *itinerant Methodist Preachers* for the high position she now occupies . . . than to any other class of men.

We might note that prior to the year 1847, half of all preachers died before reaching age thirty. Of the first 672 preachers of whom records were maintained, 199 died before five years of service, and around 350 died before serving for twelve years.

In Indiana the population grew from 24,520 residents in 1810 to 144,178 residents just ten years later. In that same period, the number of Methodists in Indiana grew from 755 to 4,410. At that time Indiana was part of the Missouri, later the Illinois Conference, which met in Charlestown, Indiana, and was attended by every preacher in the conference, all arriving on horseback. The Reverend

John Shrader was ordered to go to New Albany to preach to a class of seven people, where his first sermon was preached in a saloon. In 1832, the Indiana Conference was officially organized in New Albany. The Reverend Joseph Tarkington wrote in 1835: "A camp meeting was held in the woods near my home, Elijah Whitten preached at nine o'clock. Enoch G. Wood—father of our Dr. Henry Wood whom you know—preached at eleven o'clock. At one o'clock the presiding elder, Calvin Ruter [one of the founders of DePauw]; at three P.M. Edward R. Ames [bishop later]; and at early candlelight I held forth. Leaving out of the calculation the night service it was the best pulpit performance I ever heard or witnessed."

~

The Second Great Awakening in the 1830s left a profound stamp on the character of the Methodist Church. Charles G. Finney a Presbyterian-Congregational preacher became the focal point of this movement with his emphasis on Wesley's concept of the holy life. Revivalism swept the country, becoming more emotional the closer to the frontier it reached, though it was not totally a frontier movement. Under Timothy Dwight, one third of the students at Yale University were converted. But among the early western settlers whose lives were mainly isolated, the camp meeting and the revival meeting met many needs. It was a rare opportunity to be together with many other people. In the early stages, emotionalism was rampant. But this began to subside as the movement progressed. These meetings, sometimes attended by thousands of people, were often an attraction to those who were always referred to as "rowdies." These men would try to disrupt the meetings, which were usually held on Saturday nights. However, most preachers of the time were adept at handling these fellows. One preacher remarked that he could turn the other cheek when he was threatened, but when the church was threatened "it arouses the lion in me." One revival preacher used to put together a company composed of choir singers and other volunteers. Preceded by a trumpeter, they would parade through the crowd, slowly forming a circle around the troublemakers. They would ring them in to the center of the crowd where the announcement was made that while the other people in attendance were joined in the holy life, there were some who were not yet sanctified and who might therefore take action against the rowdies. Nearly always, the rowdies would slink away, their cowardice evident by their actions.

~

About that time, Reverend Rezin Hammond entered the scene and delivered the first sermon in Indianapolis by a Methodist preacher. It is recorded that he spoke from a log and his hearers sat around on fallen trees and stumps. This took place on the location of the present Soldiers' and Sailors' Monument. Most histories date this in 1820, though the records in Roberts Park Church date it in 1819. Hammond was buried in Charlestown. Reverend William Cravens was assigned to the congregation in 1821.

In Indianapolis, a log church was built on the south side of Maryland Street between Meridian Street and Illinois Street. In 1829, the brick Wesley Chapel was built on the southwest corner

Roberts Park Church.

of what is now Monument Circle. Records indicate that some 635 Methodists resided in Indianapolis which had recently been chosen by the Indiana legislature to be the capital city of the state. They were gathered in two congregations, divided by Meridian Street. The one on the west side became Meridian Street Church, the one to the east became Roberts Chapel, destined to later become Roberts Park. Located on the northeast corner of Market Street and Pennsylvania Street, the cornerstone of Roberts Chapel was

Reverend Rezin Hammond.

laid by the same Bishop Matthew Simpson who would later preach the funeral sermon for the services of Abraham Lincoln. The church was named after Bishop Robert R. Roberts, the first Indiana bishop. If we read the histories of those two churches today, we discover that both congregations claim to have been the first Methodist Church in Indianapolis.

~

In 1851, the preachers of the North Indiana Conference, formed in 1844, petitioned the General Conference to be allowed to divide into two conferences. This was approved and, accordingly, the Northwest Conference came into being. It is reported that one reason for this change was to keep the number of preachers small enough that the communities where the meeting was held would be able to, as one author put the matter, see to "the entertainment" of the delegates.

CHAPTER THREE

That execrable sum of all villainies, commonly called the slave trade—go on in the name of God, and in the power of his might, til even American slavery, the vilest that ever saw the sun, shall vanish away before it.
—John Wesley

The Black Church and the Civil War

It was during the mid-century that many Negro spirituals were written, and it was reported that long after the white folks had given up and gone to bed, the black worshipers were still going strong. As Norwood reports, "Around the campfires were heard the rich harmonies of 'Roll, Jordan, Roll;' 'O Sinner, Run To Jesus,' and 'Hark, from the Tomb the Doleful Sound.'"

One fifth of the population of America was black in the year 1800. Ninety percent were slaves. The slave population doubled by 1830, though by then one in seven black persons was free. As reported by Frederick Norwood, the black church has always had five definite characteristics: (1) They are black controlled, (2) they have been involved in the everyday life of the people, (3) they have given members a sense of worthiness, identity, and "somebodiness," (4) they have emphasized evangelism with direct witness to saving love in Jesus Christ, and (5) they have adjusted to the changing conditions of society over the long run.

The westward moving forces which so shaped white Methodism had far less effect on the black church. At one point, in the early part of the nineteenth century, only 12 percent of black Americans were members of a church. The Baptists and the Methodists quickly moved to include blacks in their membership. The Baptist Church appealed because its church polity allowed local control, unlike the Methodist Church with its bishops and presiding elders. Methodist worship, however, attracted black worshipers because early Methodist worship was emotional, evangelistic, and encouraging of free expression. By the eve of the Civil War, there were 215,000 black Methodists in America.

In the north, blacks were welcomed into the congregations and were not required to sit in any special part of the church. In the south, however, as the movement grew, separated seating came into fashion. A Reverend Pilmore reported preaching in one church where the ushers prohibited any black person from entering until all whites were seated. As the service began, the pulpit collapsed, and the services had to be moved outside. Some felt God's sense of humor was evident that day.

In 1800, black preachers were ordained in the Methodist Church as deacons, and by 1812 as elders, though this rule was never written into the *Discipline*. Regrettably, as slavery became more and more accepted, especially in the South, the prejudiced treatment of black Methodists became more common though abolitionist groups did begin to flourish. As early as May 26, 1785, Bishops Asbury and Coke of the Methodist Episcopal Church visited George Washington in Mount Vernon to appeal for the abolition of slavery in America. One of Asbury's favorite preachers was a black circuit rider Reverend Harry "Black Harry" Hosier who traveled with Asbury at times and was obviously an effective preacher.

It is of interest to note that foremost among the explanations of the beginning of the term "Hoosier" for an Indiana resident relates to Reverend Harry Hosier. Hosier was a powerful Methodist preacher, widely acclaimed at the time. Born in the 1750s as a slave, he was one of the most prominent evangelists during Asbury's years. Although midwestern camp meetings joined blacks and whites in worship, southerners disapproved. Linking Reverend Hosier with midwesterners and especially people living in Indiana territory, they began to refer to residents with a slight corruption of the name, somewhat disparagingly, as "Hoosiers." If this is true, it entwines our Indiana heritage with black history.

One early record states that Hosier "acted as a servant, or 'driver' for the eminent itinerants, but excelled them all in popularity as a preacher, sharing with them in their public services, not only in black but in white congregations." Of Hosier's popularity, Reverend Abel Stephens, writing in the mid-nineteenth century, reported that "Asbury acknowledges that the best way to obtain a large congregation was to announce that Harry would preach; the multitude preferring him to the bishop himself."

It seems Hosier temporarily took to drink and was gone for a time. But "God restored him to the joys of his salvation" and Harry quit drinking and rejoined his preaching friends. Of his death in 1810, Stephens wrote that he "was borne to the grave by a great procession of both white and black admirers, who buried him as a hero, once overcome, but finally victorious."

Many black people, however, wanted their own denomination, a church which could meet the specific needs of the black man and woman in the Americas of the early–nineteenth century. Two main denominations resulted, the African Methodist Church, founded in Philadelphia, formed under the leadership of one of the great early black leaders, a former slave named Richard Allen, and the African Methodist Episcopal Zion (AME) founded in New York under the leadership of Peter Williams. Both churches refused to allow segregation in their services and both had a few white members. The AME Church became a force for justice, with Bishop Allen leading a movement to refuse the purchase of slave-made goods. As the Civil War approached, many blacks in the north left the Methodist Episcopal Church to join one of the black denominations, whereas in the south, blacks remained in the ME Church. Thus the stage was set for the slavery issue to divide Methodism.

Though several years of turmoil underlay the slavery issue, most—though not all—northern preachers adamantly opposed slavery, while most—though not all—southern preachers supported slavery. One southern bishop James Osgood Andrew married into a slaveholding family and was ordered by the leadership of the Methodist Episcopal Church to either set his slaves free or resign as bishop. He refused, and in the end, a plan of separation was created in 1844 which resulted in the separation of the southern conferences from the church and their reorganization into the Methodist Episcopal Church, South, on May 17, 1845. That church's structure mirrored the northern church. While the reader is presumably shocked to think that Methodist pastors favored slaveholding, a word may be spoken to explain that they did urge slaveholders to treat their slaves with respect and kindness. In the New Testament book Philemon, one finds this very situation in which Paul commends to the slave that he be respectful of his master and that the master be respectful of his slaves. Nonetheless, the northern conferences all accorded with the words of John Wesley when he spoke of "that execrable sum of all villainies, commonly called the slave trade. . . ." Many a Methodist in the South helped build the Underground Railroad. The name of Harriet Tubman stands forth among the courageous people who made this work. Tubman made nineteen trips down into slavery country and is known to have helped some three hundred slaves make their way to freedom.

In 1895, Booker T. Washington wrote *Up from Slavery,* and a few years later, William E. B. Dubois wrote *Souls of Black Folk.* In 1910, the National Association for the Advancement of Colored People (NAACP) was formed. Writers like Countee Cullen and Langston Hughes followed. All were calling for a new understanding of the black consciousness, both by blacks and by whites. By the late 1940s, black history was becoming a movement. Other organizations were formed to band black people together, to empower them in their move toward freedom—not just freedom as the absence of restraints, but freedom as inclusion in the American dream as full-fledged partners. Then came the Congress of Racial Equality and the Student Nonviolent Coordinating Committee. Black churches grew rapidly. Frederick

University Methodist Church, Indianapolis, was established as a biracial congregation in 1966. Photo by Lynne DeMichele.

Norwood observed that the role of the black church in black communities was unique and different from the role of white churches. "The church was 'home' to the black person in a very special sense," he wrote. "They have found a larger and more significant share of their lives in their churches: hence, their minister has played a larger place in their communities." Norwood cites Adam Clayton Powell and Martin Luther King Jr. as two examples of the centrality of the role of the minister in the black consciousness.

In 1966, an attempt was made to start a new Methodist Church in Indianapolis, designed to have an evenly divided black and white membership. The church, University Methodist Church at Fifty-ninth and Grandview, was patterned after a then successful church in Chicago. With high hopes, a building was constructed, a black man named Reverend George Rice was assigned as pastor, an administrative board was created, another church was closed, and the congregation was moved with the hope—on the part of the white cadre—that a successful black and white church could be built. A number of dedicated laypeople, like the Halbert Kunz family who transferred there from St. Luke's Church, Melvin Chestnut, and Mrs. Robert Lee from University Church, made gallant efforts to make this work. It was not to be. Word drifted down that the Chicago church had become all black. A few determined whites attended University Church, but while they were treated graciously, the desired warm sense of communal fellowship did not take place. Robert DeFrantz, executive director of the black community center Flanner House, gave this explanation: "In most black people's lives, white people call the shots. At work, in government, in the marketplace—in every area 'Whitey' runs things. The one place where the black man is in charge is his church. He wants to keep it that way." DeFrantz went on to explain that only if virtually all officers of University Church were black could a harmonious blending be possible. Mr. Carnell Scott, a black leader in the North Conference, today feels there were other issues beyond DeFrantz's explanation. Nonetheless, while University was a fine church with a strong congregation, it did not become the mix of blacks and whites which was intended.

Indiana was not a slaveholding state. The population of Indiana in the 1860s was relatively small, and the church was in its formative stage. There isn't much evidence of Indiana's involvement in the issue of slavery until the advent of the Civil War. Perhaps the supreme commentary regarding Methodist involvement in the Civil War comes from Abraham Lincoln: "It is no fault in others that the Methodist Church sends more soldiers to the field, more nurses to the hospital, and more prayers to heaven than any. God bless the Methodist Church."

An important footnote to the Civil War's tragic division between Americans—and between Methodists—is the fact that one memorable day in 1876, a delegation of leaders from the Methodist Episcopal Church, South, attended the General Conference of the Methodist Episcopal Church at Baltimore. This reestablished harmonious relations between the people of the two churches. An effort was finally being made to effect reconciliation between the two churches, North and South.

In the course of the development of the Methodist Church, there were numerous squabbles and many divisions. In addition to the separation in 1844–45, there was another break off which created the Methodist Protestant Church, established in 1828 over the issue of lay representation. Because of the slavery issue and some disagreements about the episcopacy, a second group broke away and called themselves the Wesleyan Methodist Church. Still another was the Free Methodist Church. One of the remarkable facts about Methodism is that it is a hierarchical, authority-driven organization which surprisingly seems to attract men and women with strong beliefs and opinions and a great deal of courage in asserting such beliefs. Like a large, thoroughly devoted family that loves a good battle, Methodists through the ages have brought about a strong church by honoring the opinions of those with whom we disagree and by allowing the free expression of diverging opinions and beliefs in the public arena.

~

It was the way of the world in the times we have reviewed that men did the outdoor work for the church. It is only right that their heroic works be remembered. It would be easy, however, to overlook the yeomanly (or is that yeowomanly?) efforts on the part of Methodist women, who in many ways made the circuit-riding ministries possible. Most society meetings were held in homes, and it was the women who made the preparations. As Reverend A. T. Goodwin pointed out in an address to the Methodist Historical Society at Indiana Asbury University (now DePauw University) in 1869, many a housewife had to spend hours— maybe days—getting her place ready for the arrival of a preacher and his locally acquired entourage who, once the services were concluded, very often accepted her invitation to remain for dinner. The visiting preacher, Mr. Goodwin pointed out, never thought to invite the good reverend and the long-suffering hostess to his own dinner table.

Goodwin also reminded us that married circuit riders, who were the majority in the later years of that ministry, were able to do their wonderful work because of the support they received at home. Writing about one rider, Allen Wiley, who served in the Fort Wayne circuit of the North Conference in the 1820s and '30s, said:

> But what of his wife whom he left in the cabin, two miles from any neighbor, with five small children, not one of whom was old enough to render any aid toward the support of the family? And it was not grudgingly, nor of constraint that she gave him up to the work of ministry, but, on the contrary, knowing the desire of his heart to be wholly devoted to the ministry. Leaving the heroic husband, the growing and popular preacher, to travel long journeys, to preach to large congregations and to be caressed everywhere by loving and adoring friends, pursuing congenial studies under more favorable surroundings than his farm could ever have afforded, let us look in upon that heroic wife with her family of five children . . . for many years unaided by the presence or counsel of the husband, or by any considerable material aid from him. It was hers, there alone on that farm, not only to spin, and weave, and make, and cook, and wash for those children, but to train them for the church and for God. Was she not the greater hero of the two?

Not all wives served in domestic ways. Reverend Goodwin also spoke of another circuit rider Joseph Tarkington. A heroic servant to be sure. When he married, Goodwin added: "But when Maria Slawson mounted her horse with her bridal outfit on her back, and in her saddle bags, for a tour from Switzerland County to Monroe County—when she rode all day in the rain, and sat up all night in a salt boiler's shanty with nothing to eat but a biscuit in twenty-four hours, she displayed the material that heroes are made of." Yes, we do well to remind ourselves that the building of the Methodist Church through those trying though wonderful years was a joint effort of men and women of faith. Goodwin remarked that he could not by any means record the names of all the gallant women of whom he knew. He did, however, choose to leave in memory these names: "Mrs. Isaac Dunn of Lawrenceburg; Mrs. Caleb A. Craft of

Rising Sun; Mrs. Charles Bashett of Madison; Mrs. Roland T. Carr of Rushville." So may they be honored to this day.

∽

Indiana was a very patriotic state during the Civil War, featuring rallies, political speeches, and sermons that supported the antislavery motives of the Union Army. Abraham Lincoln once paid a visit to Indiana, a long-remembered event. Until more recent years, Memorial Day celebrations were held in every small town in Indiana. Replete with red, white, and blue bunting and patriotic speeches, veterans and their families, as well as people who had forebears in the various wars, along with many a patriotic citizen attended. Held in the local park, these celebrations usually included ice cream and hot dogs, both a dependable attraction for the kids. Veterans solemnly stood at attention before the flag for which they had fought. Until the mid-1960s, patriotism was held to be an honorable sentiment. Only in the sixties was the word *chauvinism* substituted for *patriotism*.

In the years following the Civil War, changes were taking place within the church as well as in nearly every facet of American life. One change was in worship, which was a result of the increasing amount of education required of clergy, many of whom were now attending Biblical institutes. This naturally affected church worship, which began to move toward a less emotionalistic, more reasoned style. Not all the old-timers applauded this change. Peter Cartwright did not like these "newfangled ideas." At the General Conference of 1860, he signed the autograph book of John Scripps with this remark: "I am a good old Methodist preacher, and am fully opposed to all innovations." As one biographer observed, "Some young ministers of 1860, already being trained in the new biblical institutes, found this tough old curmudgeon hard to take." And so as usually happens when a new generation comes along, the circuit riders with their independent spirits and their ingrained styles, which were so effective on the new frontier, were stepping aside for a new breed of ministers who would face Reconstruction and the new day to follow the Civil War.

~

Some interesting insights remain from this period thanks to Reverend William Graham who left some roughly written memoirs from his years as an Indiana pastor from 1844 until his retirement in 1894. Graham established himself early by leading the congregation of the La Porte circuit in a building program which succeeded despite the assurance of the district superintendent that Graham could not do it. Some time later, Graham was appointed to a charge in Lafayette. One of his responsibilities was to oversee the moving of the church building. We learn quite a bit about the life of a preacher in those days by observing some of Graham's problems. Graham noted:

> At that time the people here were peculiarly contentious, and I could not but note the difference between them and those of LaPorte. The people of LaPorte were divided in opinion but conciliatory, while those of La Fayette [*sic*] contended with malignance of feeling—in short, they were inclined to be quarrelsome, not only the officers, but the private members, and the women.

He did, however, succeed in convincing the people to make the move—at which point his troubles apparently really began.

Mr. Graham left some lengthy descriptions of his difficulties, including an illness called "milk-sickness," common in those days. The physician gave him Calamon, a then current medicine which should have killed him, but didn't. So, in due course, Graham stood and watched as a hopelessly incompetent carpenter ("favoritism gave it to him") struggled to have some roof trusses raised into place, completely without success. The editor of Graham's memoirs noted that merely because one is a good Methodist does not mean he or she is a good carpenter.

A large group of men was present, none of whom could think of any way to get those trusses into position. Graham reports:

Fletcher Place Methodist Episcopal Church Sunday School picnic circa 1888.
Photo courtesy of DePauw University Archives and Special Collections.

> I finally took the contractor to a side and told him that if he
> would give me charge of the hands, I would raise the two bents
> [trusses] he had put together. He could do nothing else, and told
> me that I might try, but that he knew it could not be done.
> Mindful of my experience in such matters, I made sure that all
> parts, ropes, pulleys, and guys were all properly arranged, and
> proceeding deliberately, raised the two bents and anchored them
> on the wall. After that there was no more trouble.

One gets the impression that a mid-nineteenth-century preacher
needed somewhat different skills than are expected of a preacher
today.

Another example of this truth is the life of Joseph Collins, an
early preacher about whom the other preachers loved to tell
stories. One story told of the time Collins was riding to a camp
meeting and encountered a rather angry young man who said he
was also heading to the meeting because he had a grudge against
the preacher. He and Collins rode for some time. Finally, Collins

asked the young fellow why he was so mad at the preacher. The young man gave some reason lost to history but then said that it was a Reverend Collins whom he was going to give a beating. Collins thereupon identified himself and stated that it would be best if the matter were settled before they reached the camp meeting. The two dismounted from their horses, and Reverend Collins grabbed the young man by the scruff of his neck and the seat of his pants and threw the poor guy over a fence. The young man got to his feet, straightened his clothes, and said, "If you'll just help my horse over the fence, I'll be on my way." Mr. Collins often quoted a passage that he was "strong in the Lord." He obviously meant more than strong in the faith.

It is significant that little reference is made in Graham's memoirs to the Civil War at all. It would seem, if one were to use this pastor's recorded experiences, the war was not uppermost in people's minds. He did refer to the death of Lincoln. He wrote:

It was during this conference year—on the memorable 14th of April, 1865, that the assassination of Lincoln occurred. Never before had I witnessed such universal expression of deep grief and profound excitement as that morning, when the court house bell was tolled and the citizens gathered on the public square by the thousands. The excitement was intense.

By this time Graham, having served in Crawfordsville since his time in Lafayette, was appointed to Asbury Chapel, Terre Haute, by Bishop Osman C. Baker.

Apparently, as the end of the war seemed to be in sight, the Union forces were short of men. Each county had a quota of men for service. If a county failed to produce enough volunteers, conscription was the answer. Graham was forty-five years old and subject to the draft. Vigo County had fallen short, so Graham faced a call up. The law provided that a man could pay to have a substitute serve in his place. As a result, many men waited to volunteer until someone was willing to pay them. Graham arranged to pay twenty five dollars as a first installment to have someone else take his place in the service. He observed that he was frequently in the office of the provost marshall, a member of his church, "which in itself was enough to make one sick of the rebellion." By the standards of our own time, Mr. Graham appears something less than a patriot, having paid a substitute to fight in his place, and then writing of the unnamed man: "I hope my substitute was not killed, but if he was it was the result of his own contract, rather than mine."

One other memorable historical event is recounted by Graham. Presiding Elder Benjamin Winans of Indianapolis, a close friend of Graham's, held a quarterly conference at Strange Chapel, Indianapolis, then boarded a train to return to his home in Lafayette. The train was hit head-on by an unscheduled cattle car driven by a substitute engineer, and thirty men were killed, including Reverend Winans. Most of the other casualties were Union soldiers travelling home on leave. The bodies could not be identified, so all were buried in a common grave in the northwest corner of Greenbush Cemetery.

CHAPTER FOUR

*They pray, they sing, they
preach the best.
And do the Devil most molest,
If Satan had his vicious way,
He'd kill and damn
them all today.
They are despised by
Satan's train,
Because they shout and
preach so plain,
I'm bound to march in
endless bliss,
And die a shouting Methodist.
—Old Camp Meeting Song*

Turn of the Century: Post–Civil War to World War 1

The Methodist Episcopal Church grew rapidly in the early years following the Civil War. One issue which plagued the clergy was the role of a bishop. Is a bishop someone of a higher order than an ordained elder? Or is a bishop an ordained elder given a specific job? The answer to this question addressed the issue of democracy versus authority. As the years passed, the Methodist Church became both more democratic and more authoritative. Laity were finally allowed to vote at Annual Conference and at General Conference. At the same time, anyone who has served on a parish personnel committee (the names change from time to time) is aware that when it comes down to the choice of a pastor to replace an outgoing pastor, the church is very authoritative. On the other hand, any bishop who acts in a way which may appear high-handed to a congregation will discover how tight finances can become if a congregation of some size decides not to pay their apportionments. Mercifully, authority has been exercised responsibly, with rare exceptions, and cooler heads tend to rule when upset parishioners counsel financial rebellion.

Culver Methodist Episcopal Church Ladies Aid society, circa 1895.
Photo courtesy of DePauw University Archives and Special Collections.

As the national economy of America began to prosper more and more, Methodists prospered as well. As this happened, the demand for educated clergy and for a more rational style of worship developed. The demands made on members began to appear excessive to some. "The class meeting was in real trouble," wrote Frederick Norwood. "The decline which had set in about mid-century continued its erosion. . . . Since people didn't attend regularly, attendance was made voluntary instead of compulsory, the decline of the class meeting and the decline of the itinerancy were related." As clergy moved into parsonages instead of showing up every few weeks or months on horseback, the need for talented laity to run the church declined. This had the effect of reducing the leadership involvement of the laity, and in all likelihood explains, at least in part, the decline in participation in the class meetings.

Also, the style of ministry of the circuit riders with Bible and hymnal gave way to the educated clergy. "In the same way the camp meeting was domesticated into the summer Chautauqua," wrote Norwood, "the plaintive voices of those struggling under conviction and glad cries of those rejoicing in salvation faded into the distance, while the Chautauqua lecturer dispensed popular culture and the preacher preached what he had learned in the new liberal-minded seminaries." Referring to this new style, William Graham, the old circuit rider remarked, "Less thought and more sound would have been preferred by the people generally." Perhaps today's preachers can understand this inclination to appear knowledgeable on the part of neophytes of all professions. I'm embarrassed to recall the opening line in one of my very early sermons in my student church which went like this: "As we all know, it is written in the Pentateuch that . . ." Now the truth is, I had never heard of the Pentateuch until three days earlier, and I'm sure none of my parishioners had ever heard of it either. I was showing off.

The issue of education was a divisive one in the mid-nineteenth-century Methodist Church. In a biography of Reverend Joseph Tarkington, a circuit rider until his appointment to the church at Milroy, and later to St. Omer, Greensburg, Belleview, and Westport, author David Kimbrough wrote: "The growing wealth of the Methodist Church and many members of its congregations often conflicted with the Methodists' earlier emphasis on egalitarianism. The upper class Methodists often resented the traditional and poor church members." Sadly, class distinctions marked the early church just as they all too often do today. And another effect of this increasing emphasis on education was, in the opinions of many of those less-educated Methodists, a decline in the fervor of the message. Supervisor Allen Wiley, decrying the changing effectiveness of Methodist revivals, wrote in 1846: "There was much more preaching talent at those meetings than the former; but there was not the same zeal in the preachers or the people." Bishop Edwin Holt Hughes, former president of DePauw University, put it this way: "To conservatives, liberals lacked piety; to liberals, conservatives lacked scholarship."

In a somewhat disturbing assessment of the move toward an educated clergy, sociologists Roger Finke of Purdue University and Rodney Stark of the department of religion at the University of

Washington recently published an evaluation of the religious situation at the turn of the century (into the twentieth century) this way:

> Thus we see the Methodists as they were transformed from sect to church. Their clergy were increasingly willing to condone the pleasures of this world and to de-emphasize sin, hellfire, and damnation; this lenience struck highly responsive chords in an increasingly affluent, influential, and privileged membership. This is, of course, the fundamental dynamic by which sects are transformed into churches, thereby losing the vigor and the high octane faith that caused them to succeed in the first place.

Finke and Stark quoted George W. Wilson who, writing in 1904, put the matter even more directly, charging that "empty speculative babblings are uttered from pulpit, rostrum, and professor's chair . . . sermons are preached without a single appeal to the sinner to accept Jesus Christ now."

This disagreement between those who fervently urged the church to return to the fundamental theology of Wesley and the early church and those who pointed to archaeological research of the late–nineteenth century which revealed many underlying misunderstandings in the theology of the early Methodist Church was destined to smolder and eventually burst once more into flame in the latter part of the twentieth century.

~

Reverend Graham, by this time serving as presiding elder in Valparaiso, took a train to Chicago to hear the famous evangelist Dwight L. Moody. He was only marginally impressed. "Moody is not an orator but a plain blunt talker on the Bible and religion," he observed. "All around him on the platform sat pastors of the city churches, in every way his superiors in scholarship and oratory." One interesting consequence of this event was the emergence of a number of young preachers, some of them only recently ordained, who sought to emulate Moody's style and to gain entrance to the established Indiana churches in the North as evangelists. "Shallow imitators," Graham called them, "sorry and ridiculous caricatures." These fellows pestered the local clergy for a year or so before disappearing. Ministers of every era are familiar with the suddenly zealous young convert who seeks to explain to the pastor how wonderful God is, as though the pastor had not really learned this truth until the bright young thing arrived. They must, of course, be dealt with gently.

A presentation of the Methodist Church, "warts and all," suggests that we include a brief reference to the story of Reverend William Fred Pettit, pastor of Shawnee Mound Methodist Church in southwest Tippecanoe County, who became the object of widespread pity upon the death of his wife, Hattie, in 1889. Unhappily, a short time later, indictments were brought against Mr. Pettit and a local widow Elma C. Whitehead, who were revealed to have added strychnine to Hattie's tea. The upshot was that Mrs. Whitehead was released but Reverend Pettit went to prison and died there three years later. Reverend Graham had appeared as one of the witnesses.

～

In 1874 a new word entered the lexicon of the Methodist Church: Chautauqua. An Indian word meaning, literally "bag-tied in the middle," it is also the name of a lake northwest of New York City. The leaders of the church had begun to recognize the need for education, not only of its preachers and members, but most particularly of its Sunday school teachers. Some two thousand people met under the maple trees along the lake on August 10, 1874, to decide how to alleviate this growing problem. John Heyl Vincent, a preacher in charge of the Sunday schools of the Methodist Episcopal Church, North, presided. Thus was born a much loved Methodist institution. It had two dimensions. As a camp, Methodist families gathered there for innocent recreation and learning opportunities while spending time together in the pleasant surroundings of Lake Chautauqua—and this tradition continues today. Also, entrepreneurial religious leaders, not all Methodist, began leading weeklong tent meetings in small towns across

DePauw University, originally Indiana Asbury University.

America with preaching and teaching services, using the name Chautauqua. These meetings did not always have the high standards of the original, but nonetheless established an American religious tradition.

This was all part of a growing sense of need for education. In 1871, a seminary became the first department of Boston University. Other schools followed. The Methodist Episcopal Church, South, started what became Vanderbilt University. There followed Duke, Southern Methodist, Emory—today nearly 50 percent of all students in Protestant-related colleges are in Methodist-related institutions.

As the need for education grew, one of America's finest universities was founded in 1884: DePauw University. Actually, the institution was founded in 1837 with the name of Indiana Asbury University. The early institution was devoted more to character development and to religion than to scholarship. It seems the early Methodist leaders were concerned at the lack of any educational institution under the auspices of the Methodist

Church, particularly since the Presbyterians had already established two schools, Wabash College and Hanover College, and they felt it was time for Methodists to place a greater emphasis on education. The new institution was authorized at a meeting in October 1836 under the leadership of Bishop Robert R. Roberts. Referring to the institution as a seminary, twenty-five trustees were authorized, and a search for a location began. Greencastle was chosen because the good citizens of that city donated twenty-five thousand dollars to the project, a large sum at that time. Unofficial reports insist that another reason was the contention by one Dr. Tarvin Cowgill that "people never die in Greencastle, although for convenience they have a cemetery there." It is interesting to note that in 1837, Greencastle was a tiny frontier village with unpaved streets. The school's function was somewhat different from what it would eventually become—records show that the first class was composed of forty male students with an age range of thirteen to thirty-eight.

At the outset of the Civil War, a large percentage of the student body left school and formed the Asbury Guards. Moved to Camp Morton in Indianapolis, the majority lost interest when they learned they must enlist for three years, so they returned to Greencastle. However, a few enlisted in the 10th Indiana Volunteer Regiment and fought in Virginia, Kentucky, and Tennessee. All told, 450 Indiana Asbury men served in the Union army. A few served in the Confederate Army. Shortly after the end of the Civil War, women were admitted to the school.

This institution has a grand history and was destined to gain nationwide recognition for its splendid scholarship and its successful graduates. But in the early 1880s, Indiana Asbury University had serious financial troubles. The head of the board of trustees, Washington C. DePauw, offered to make a major financial donation to save the institution. In appreciation, the school was renamed DePauw University in 1884. The change may very well have been significant as, though religion remained a major force on the campus with a well-established YMCA, the school had really begun by this time to make education its primary emphasis. There were probably psychological as well as economic benefits to the

change. One disapproving author, however, troubled by the less-
ening influence of religion at DePauw, theorized that Bishop Asbury
probably breathed a sigh of relief somewhere in heaven at the name
change. As recently as 1937, the minutes of the Annual Conference
included this observation: "DePauw has one reason alone to justify
her existence and that is the specific function of Christian education. At this point she has to make her unique contribution." In
modern times, Eugene C. Pulliam, one of Indiana's premiere jour-
nalists, said that he was "quite sure there was no college in
America, which on a per capita student basis has produced as many
outstanding newspaper men and women as have come out of
DePauw University." By the year 2000, DePauw was ranked thirty-
ninth among the top fifty private colleges in America, according to
U.S. News & World Report. President Robert Bottoms's reaction
was to the point: "We're tickled to death."

In 1854, shortly after the founding of Indiana Asbury
University, a small Methodist college was started in the town of
Moore's Hill by a man named John Moore. Known as Moore's
Hill College, it catered mainly to local people in southern
Indiana, plus a few students from Kentucky. Financial problems
plagued the school, and the trustees realized a relocation was
necessary. Thus in 1917, the decision was made and sanctioned
by the Annual Conference to move the school to Evansville. On
September 16, 1919, the doors opened to Evansville College, and
104 students enrolled the first day. Like DePauw, Evansville
College (later the University of Evansville) would distinguish
itself by its fine academic record and the achievements of its
many graduates.

One result of the growing emphasis on education would be the
effect of science on theology. Older generations of bishops and
clergy opposed the secularization of the universities, a phenomenon destined to grow in most religiously founded colleges. But
while some of the very conservative educational institutions would
hold their ground, most Methodist schools would experience
weakened denominational ties. This did not mean the schools
would totally eschew support from the Methodist system. It did,
however, mean that while a friendly and supportive relationship

between church and school remained, the schools very rightly insisted on educational freedom without any dictation by a religious body. So evolution was taught. And as the sciences raised questions about previous assumptions regarding biblical history, educated clergy within Indiana Methodism began to move slowly but surely away from ultraconservative theology. The trajectory of this movement would reach dramatic proportions in the later part of the twentieth century.

~

Life in Indiana was not easy as the nineteenth century drew to a close. Farming was the dominant vocation among Hoosiers, except for those living in Indianapolis and in the extreme northern cities adjacent to Chicago. Indianapolis eventually

Riverside United Brethren Church, circa 1903. The twenty-eight charter members, organized by Henry C. Marsh, first met in a bakeshop. After two denominational mergers, the current congregation is known as Riverside United Methodist Church in Muncie. Photo courtesy of DePauw University Archives and Special Collections.

became known as the Crossroads of America. Indiana was divided between rural farmers and the growing number of people engaged in manufacturing, particularly in new developments occasioned in the Calumet area by the invention of the horseless carriage. Cities like Whiting, East Chicago, Gary, and Hammond built tenements, and men seeking employment in the coal, steel, and automotive industries arrived in growing numbers. Jack Detzler wrote of the Northwest Indiana Conference at that time:

> This conference achieved its individuality by successfully shifting from its pioneer setting into a rural conference which embraced the highly industrialized northwest Indiana cities. The varied problems of the rural and urban areas were courageously met with a humanitarian social creed. The Conference came to stress social doctrines almost exclusively—parishioners were no longer interested in fine theological points.

In Indianapolis, the southern suburb of Beech Grove became a central location for the railroad industry. The downtown area was graced by a slaughterhouse and meat packaging plant, whose presence was especially noticeable on a breezy summer day. Small businesses were begun in growing numbers, many of them foundry operations. Department stores arrived with names like Ayres, Wassons, and Blocks. Down in southern Indiana in the vicinity of towns like Bloomington and Spencer, extensive limestone deposits were discovered, and Indiana was thus destined to be the center of the limestone industry nationwide. Indianapolis soon had a reputation as a quiet, rather unexciting but fairly safe place to live and work. A growing black population lived in areas referred to as inner-city neighborhoods, most of them poor. Indiana Avenue came alive with a rich black culture which still thrives. Madam Walker, reputed to be the first black woman millionaire, proved that in spite of the many barriers placed before energetic blacks, success for them was still possible.

So began the building of Methodist churches in every small and not-so-small town in Indiana. Membership grew rapidly and

The Methodist Children's Home, originally located in Greencastle, 1955, is now in Lebanon. Photo courtesy of DePauw University Archives and Special Collections.

by 1924 there were about 300,000 members of the approximately thirteen hundred churches in what was then called the Indianapolis area (which covered the entire state of Indiana, later called the Indiana area). It is interesting to note that most of the members, some 280,000 people, were enrolled in Sunday schools. Methodism continued to place great emphasis on outreach and by 1924 had already established thirty-six homes for the aged, forty-five orphanages, and eleven homes for working girls nationwide. Bible schools were still much a part of Indiana churches. Weekday religious education programs were also established nationwide. The Cincinnati area had the largest Methodist membership in the nation. The Indianapolis area was second.

In Indianapolis, Roberts Chapel Church members decided to move to a new location, and the present location at the corner of Vermont Street and Delaware Street was chosen. This project began in 1868, and the building completed, less some later additions, on August 27, 1876. The dedication was performed by

Epworth League, 1890, of the German Methodist Episcopal Church in Bedford. The congregation was founded in 1872 by German immigrants; today it is Grace United Methodist Church. Photo courtesy of DePauw University Archives and Special Collections.

Bishop Simpson who had also laid the earlier cornerstone in 1845. Simpson was DePauw University's first president.

One event worth remembering was the fourth international convention of Epworth League, which was convened in Indianapolis in July 1899. The hosts were the Methodist youth of the church. In attendance were well over a thousand black youths. To fully appreciate the Christian spirit of those young people, one must recall that segregation was taken for granted at that time. Some news reporters asked the kids where they planned to seat the Negro delegates. After talking to the leaders, the kids wrote: "There was no plan to segregate the blacks attending the convention, and the Negro delegates will come and go as they please and sit where they please just as the other delegates will."

Bill Loveday, current president and CEO of Methodist Hospital in Indianapolis, also reports the splendid fact that the proceeds from that successful gathering of young people, some

$4,750—a very large sum at that time—was donated to the fund for the building of Methodist Hospital. The hospital was completed in 1908. Now, as part of Clarian Health Partners, it is the third largest hospital in America in terms of admissions. Methodist young people have always been an important source of energy and good spirit on behalf of all that matters most.

~

World War 1 sent thousands of young American boys to the trenches of France with the usual disruption of farming and industry. The first soldier killed in that war was a Methodist, Corporal James B. Gresham, a member of Simpson Sunday school in Evansville. Unfortunately, many more of Indiana's sons would die in France. A note in the 1924 conference report stated that "in the recent great conflict no church exceeded the Methodists, either in the number of soldiers, sailors and nurses furnished, or in the enlistment of resources."

CHAPTER FIVE

Those who benefit from social injustice are naturally less capable of understanding its real character than are those who suffer from it.
—Reinhold Niebuhr

The Depression and Beyond

One tragic chapter in Indiana history was the reign of the Ku Klux Klan under the leadership of D. C. Stephenson who actually stated at one court hearing, "I am the law in Indiana." For a time it appeared there was truth to that outrageous assertion. Stephenson was unquestionably riding high for a time. Secretary of State Edward L. Jackson, who became governor in 1924, was linked with the Klan. Finally, thanks in large part to the courageous work of the prosecutorial staff led by Asa J. Smith, a DePauw graduate, Stephenson was found guilty of kidnapping a woman named Madge Oberholtzer, taking her on a train, and abusing her so that she committed suicide "to spare her mother the disgrace." Stephenson went to prison in 1925, and the Klan in Indiana collapsed. However, a dark note relates to the Methodist Church. Asa Smith, a Methodist, reported that one day he was invited to a meeting at a Methodist church in Wabash where he had been raised. When he arrived, he was shocked to realize it was a meeting to recruit a group of Klan members. He further reported that many Methodist churches in the Indiana area were reputed to be sympathetic with the Klan.

In the Northwest Indiana Conference, one pastor told of being invited to a Klan meeting by two of his parishioners. At the meeting, the pastor became incensed and shouted his anger at the hateful words and attitudes that were displayed towards Catholics and Negroes. He departed the meeting and reported that the two church members never returned to his church. It was also reported that the Montrose Church in Terre Haute was divided over the issue of the Klan. Reverend George B. Jones refused to accept any money from the Klan, despite his congregation's financial problems. According to a history of that church, "This caused so much strife that it did not seem advisable for him to return for a second year." Fortunately, those days are long gone and few Methodists in later days would have approved such conduct. One would like to think that many

Methodist Hospital, 1808. Photo courtesy of DePauw University Archives and Special Collections.

people failed to realize the evil nature of the Klan, assuming it to be more of a fraternal organization. If so, they were dead wrong.

~

In 1929 the stock market crashed. Large fortunes were lost. Not only paper fortunes, but actual fortunes since stock was often purchased on margins, and shareholders lost not only the values of their stock but the margin amounts they were required to produce. Suicides were not uncommon. Businesses failed. Unemployment spread. Educated, successful people were reduced to seeking out menial employment which, in turn, reduced less educated people to standing in long bread and soup lines. Thank God for the Salvation Army and many other church-related institutions that did everything they could to keep the hungry populace alive.

Physical hunger was not the only consequence of the Great Depression. Formerly successful or at least upward-striving men and women experienced devastating losses of self-esteem as they found themselves unable to maintain their living standards. Many were forced to go with hat in hand to friends or former colleagues who had survived more successfully to ask for small loans to provide food for the table. My own father, a sales manager for an insurance company, had invested in a grocery company that failed. He lost his investment but came home with a carload of canned cherries and green beans. The day our lights were turned off because Dad couldn't pay the light bill, we had beans and cherries by candlelight. We laughed and thought it was fun. Shortly after, he was critically injured in a car accident but remained in bed at home because he had no insurance for medical care. Long before he should have done so, he was up and trying to sell life insurance so we could remain in our home. That kind of courage was widespread as men and women all over America realized they could stand tall in the face of calamity. Where did they find the courage and faith for this? In their churches. Millions found it in their Methodist churches. Preachers reminded

Vacation Bible School class, 1920, Sacred Heart Methodist Episcopal Church, South Bend. Photo courtesy of DePauw University Archives and Special Collections.

people of words such as those of Saint Paul who wrote: "suffering produces endurance, and endurance produces character, and character produces hope, and hope does not disappoint us. . . ." (Rom. 5:3–5 NRSV). They told people about the words of Jesus, words which had slipped by many parishioners in the past, but which brought hope now: "Ask and it will be given you; search, and you will find; knock, and the door will be opened for you" (Matt. 8:7 NRSV). People learned that they could endure, that sometimes the simple things of life are best after all, and that the hope of which Paul wrote would apply to their own new futures. In the churches, the collective Methodist belt was tightened, and the people, realizing that when incomes stop at home they stop at church, began to find other means to keep their congregations intact. Trinity Church in South Bend cut its budget 45 percent. The members of Pittsboro Church cleared a swamp and were repaid with enough firewood to keep the church warm through the winter. It was a rare church that did not have to resort to strenuous efforts to meet operating budgets.

Methodist preachers shared the hard times. The typical minister was paid a small stipend, and beyond that, many depended on the occasional largess of farmer-members who would drop by with tomatoes, green beans, corn on the cob, and on rare occasions, some fresh meat. It was the custom then to include a 10 percent discount on local purchases, a small fee for the performance of a wedding, and the enclosure of a dollar bill in the preacher's Christmas card. Only thus did many clergy contrive to support their families, which often tended to be large. The preacher's home was always provided, which—in the private thinking of most clergy—was a mixed blessing. It spared the parsonage family the necessity of paying for the upkeep of the home, but the embarrassing custom of frequent walk-throughs by trustees and concerned women members was often viewed as a nuisance by clergy wives. Fortunately for the churches, prior to the modern mind-set of clergy wives and husbands, most clergy wives allowed themselves to become unpaid assistant ministers, making house calls, teaching Sunday school, playing the piano, and generally pitching in when there was work to be done. This is not to say that clergy spouses don't pitch in today, but back then it was taken for granted. Today it is optional. That's how it was—until the 1960s. As long as the average minister moved to a new charge every few years, the parsonage system was necessary for smooth transitions. It would take the raging inflation of the mid-seventies for congregations to realize that when a minister retires, he or she could be very hard pressed to find housing in an inflated market unless permitted to purchase a home while serving the church. Thus, pastorates lengthened, the housing allowance was born, and a growing percentage of clergy were enabled to buy homes of their own while serving the church.

~

The consequence of the Great Depression was twofold. It brought forth the best character traits of a nation of people who had learned how quickly bright dreams can end in darkness, yet how personal courage and faith could see them through. It also created in those people a deep awareness that nothing could ever be taken for granted. This deep, smoldering anxiety would play an important part in the events which lay ahead beyond World War 2. The children of the depression would be haunted by an inner sense of economic uncertainty to the end of their days. Author Kurt Vonnegut, who grew up in Indianapolis during the latter depression years, recently observed in an interview, with his typically salty directness, "I think our parents were so upset and confused and lost, not knowing what the hell to do with a failed capitalism, that because our parents were so unhappy from 1929 to 1941, we got out of town."

The social action impulse of Methodism, the social gospel, drove many a Methodist church to design new outreach programs, not just for members, but for the poor of every community. People today who have televisions, VCRs, cars, and government subsidies, yet can be defined as "below the poverty line," would be appalled to realize what poverty was like in the America of the thirties. Children literally sold apples on the street. The story was often told of a man who found a little girl crying on a street corner one cold afternoon. He asked the child what was wrong. She replied that her mother had sent her to the store with her last dollar, and she had somehow lost the dollar. The man thereupon took a dollar bill from his pocket and gave it to the child. As she headed toward the store with a smile and new hope, the story concludes that the man went down the street hoping to find another little child who needed a dollar. That spirit of generosity and compassion would characterize the Methodist churches throughout the depression years.

In Indianapolis, strong downtown churches like Roberts Park, Meridian Street, and Central Avenue Methodist Churches drew crowds. Broadway Church on the near north side joined them. Other denomination churches such as Second Presbyterian, First Baptist, and Christ Church Episcopal made the central city a locus for Christian outreach. People had cars. Thanks to Henry

Roberts Park Church, Indianapolis, was founded in 1821. Photo courtesy of DePauw University Archives and Special Collections.

Ford, the Model T followed by the Model A made local travel easy, and thus a few major downtown churches were prominent on the religious scene. The suburbs as a category did not yet exist. Neighborhoods existed. Broad Ripple was the end of the trolley line on the north side. Irvington Methodist Church was the "big steeple church" on the east side, located in a posh town within the community of Irvington. The west and south sides had not yet attracted the fine communities located there today. Neighborhood churches were built, and they concentrated their emphasis on Sunday schools and youth programs such as Epworth League, later to become the United Methodist Youth Fellowship. Women's groups took over such leadership roles as Women's Christian Temperance Union (WCTU). In 1924 the WCTU state president was a Methodist woman, Mrs. Culla Vayhinger. On campuses of state universities, the Wesley Foundation was active: at Purdue University through First Methodist Church, West Lafayette; at Indiana University through First Methodist Church, Bloomington.

By and large all was well. Or at least, all was getting better. America was beginning to dig its way out of the depression. Other nations were having problems. The Japanese were plaguing the Chinese with military depredations. The defeated Germans were said to be building a great new industrial complex. Average Americans did not pay a lot of attention to the other countries of the world. Isolation was in. "America first" was a byword. President Roosevelt assured Americans that the only thing we had to fear was "fear itself." Government programs like the Works Projects Administration (WPA) and the Civilian Construction Corps (CCC) were providing employment for the least employable of America's men. The churches were now free to devote their energies to evangelism and religious education.

Until December 7, 1941. Our world exploded that morning as Japanese planes bombed Pearl Harbor, Hawaii. America once again entered into a time of transition which would leave us dramatically changed. The new patriotism was far more ethical, enhanced by millions of young men who rallied to the armed forces and by mothers and fathers who proudly displayed little flags in their windows bearing blue stars which signified a son in service. A growing number of gold stars also appeared reminding the nation of the price it was paying for doing what was right. Rationing soon meant hardship and privation for most Americans. But it was generally accepted with good humor

Chaplain John D. Wolf conducts Christmas Eve worship, 1944, on the deck of the USS Funston in the Admiralty Islands (Western Pacific). During all wars of the past century, many hundreds of Indiana Methodist chaplains brought comfort, compassion, and courage to those in U.S. military service around the world.

and a sense of solidarity. As men left for service, women stepped up to fill their roles. Rosie the Riveter was a national symbol. Women were in aircraft factories; women were making tanks and artillery, and women were driving ambulances. True, they would have to return home when the men came back, but a new self-image had been born, one which would reemerge when their children came along. Women now knew they could do what men could do. Men and women of that generation stepped up, didn't flinch, paid an exorbitant price to preserve freedom, and never thought they had done anything special. Eighty-seven Methodist pastors from Indiana volunteered to serve as chaplains during the war. Most are deceased now, but several, including John Wolf (who is now retired and was once the youngest chaplain in the United States Navy), were able to participate in a North Conference celebratory service honoring these chaplains by

Bishop Woodie W. White in 1995. The oldest living former Indiana chaplain is Reverend Arthur Dale Giles who served in the Army Air Corps through World War 2. Ninety years old, he lives in Muncie. As for the churches, many of them established service organizations for servicemen home on leave, or as in Indianapolis, for men stationed at Fort Harrison.

The end of the war brought with it the proliferation of low priced, prefabricated homes clustered in outlying areas of all major cities—the flight to the suburbs had begun. That newfangled entertainment medium, television, had arrived. Neighbors gathered around the living rooms of friends who had one of the early sets. Live television produced some memorable moments, like the time one villain forgot his lines toward the end of a high tension thriller, just as he was about to commit a murder. Stumped, he turned toward the screen, shrugged his shoulders and, with an embarrassed smile, admitted he didn't know exactly what he was supposed to say. Someone must have been frantically developing video tapes at that point. But television introduced a new dimension to current events. People watched Senator McCarthy make a fool of himself while destroying innocent lives with his paranoia. Early news shows brought the harsh realities of the world into living rooms. People were slowly drawn together by a common culture as Milton Berle, Captain Kangaroo, Lucy and Desi, and so many other entertainers were shared by millions all over America at the same time. To a nation that still retained vivid memories of World War 2, it seemed to be a wonderful era—one which need never end.

The effects on the Methodist Church were immense. New church starts were numerous. While large downtown churches began to decline in membership, new congregations proliferated. Formerly small outlying churches experienced sudden growth. Forest Manor Church with Lawrence Cooper as pastor in Indianapolis, for example, grew from two hundred members to more than sixteen hundred members in just a few years. Old Bethel Church, a small, semi-rural congregation gained a thousand new members in a short time under the leadership of Ralph Henard as new neighborhoods opened up on the far east side.

Writing around 1950 about the history of the Northwest Conference and anticipating the changing role of the clergy as the country became more sophisticated, Jack Detzler noted: "I fear that the demands upon our pastors to meet quotas and aid in special financial campaigns, to fill every conceivable job from taxi-driver for the Ladies Aid, to lecturer for men's clubs; from teaching a Sunday School class to business manager and promoter and advertising agent, has robbed the pastor of his passion for souls and drained his physical vitality until our church is without an evangel." But times seemed quiet, peaceful.

Church growth did not happen by accident. Reverend Lawrence Cooper, who led Forest Manor Church through its impressive growth in the 1950s and early 1960s, displayed the combined talents of preacher, pastor, and building contractor. Cooper was from Kentucky and managed to use a farm boy manner to conceal the fact that he had graduated with honors from a fine university. My dad would have said they broke the mold on Cooper.

Lawrence Cooper rose early in the mornings to put in half a day's work doing such things as mowing the lawns of his shut-in members, or when one of several building expansions was in progress, laying concrete blocks along with the workmen hired for the job. Then after a quick shower, he was out calling on his members. In later years, he was proud to say that he averaged thirteen calls a day every day during his years at Forest Manor. Cooper was only known to take one vacation during his thirteen years there. That one was paid for by the congregation as a gift. It was to last two weeks, but he and his wife, Nellie, also a tireless servant of the church, returned in one week. When Reverend Christian Coker followed Cooper in 1963, he told his pastor-parish committee of his plans for a vacation that summer. He was horrified to learn that they were unaware that their pastor was entitled to a vacation. When Cooper was finally moved to become district superintendent of the Vincennes District, he broke down in tears during his final sermon and Reverend Phil Mercer had to finish for him.

A different approach was begun in a new congregation called Church of the Savior located on the east side of Indianapolis.

Begun in 1961 by founding pastor John L. Carr, the church was patterned after a then-famous church in Washington, D.C. of the same name. That church, founded by Gordon Cosby, had become well-known because of one of Cosby's books which extolled the virtues of the small, intimate, highly dedicated congregation in which each member undertook a specific and demanding mission responsibility. Reverend Carr was a former member of the Yale Glee Club and an exceptionally bright young man. Along with his wife, Adrienne, also a seminary graduate who played a major role in the church's formation, Carr brought an unusually wide range of talents to the church as it saw to the construction of a building with a round sanctuary. This was designed to foster intimacy of worship, which destined the congregation to remain small in size. The approach was experimental in nature, and while this particular congregation has remained loyal to the concept, the concept itself has failed to become a widespread style of church. By 1999, the membership of Church of the Savior was still less than 150 members. As years continue to pass, the future appears to belong to very large congregations.

∼

Professor Al Lindgren taught church administration at Garrett Seminary, and he insisted that if a minister hopes to have the trust of his or her congregation, he or she must show them that he or she trusts them. This was brought home to me in 1960 in my first year as a minister when I was the student-pastor of the Waynetown-Wesley charge. One day the members of the finance committee at Waynetown Church, faced with a serious financial shortfall, discussed the idea of holding back on payment of their apportionments. I found myself feeling several emotions as I listened to first one, then another member show approval of the idea. I felt this was not good stewardship. Self-interest also reared its ugly head, as I realized what the district superintendent might think and, ultimately, what the bishop might think if I allowed my very first congregation to fall short in this responsibility. My impulse, therefore, was to quickly urge them to reconsider. But I remembered Dr. Lindgren's advice, so I remained silent. Soon, Merle Sennett the chair of the committee spoke. Quietly, he reminded the members that we were part of a connectional system which relies on the integrity of its members to pay those apportionments in spite of any other problems they may face. "No," he said. "We must pay them." Everyone was quiet for a moment, then they all agreed. I realized Lindgren was right. I had trusted them and found them not to fail. This sentiment remained with me through all my years, and I was never disappointed.

∾

Racism was barely recognized in the fifties by the average white person; but prejudice prevailed. But the typical Methodist assumed with little self-criticism that each person's place was determined by birth. Black people, then called colored people, were obviously created for a lesser station in life and were to be treated with kindness. That didn't mean, however, that they were equal to white people. My own family never spoke a bigoted word. My father always spoke respectfully of black people. The "N" word was never, ever heard in our home. To have used it would have brought severe and memorable consequences. However, the several colored people of our acquaintance were employed in menial vocations, and that was never questioned in our homes either. Jews received the same treatment in a more subtle way. It is said that Senator Barry Goldwater, widely celebrated and respected, was nonetheless denied membership in Chevy Chase Country Club because he was Jewish. He entreated that since he was only half Jewish, couldn't he at least play nine holes? One pledge in a fraternity at Butler University, a very popular young man, was found to be part Jewish. Reluctantly, he was depledged. All of this sounds so unbelievable, so heartless today. It was hardly questioned in the 1950s.

∾

One undeniable and grotesquely harsh reality confronted America, indeed, the world during these years. The Bomb. And the Russians had it. If men and women of the forties based their anxieties on the economy, the children of the fifties based their anxieties on the bomb. Movies like *On the Beach* gave graphic visions of a world devastated by uncontrolled atomic power. Entrepreneurs sold thousands of people on the wisdom of building bomb shelters. One favorite topic for high schoolers to discuss in Sunday school (then being rebaptized as church school), was this: Suppose a dozen people (or however many were in the class) were marooned in a shelter following an atomic attack. Suppose a scientist among them estimates that there is one too many people in the shelter. The rest can survive on the amount of air available if one leaves, and therefore dies a terrible death. Who should leave? Such speculation, while provocative, taught young people to view the threat of atomic power with fear and trepidation. Those fears were not completely unfounded. Sociologists would argue that many kamikaze attitudes on the part of young people were a direct result of their deep-seated fear that the world would come to an explosive end.

Racism still haunted America. In 1942 thousands of Japanese were sent to what were virtually concentration camps—not because they had done something wrong, but because they were Japanese. Black American soldiers returned from World War 2, but no one talked about the Tuskegee airmen, those gallant black fighter pilots who, once they were finally allowed to escort American bombers over Germany never lost a single bomber. Sixty-five of those men died in battle. No one talked about the Red Ball highway, an unprecedented transfer of millions of gallons of gas to General Patton's thirsty tanks by black GIs. They worked with little sleep for days on end, driving huge army trucks over dilapidated roads at speeds up to seventy miles an hour in near darkness to enable one of the most crucial battles of the war. No one talked about the Japanese 442nd Infantry Regimental Combat Team, composed entirely of Japanese-American volunteers, which eventually became the United States Army's most decorated regiment. Only in the year 2000 would twenty-two of those men, many already deceased, receive the

The Confirmation Class of Emmanuel Methodist Church, circa 1950.
Photo courtesy of DePauw University Archives and Special Collections.

medals of honor they had won but been denied. GIs came home and innocently—they knew no better—reported that black soldiers always avoided combat. More than fifty years after World War 2, seven black men, nearly all deceased by then, were awarded the medals of honor which they had won but been denied. Black Methodists were mostly members of the Lexington Conference in Indiana, a kind of second-class Methodist citizenship. But America was destined to be called to account for all of this before long.

Professor Todd Gitlin of the University of California, Berkeley, in his insightful book *The Sixties: Years of Hope, Days of Rage,* calls the fifties "the dead, dreary fifties." Think of a garden newly planted. It is flat, plain, and serene, with only a few quiet buds showing above the surface. Gentle rains and warming sun give promise of new growth. But underneath, a profusion of bulbs and seeds of tomorrow's flowers and plants—and voracious weeds—all gather strength for the new season's dawning. Only the knowledgeable gardener suspects what the future will bring.

So with the fifties. Veterans with free (though richly deserved) educations afforded by the GI Bill behind them, married and moved to the suburbs, which nearly all could afford. In Indianapolis's far east side, thousands of prefabricated homes were built—a mass production of affordable housing for the masses. "Sweat equity" arrangements allowed one to do much of the interior finish work and thus avoid a down payment. Men and women from poor and not-so-poor backgrounds, wanting to escape the dreary neighborhoods in which they were raised, saw these brand-new homes in clean new neighborhoods, and having little or no concept of the additional expenses which go along with mortgage payments, they swarmed into these new homes. Other similar neighborhoods grew up on the far reaches of the city. It was the new melting pot. Municipal court judges, city planners, insurance salesmen, truck drivers, policemen, secretaries, teachers, carpenters, transplanted farmers, electricians, school custodians—people from all walks of life—young people, newly married couples, and families with new babies all gathered together in close proximity. And most had no idea how to build the sense of community which such conditions require if a peaceful future is to be built.

Enter the churches. Some established churches stepped in. In Indianapolis, Old Bethel, a longtime small church, was besieged with new members. Irvington Methodist Church experienced a growth surge as newly arrived east siders sought a large church. Asbury Methodist Church was established in 1962 near Fort Harrison and soon grew to more than five hundred members after starting in an incompleted home. Saint Paul's Church was built on the far east side. Christ Church was started on the south side and experienced immediate healthy growth. Carmel Methodist Church in the north suburb of Indianapolis set forth on a rapid period of growth. In about 1965, a speech was delivered at St. Luke's Church during a program sponsored by Christian Theological Seminary. The main speaker, a noted psychotherapist, declared that though he himself was not a practicing Christian, he gladly acknowledged that the churches were the one means by which families on the move could find a healthy adjustment to their new locations. He said that while a husband moving to a new locale usually had a made-to-order circle of support within his organization, the wife was usually left to find a new grocery, a new cleaners, and a new circle of friends. The speaker had come to realize that the one place the newly arrived family could go for immediate acceptance—to feel at home almost at once—was the local church. And that, he assured us, was our primary role in the fast changing culture of the times.

In Bloomington, First Methodist Church was filled to capacity week after week under the ministry of Merrill McFall, a man at once grandfatherly and charismatic. A large man with silver hair and widespread arms, he drew hundreds of Indiana University students every week. "Mac" was a popular preacher throughout America by virtue of having preached to so many IU students who went on to become educators. Thus, he was invited to a variety of educational institutions to preach. He was a memorable character, but he also ran the church. The story is still told about the time a meeting of the administrative board was called to vote on the question of whether the sanctuary should be air-conditioned. As the members were arriving at the church for the meeting, the chairman of the board happened to enter by the sanctuary door rather than the main entrance where one normally entered for a meeting. The place was dark, but the chairman decided to carefully find his way through to the office area. In doing so, he tripped over something in the aisle. When the lights were finally turned on, it was discovered that the board chairman, on his way to the meeting to decide whether to air-condition the sanctuary, had tripped on the pipes which Mac had already had delivered to begin the air conditioning installation.

Richard Hamilton, one of the young conference leaders, established St. Mark's Church on Bloomington's east side when it was apparent First Church was filled. Hamilton's strong voice soon drew crowds to that church. Down in Evansville, Methodist Temple was filled with students on Sunday mornings when Reverend Guy Carpenter was preaching.

One consequence of the move to suburbia was the deflation of the major city churches. The congregation of Meridian Street Methodist Church moved from their downtown location to what in 1956 was the far north side of Indianapolis. Second Presbyterian Church and First Baptist Church also moved four years later. Those which did not move were destined to suffer dramatic decreases in attendance.

Roberts Park Church, for example, one of Indiana's most historic congregations, had more than thirteen hundred members in 1959. By 1999, the membership was barely four hundred. Reverend Cyndi Alte started building on the work of earlier pastors and has helped to create a splendid outreach program for people in need. The program includes free meals on Sundays, a caring ministry to children, the creation with other local congregations of the "Shalom Zone," a neighborhood area devoted to bringing peaceful coexistence among the nearby residents, and a "Shalom Wellness Center," staffed by doctors and nurses from Indiana University Medical Center, which helps people who have no other access to medical care. It is this commitment to the downtown neighborhoods which commends the people of Roberts Park Church and the Methodist Church as times have so drastically changed the city.

These trends were true in the North Conference as well. City Church in Gary, for example, was what today would be called a megachurch with more than thirty-six hundred members in 1960. But that changed. People moved away and were replaced by lower income ethnic residents, many of them Roman Catholic. In very short order, City Church lost most of its members. In 1968, the formerly powerful church was closed. Trinity Church in Elkhart relocated, thus remaining a strong congregation. In Fort Wayne, the two downtown churches, First Church and Wayne Street Church, merged to become First-Wayne Street Church. Even so, in the years since, that congregation has declined as the suburbs have grown. Meanwhile, churches like St. Joseph's, Aldersgate, Christ Church, Good Shepherd, and Waynedale have thrived in suburban settings. The change was general. Mishawauka First Church's attendance dropped by half, and First Church South Bend declined, as did attendance at Hammond First Church when Woodmar Church was built in the suburbs. It became obvious that apart from a few extremely loyal members, most people, especially if a well-liked pastor moved, found it easier—and safer—to attend where parking was easy and where people attending mid-week programs, particularly those held in the evenings, felt secure. For all but a very few city churches, it was to become a losing game. I still remember one new member at St. Luke's who had been mugged on the way to a board meeting in a downtown church in Indianapolis one previous Sunday. Her family insisted she quit going there.

There were exceptions. In the north, First Church, Anderson, remained healthy as Reverends Don LaSuer and then Virgil Bjork proved strong enough to maintain them for awhile. Those two men later served as district superintendents. In the South, Broadway in Indianapolis, a church near downtown, managed to retain a large attendance by virtue of the exceptional preaching of Robert Pierce, then James Armstrong who was destined to become a bishop. But churches like these were few.

~

In 1953, a small contingent of leaders from Central Avenue Methodist Church, located near downtown Indianapolis, decided to start an annex to the main congregation on the far north side. They all lived north and wished to worship closer to their homes. This was a crucial time in the history of Central Avenue Church, which was founded in 1854. Once one of the city's leading congregations, the loss of several key leaders along with nearly a hundred regular attenders dealt the congregation a severe blow. The breakaway, led by prominent attorney Francis Hughes, whose father had been a bishop and president of DePauw University, began worshiping in the American Legion building in Broad Ripple. Reverend William Imler was appointed pastor. The group

Merrill McFall.

approached Union Chapel Church leaders, seeking a merger once it had become clear that to remain part of Central Avenue was impractical. That congregation decided against the idea, so property was purchased at the intersection of Eighty-sixth and Illinois Streets and thus was founded a new congregation, St. Luke's.

Several coincidences were related to those congregations. Mrs. Henrietta Leete, daughter-in-law of Frederick Leete who served as bishop of Indiana from 1921 to 1924, was one of the group who chose to remain at Central Avenue. Thus, a bishop's son and a bishop's daughter-in-law led the two groups: those who left and those who remained. While the Central Avenue people continued to be social friends, there was some strong resentment among them for a long time following the breakaway. Meanwhile, the new pastor of Central Avenue, assigned just following this departure, was Reverend Frank Hamilton, one of the denomination's well-regarded pastors. His son, Richard Hamilton, who had been pastor of the new St. Mark's Church in Bloomington, was assigned as pastor of St. Luke's in

1959. This new congregation would grow to become the largest
Methodist Church in the jurisdiction, and within thirty years it
was the eleventh largest Methodist Church in the nation.
Central Avenue Church, now renamed Old Centrum, was
destined to become a historic building and has served admirably
in recent years as a new concept community center and church
in downtown Indianapolis, presently under the ministry of
Reverend Robert Johnson.

The exception among the downtown and inner-city churches
was Broadway Methodist Church, also a historic congregation
founded in 1873, whose splendid preacher Robert Pierce maintained a central presence in Methodism. Broadway and First
Church, Bloomington, were the two largest Methodist churches
in Indiana, based on worship attendance. When Dr. Pierce
finally moved to Detroit in 1958, there was despair that
Broadway would now go the way of the other inner-city
churches. But another equally brilliant young man, the very
personification of a charismatic personality, was found to be
serving as an associate pastor in a Florida church. James
Armstrong was quickly summoned by Bishop Richard Raines,
and the parishioners of Broadway Church celebrated the new
preacher who was an immediate success. Dr. Armstrong's
sermons were quoted in the Indianapolis papers, he was chosen
as the city's outstanding young man by the Indianapolis Junior
Chamber of Commerce, and the Methodist Church became a
strong voice on the Indiana scene.

Down in Bloomington, a young man drove up to First
Church in a Jeep and alighted to be seen in all his splendor,
wearing a well-worn T-shirt and a pair of plaid walking shorts.
Common as those may be today, they were not worn in public by
any self-respecting adult male in the year 1957. Apparently no
one had told brash young R. Benjamin Garrison, who had just
arrived from New Jersey to interview for the associate pastorate
of First Church. Of course, ministers do not really interview for
appointments in the Methodist system. At least not officially.
But, this was First Church, and Merrill McFall was a friend of
Bishop Raines. Some of the interviewing committee were, to put

it mildly, taken aback at the temerity of a young man showing such impertinence as to arrive in a Jeep wearing Bermuda shorts for an interview with gentlemen wearing suits. Others, though, were charmed. Before long, everyone fell in love with Garrison, and he was appointed to First Church. The results of this appointment would be beneficial in some ways, quite chaotic in others.

Garrison happened to be a splendid preacher. Having two splendid preachers in one church usually does not work very well. Many people felt that Garrison was the better preacher though just the associate pastor. After all, preachers first start out as human beings. As such, they are prone to all the emotions and all of the sins of the rest of humanity. Try as they will, they do not automatically become sanctified just because they are ordained. This is not to anyone's discredit, but people began choosing sides. Someone had to go. It was all in good spirit, of course. But Dr. McFall was ready for a new challenge anyway and was moved to Irvington Church in Indianapolis. Garrison was preaching to three packed services every morning. With Garrison at Bloomington and Armstrong at Broadway, preaching in Indiana was at its zenith. There were, of course, several other fine preachers in the state as well.

Garrison's appointment as successor to McFall was perceived by some as favoritism on the part of the bishop. Ed Garrison, the bishop's assistant, was Ben Garrison's uncle. Several cabinet members tried to block the appointment, but people did not easily block appointments which Raines wished to make. The truth is, the leaders of the church used every bit of persuasion they could muster to convince Raines to make the appointment. The congregation was delighted when the announcement was made. However, it thereafter became an unwritten rule that no associate pastor could succeed the senior pastor.

⁓

What about America? The realization of several truths was dawning on an increasingly anxious population. Psychologist

Central Avenue Methodist Church, once a preeminent urban congregation in Indianapolis, shrank over the years as people moved to the suburbs. Today the enormous old church building is being transformed. Now known as Old Centrum Urban Life Center, it houses various community service agencies along with the remnant congregation. Photo by Lynne DeMichele.

Rollo May would define the '50s into the '60s as "the Age of Anxiety." People had begun to realize the price that had been paid to achieve this power-mower-barbecue-grill-two-car culture. Life was being sucked out of once thriving cities, driving property

values down, depressing the tax base, and spawning slum neighborhoods. If new people were welcome in these new crowded
neighborhoods, that welcome did not extend to Negroes. As far
as other ethnic minority residents were concerned, hardly anyone
knew if there even were any minorities around. Trolley cars disappeared, and bus routes were established based on ridership. This
meant that many people had no access to public transportation,
hence to jobs far from home.

Despite all, it was a great and heady time to be alive for
most church people. Churches were growing. New churches
were building. Both conferences had a good number of strong
preachers and leaders. Numbers were increasing. If Methodists
are prone to a somewhat disconcerting tendency to obsess over
numbers, at least that preoccupation was richly fed, especially in
suburbia and in many county-seat churches. Preachers, generally
more than capable of handling conflict, discovered there was a
virtual absence of conflict, apart from the usual minor league
arguments over the menu for the sunrise breakfast. If America
was in the eye of a storm, few in the church seemed aware of the
fact. If important categories of Methodists were still on the
fringe of all this, the average Methodist was unaware. There
were, after all, jobs for everyone who wanted to work. Business
was good. Oh, of course there was concern about the
Communist world, but we had shown the world that we in
America were number one, had we not? That Sputnik thing was
a bit unsettling, but we surely had something bigger and better
ready to go. The Korean Police Action—apparently someone
thought getting killed in a police action wasn't quite as bad as
getting killed in a war—had been settled. By 1960, America
became the first nation in world history to have more college
students than farmers. No one had quite realized what all that
education was about to unleash.

~

In New Albany, young Robert W. Gingery was establishing
himself as one of the finest preachers of the conference in the

mid-fifties. One day his career almost came to an abrupt end in what today seems an exciting adventure. Gingery told the tale this way: A member of his church, New Albany Trinity, was to retire as a sergeant of the state police. He invited Gingery to ride with him on his last day of service. As they were patrolling a stretch of Indiana highway, the sergeant received a call on his police radio about a bank robbery in a nearby town. As fate would have it, they soon spotted the car used by the bandit. The policeman immediately turned on his flashing lights and headed off in pursuit.

The pursued vehicle pulled over, the sergeant drew his revolver and approached the car. But before he could react, the bandit opened fire and the sergeant fell mortally wounded. The man then got out of the car, retrieved the officer's weapon and, with a gun in each hand, began advancing on the police cruiser where Gingery was waiting. The bandit began firing, no doubt assuming Gingery to be a police detective. Gingery realized he was in mortal danger. He saw a shotgun in the rack, pulled it loose, and found himself faced with one of life's most painful moral dilemmas. As a minister committed to the commandment "thou shalt not kill," he was seconds from his own violent death. Gingery then made a courageous and, as was later agreed by all the leaders of the church, a proper decision. He fired the shotgun at the bandit, who was firing two weapons at him. He later reported that it felt like he only fired one shell, but several empty shells littered the floor of the cruiser. The bandit was killed. Gingery survived, physically unharmed, but thereafter burdened with the frightening recollection of a terrible experience and the realization that he had taken a human life. Now retired and living in Florida, Gingery was asked in a recent interview if Bishop Raines was supportive of his decision. Gingery replied, "He certainly was!" He also commended his district superintendent Reverend Floyd Cook for his loving support at a very emotional time. Looking back, Gingery recently said, "I'm very lucky to be alive." Gingery's career continued to prosper. He became senior pastor of First Church, Bloomington, in 1966 and continued the excellent reputation of that fine church's preaching. He served there for six years, then became pastor of a church in Florida.

～

It is important that we remind ourselves of the man who oversaw events in Indiana from his arrival in 1948 until his highly entertaining retirement in June of 1968. The day Richard Raines awoke following his election to the episcopacy in the General Conference held in Roberts Park Church, Indianapolis, his first conscious sensation was that of a pillow bashing him in the face and the sound of his devoted wife, Lucille, announcing, "Good morning, Bish." And so the dashing athlete-scholar from Hennepin Avenue Church in Minneapolis, Minnesota, former amateur golf champion of that city, and piano player extraordinaire, was about to begin a historic tenure as the bishop in Indiana. Even today, Raines is still referred to by many retired clergymen of the fifties and sixties as "the bishop." Tall, erect, regal, and a natural commander of people, Richard Raines would oversee this more than thirteen hundred church area with benevolent, but iron control. There is no way Raines should be compared to other bishops because times have changed so much. It is highly doubtful that anyone today could wield the uncontested authority which was Bishop Raines's style. Universally admired, though occasionally maligned behind his back by disgruntled clergy, Richard Raines was a man no Methodist minister would defy. At least not successfully. One minister who later became a district superintendent told of the occasion when, while serving a small church, he argued heatedly with the bishop at a meeting. Many years later, as he spoke with the man who had been his district superintendent, he rather boastfully remarked that he had served that church for seven years at a time when five years was a long pastorate. His smile of satisfaction faded, however, when his friend confided that following his confrontation of Bishop Raines many years earlier, the bishop had heatedly told the district superintendent, "That man stays in that church forever." In time, the bishop relented.

David Lawson was pastor of several South Conference churches. He was elected as a bishop in 1984. But during his early years in ministry, he came to know Bishop Raines. In a recent interview, having both the insights of many years of service with Raines and his own years as a bishop, he remarked, "Everything which happened in the twenty years of Bishop Raines's term must be seen in the light of that man's leadership." Lawson placed special emphasis on Bishop Raines's vision for foreign missions. Much of today's emphasis in Indiana on world missions is a direct result of the values inculcated in young clergy more than thirty years ago.

Richard Raines was an old-school commander who rigidly preserved the barrier between himself and his clergy. One former North Conference leader recently admitted that in his circles, Raines was known as "King Richard." Fair-minded, benevolent, courageous, and of unimpeachable integrity, he nonetheless brooked no intrusion into his area of authority. Stories were often told about one minister or another who was called to the episcopal parsonage and asked how he felt about being appointed to this or that church. The man was then told "go home and pray about your decision, but be ready to move on June 12." Whether that literally happened, it was a rarity for a minister to dispute the bishop's decision as to church appointments. This firmness of mind caused Bishop Raines to take strong stands in controversial issues, no matter how unpopular. At one time, for example, he spoke before the state legislature in favor of Right to Work laws at a time when these were strongly opposed by labor unions.

I can report a firsthand observation of Raines's fairness. I happened to be seated in Bishop Raines's home one day when his phone rang. From the one-sided conversation, I could tell it was a district superintendent on the line. It seemed one of the man's pastors wanted a new appointment for which the district superintendent considered the man unqualified. Raines listened, then said to the district superintendent: "Several years ago I asked that man to take the appointment where he is now. He didn't want to go there. I promised him that if he would go where I sent him and do

Bishop Richard and Mrs. (Lucille) Raines board a plane, circa 1960. Raines served a twenty-year episcopacy, the longest in Indiana church history. Photo courtesy of Indiana Area Communications.

his very best, when the time came for him to leave I would see that he received a desirable appointment. Now it's time to keep that promise. Send him where he wants to go."

The young reader may find it hard to believe that as recently as the 1950s, few ministers knew what church they were to serve until the list of appointments was read at Annual Conference. Behind the scenes, the superintendents caucused with the bishop and last minute changes were often necessary. One clergy family on their way to a new appointment is said to have been stopped by an Indiana state trooper and told they must change their destination. It seemed the bishop had changed his mind, the moving van had been diverted, and the state trooper had the new address of their home for the following year. How ever true these stories may be, they reflect the reality of the time. While we are all glad those days are gone, something wonderful at the time went with it. The high moment for many Methodists in those earlier days took place on Sunday mornings following Annual Conferences, in Fort Wayne, Lafayette, and Bloomington. The bishop would preach to two thousand delegates and family members, then appointments were read. People who experienced one of those Sundays never forgot them. Bishop Raines was one of the finest preachers in America, and clergy always flocked to hear him preach as a role model for the rest. Every minister found someone else to preach for them on Conference Sunday so they could be present for the grand occasion.

It is also important to record that Bishop Raines was a genius at involving talented and highly placed laypeople of Indiana in causes about which he cared. In the South, he recruited people like Bud Tucker, Francis Hughes, Dan Evans, Edward Gallahue, and Herman Krannert. Up north, there were Ed Auer, Glenn Banks, Welcome Weaver, and Bruce Kephart. There were many more. Though most of those names may be unfamiliar to the average Methodist today, they were quickly recognized as the movers and shakers of yesteryear. And people like these made Bishop Raines a powerful influence for good. He demonstrated how important it is for a bishop to cultivate the friendship and support of people who have the influence and the wherewithal to make things happen. People like those trusted and respected Raines, and with their support, he was able to acquire the needed funds for many worthy projects.

Raines also caused many of the splendid charitable programs of the Methodist Church to begin. Operation Doctor, which still sends dedicated physicians to desperately needy third world centers was one such program. Raines also initiated the Indiana counseling program, the Raines Center later bearing his name. Begun at North Church in Indianapolis by Paul Johnson of Boston Seminary, it was later run by James Doty, and finally by Edward Alley. Changing times and financial limitations eventually put an end to that program, well run though it was. Raines was also quite active on the national and international scene, and many influential people from other nations came under the persuasive influence of Bishop Richard Raines. He was the first

Methodist bishop to request and receive an administrative assistant. He encouraged the establishment of an areawide newspaper which would finally become one of the finest of its kind in the country, the *Hoosier United Methodist News,* known these days to its avid readers as *HUM.*

In 2000, Lynne DeMichele, Indiana Area director of communications and editor of the *Hoosier United Methodist News,* was elected president of the United Methodist Association of Communicators. This was the culmination—so far—of one of the nation's most celebrated religious periodicals. It binds together the staffs and members of the thirteen hundred Methodist churches of the state of Indiana into something resembling a church family. It has been a source of deserved recognition for many laypeople and ordained people who have done the work of ministry to the world. It seeks out the worthy activities of small churches as well as those with more visibility, seeing to it that a cross section of Indiana Methodism is seen by and known to the people of the church.

From a very simple beginning when Reverend Harvey Kieser published a small newsletter for twenty-five cents a year back in the 1940s, the publication has evolved under the oversight of people like Reverends Warren Saunders and Wesley Brashares. It flourished due to the talented editorial work of Nelson Price, Robert Gildea, Newman Cryer, and Jim Steele, each of whom took the publication to a higher level. Now, *HUM* has entered the twenty-first century computerized, graphically sophisticated, and with a staff of news correspondents. DeMichele has brought the publication to be recognized as the premiere church publication in the denomination, as every pastor and church leader waits for the current issue of *HUM* to learn what is going on in Indiana's Methodist Church.

Raines disliked anyone having knowledge of a major appointment until the announcement was made officially. In 1958, Merrill McFall, the much loved pastor of First Methodist Church, Bloomington, who preached to a house full of Indiana University students Sunday after Sunday, was told he was to move to

Broadway Church in Indianapolis. Those were the two premiere churches at the time, and McFall, knowing it was time to leave First Church, considered Broadway to be the perfect move. Accordingly, the pastor-parish committee was told the news in the very strictest confidence, and McFall went home to pack—and celebrate. But one member of that committee had ties to a local news agency and apparently strictest confidence meant "don't tell anyone but the public." So the news was broken through the media. Raines was furious. He called McFall and told him the appointment was canceled—he was going to Irvington Church in Indianapolis instead, and a new search would be made for a replacement for Bob Pierce at Broadway.

God, of course, has a pixieish side, and apparently likes to remind all of us of our humanity. In Bishop Raines's case, this took amusing forms. When a dinner party was held at the new Episcopal parsonage on north Illinois Street in Indianapolis, Anna Lee Hamilton reports there was a heavy thunderstorm and water drained through the roof and down through the new chandelier onto the dining room table. On another occasion, Raines, always the well-dressed gentleman, was dashing to give a speech at First Church, Crawfordsville, and managed to slam the car door on his suit jacket. Time was of the essence, the door was jammed, the coat was irretrievably caught, and the only person nearby with a jacket the bishop's size was wearing a plaid sport coat. Torn between shirtsleeves and plaid, the bishop elected plaid and thus gave his speech to a crowd of admiring clergy who thought their bishop was learning to lighten up at last.

And old-timers still chortle over the novel written by one Reverend Charles Merrill Smith. Its title was *How to Become a Bishop without Being Religious*—a thinly veiled depiction of Bishop Raines said most knowledgeable readers. Whether true or not, it did not sit well at all with Raines. Smith's novel was eventually produced as a musical comedy, and Smith, nothing if not prudent, moved to Ireland.

Those who knew Raines well attest to his sense of humor. Bob Gildea, pioneer editor of the *Hoosier United Methodist News*, and himself a widely known humorist, tells of the time Raines was preoccupied by something and his assistant (later bishop) Ed Garrison smilingly informed the bishop that he had just helped Mrs. Raines zip up her dress. To which Raines replied, "Well, Ed, at least you were moving in the right direction." The story is still told of the time Raines was to preach in a well-known northside church in Indianapolis. As was the custom, the information was posted on the church's outdoor sign along with the title of the bishop's sermon. Passersby were greeted with this interesting bit of information: Bishop Richard Raines, preaching: "My God, My God, Why?"

So Bishop Richard C. Raines was a man for the times. If God raises up church leaders appropriate to times and needs, He certainly did a splendid job with this man. Remembered with affection by those who served under his direction, Raines was a man who held tightly to the reins of leadership during an unruly era. Indiana Methodism was established as the strong point of the Methodist Church in America, and those clergy who felt themselves called to stick their necks out on controversial themes always found their bishop standing behind them (assuming, of course, they were acting with wisdom and integrity). Retired Bishop Lawson of the Illinois area, who spent many years as an Indiana Conference leader under Raines, observed that Raines's style of leadership would not work today. Times have changed. But for his day, Raines stood out from all the rest.

Normally circumspect men and women who had once made virtue of prudence, and were to resume responsible behavior in due course, did foolish things in those years.
—Paul Johnson

The 1960s: The Gathering Storm

I n the late 1950s, a profound cultural change came out of the universities of America through the rejection of traditional recruitment standards. Heretofore, Ivy League schools and many of the elite universities nationwide sought students with pedigrees, kids from prep schools, and people whose families had money and prestige. That all changed as school presidents began to seek out students who had shown merit, regardless of their heritage. Changing laws also encouraged the admission of ethnic minority students, and as this process took place, a young generation began to repudiate the straightlaced styles of their older brothers and sisters. Author David Brooks, in a recent book with the provocative title *Bobos in Paradise*, noted that "The campus gates were thrown open on the basis of brains rather than blood, and within a short few years the university landscape was transformed. Harvard . . . was changed from a school for the well-connected to a school for brainy strivers." Between 1950 and 1960, the number of female students increased 47 percent. In the next ten years, Brooks reports, the number increased an astronomical 186 percent. He reports that in 1960, there were 235,000 professors in the United States. By 1980, there were 685,000. Kids from all over America were swarming into the country's colleges. And their attitudes toward authority and traditional values were undergoing profound redefinition. If conformity was the ethos of the fifties, that was about to change. Paul Tillich, a popular theologian in the seminaries, said to a college audience in 1957: "We hope for nonconformists among you, for your sake, for the sake of the nation, and for the sake of humanity." He was due to get his wish.

Brooks also reminds us of the 1967 movie, *The Graduate*, which became the most popular movie of the year. With a background of Simon and Garfunkel songs, Dustin Hoffman starred as a confused young man just out of a fine university. In one scene, he attends a cocktail party peopled by the wealthy, conventional, and influential people of his parents' circle. One overbearing man guides the young man out to the swimming pool and with arrogant self-importance murmurs his advice that the future is "in plastics." The viewer is immediately embarrassed for the completely unselfcritical gathering who, in the young man's eyes, look ridiculous. The movie concludes with a memorable scene in which a young girl is about to marry a handsome doctor who personifies all the entrenched conventionality which the movie is designed to denigrate. Dustin Hoffman's character arrives at the last moment. Denied entrance to the church, he makes his way to the balcony and screams at his beloved. She takes one look at her self-satisfied groom, then at her desperate, totally unorthodox suitor, and makes her choice. She symbolizes her own generation, looking at all that was valued in the society around her, then at the promise of an unconventional future, and throwing off all the givens of the past. She, the girl of tomorrow, dashes out of the church, and away they run. They are last seen on a bus, she in her torn wedding dress, he with a look of uncertainty as they head off into a new world together. While this movie seems exaggerated by Indiana standards, it does depict a societal change which would have a definite impact on Indiana Methodism.

~

In the sixties, a surprising thing began to happen. People got bored. Widely read books began to redefine the meaning of the times—books like Sloan Wilson's *The Man in the Gray Flannel Suit,* in 1955, in which a man encounters conflict between the drive to succeed and his family relationships. David Riesman's *The Lonely Crowd* condemned the "degradation of work," suggesting that the "outer-directed" people of America had sold out originality and independence for the sake of conformity. That was in 1953. *The Organization Man* by William Whyte in 1956 decried the conformist businessman. Vance Packard's *The Hidden Persuaders* and *The Status Seekers*, detailed the bill of goods we had all sold ourselves in order to keep the pleasant image of the comfortable suburban life alive. And so the dream began to dissipate. Some of those hidden weeds in the garden of America began to show their heads. America and the Methodist Church were about to enter the turbulent sixties. Time to fasten everyone's safety belts.

~

For the twenty-first-century reader to comprehend the role of Indiana's churches in the turbulent era from about 1955 until the end of the '70s, it is important that we first reset the stage of mid-twentieth-century America. These years produced a sociological earthquake in America. Hippies. Beatniks. Flower children. Streaking. The Pill. Burning ROTC buildings. Invasions of corporate offices by "Peaceniks." Five hundred thousand screaming, mainly drugged-out college-age kids running wild at Woodstock. The National Guard killing of four students at Kent State University. Violent school integration in Little Rock and Montgomery. The devastating, though necessary, Civil Rights movement, as Watts burned and "colored" people made it clear to the rest of us that the old ways were gone. Black was beautiful. The Black Panthers, the Black Muslims, the new black man and woman stepped forth on the American scene. A Promethean young black minister stepped to the center of history's stage, and America listened.

Young people no longer accepted authority for its own sake. "Never trust anyone over thirty," some argued. They did not define obscenity as the use of some naughty word. Obscenity was war in southeast Asia. Obscenity was prejudice. Obscenity was blindness to the need for radical change. Definitions had changed. Young people used every traditionally obscene word they knew in ordinary conversation, especially when stodgy old folks could hear. Thus the very language of the masses was corrupted. Sex was fashionable. Live-in boyfriends and girlfriends were the way to go. Communes, with group sex and defiance of authority and tradition became the order of the day for many young people. The generation gap separated cocksure children from dumbstruck parents. College students demonstrated, tried to manage their own universities, and chided their parents for being uninformed, over-the-hill, and blind to the breaking dawn. Not all students, of course. Not even most. Just a small but mightily vocal attack force, present on nearly every campus. Behind them stood a less-militant but frequently well-organized growing minority of students who supported this leadership. In 1964, Digby Baltzell of the University of Pennsylvania wrote *The Protestant Establishment*. In that tome he coined the phrase WASP: White Anglo Saxon Protestant, a definitely pejorative reference to the eastern Ivy League establishment. Of course, the term was soon applied to anyone who fit the description.

Many adults, set adrift from a culture that was rapidly being overthrown, began to cater to this new movement. "If you can't beat 'em, join 'em." Staid forty year olds dressed in outrageous new styles. Businessmen bought garish colored jackets. "Trophy wives" were sought by many middle-aged men as divorce became common, and mainline churches relaxed their opposition. Mothers of teenagers began learning their kids' lingo, copying their dress styles, and attempting to be their friends, rather than their parents. It is all very embarrassing now, but back then everyone was trying on new lifestyles. One well-known professional counselor who specialized in helping Indiana Methodist clergy remarked that were it not for the risk of job loss, the prevailing statistics of 43 percent of all marriages ending in divorce would apply to clergy as well. One cartoon in a popular magazine showed a disconsolate middle-aged couple staring out a window. The sad-faced man said to his frumpy wife, "Just remember dear, we missed the sexual revolution together." It was a time for "doing your own thing."

The very people who should have brought balance and reason were often cast adrift in a sea of cultural change. Many clergy joined the fray. Pastors showed up in the latest styles. Sermons on controversial issues were in vogue. Many young pastors took pride in the number of members who left their congregations as evidence of their courageous preaching. Seminaries eliminated courses on preaching in favor of courses on community political structures. An early concept of preaching as evangelism gave way to preaching as a means of righting the wrongs of a sinful society. Many ministers took to the streets to stand arm in arm with militant advocates of societal change. Several ended up in jail. One national publication featured a front page photograph of the pastor of a very large congregation, attired in a multi-colored clerical robe, dancing down his center aisle with a beatific smile on his face. Kindly old pastors, utterly nonplused by all that was happening, all too frequently lost their certainty. Some positive change was taking place, of course, despite the anguish of many a loyal Methodist. Finally, the church would give leadership to the Civil Rights movement, opposition to the war in Vietnam, and encouragement for new social agencies designed to help the poor and underprivileged.

But it wasn't going to be easy. *Honest to God*, a 1960s book by the bishop of Woolwich, England, questioned the very existence of God, and *Situation Ethics* by Joseph Fletcher caused theological uncertainty among many clergy. The latter book, published in 1966, was all the rage among clergy and became fashionable in church study groups. Its premise held that hard and fast ethical rules do not work. What we need is love, pure love. The author used several persuasive examples of situations in which one or another of the traditional rules of moral conduct must be violated for the higher ethic of love. The argument was persuasive. Unfortunately, it seemed to overlook the degree to which self-interest infects love, even among the most devout. As a result, the church for some time became a ship without a moral rudder. All kinds of disruptive behaviors were justified on the grounds that love was simply above rules. Sometimes such behavior produced good results. Just as often, people were hurt and little good resulted. Only God can judge the motives of the people. History must judge the outcome.

There was a period of time in which the church seemed to many to have lost its sense of direction. We would eventually be reminded that Saint Paul was right: "Suffering produces endurance, and endurance produces character, and character produces hope." But first, there would be a time of social cataclysm and lost bearings. For awhile Paul's other words—"the whole creation groans in pain"—seemed to characterize the times. Perhaps an insight for the future, however, came from John Glenn. He returned from outer space in 1962 and later observed, "To look out at this kind of creation and not believe in God is to me impossible. It just strengthens my faith."

~

Not everyone was confused. Shortly after Leroy Hodapp arrived as pastor of First Church, Bloomington, in 1961, a group of fraternity students approached him about a professor at Indiana University who was an avowed and outspoken atheist. They asked if Dr. Hodapp would consider entering into a debate with this professor. For the man who was destined to become a bishop, this was an offer he couldn't refuse. Accordingly, the time and place were set, and the two men—the atheist and the Methodist pastor— opened the debate. The professor wasted no time in announcing that not only did he have no regard for Christianity, but neither did he have any regard at all for the intelligence of anyone who

*Leroy C. Hodapp. Photo
courtesy of Indiana Area
Communications.*

believed in the Bible. He especially had no regard for anyone who taught such nonsense. Hodapp was aware that the intellectual debate, which was the scheduled topic, might be secondary to the attitudes and spirit of the combatants.

Hodapp allowed the professor to carry on at great length, producing his erudite quotations and presenting his overwhelmingly persuasive argument for atheism. Or so the man thought. When he was done, Hodapp thanked the professor for his forthright approach. Then Hodapp stated that while he disagreed and believed most profoundly in the existence of God and in the Bible, he realized that no one can be persuaded by argumentation. But what he did propose was this: "Since you and I both want to see the ills of our society overcome, and since both of us wish very much for the welfare of everyone in our community, can we join hands—you from your admirable insights from the field of science, me from my insights of my religion—and can we then join our energies, each according to our understanding, in making this world a better place?" Point, set, and match to Hodapp.

As a result of this contest, Hodapp became a popular figure on the Indiana campus, and he participated in a number of similar discussions. Interestingly, he built a grudging (on the professor's part) friendship with the other man. One day Hodapp received a note from the professor. It concluded with the sentiment, "God bless."

Another incident provides additional insight into this man destined to be our bishop. In the fall of 1967, while superintendent in Indianapolis, Hodapp joined Bishop Raines in the dedication of the new sanctuary of St. Luke's Church in Indianapolis. After the ceremony in which former pastors Bill Imler and Dick Hamilton, along with the new pastor—me—were participants, we all gathered with our spouses for a private reception. However, Hodapp was running late for another appointment and had to leave. He was meeting Hugh Hefner at the Playboy Club in Chicago. It seems Hodapp had challenged Hefner on some theological issue because Hefner portrayed *Playboy* magazine as having a theological basis. They had then become good friends. Hodapp would much later be invited to Hefner's sixty-fifth birthday party in California. In fact, Hodapp had two interesting and valued friends: Hefner and Bobby Knight.

∼

There were others who were not dismayed. Not all were caught up in the conflict. If the word *saint* is a good Protestant word describing someone—anyone—who loves Jesus, it still implies a special quality when used about someone like Reverend Guy Tremaine. Guy was a supply pastor. Those were men who did not have the wherewithal to attend a university or a seminary. But they were clergy nonetheless. Supply pastors are the nearest thing we now have to the people who held the church together in the circuit rider days when the ordained minister only showed up once every three months, and the local leader saw to the church the other eleven Sundays and all through each week. Such was Guy. He was born some time in the late 1870s and served a variety of small churches. People like Guy rarely received honorary degrees or conference honors of any kind. I have a good idea there are other, greater honors awaiting people like Guy.

By the time I met Guy Tremaine, he was long since retired. Having served Wesley Methodist Church, located between Crawfordsville and Waynetown, for his last appointment, and having fallen in love with the people there, he bought a farm and retired at the bottom of a gentle hill just south of that old church. Guy could often be seen driving his tractor or working in the enormous garden which enabled him to feed himself and his wife, Merlie, and to share with anyone who was in need. He had an old hat which he had worn for many years. One day I drove by Guy's farm and noticed that his hat was torn and ruined. Guy, then in his mid-eighties, laughed and explained that he'd driven his tractor under a tree, a limb had knocked his hat off, and the mower blade had run over it. No matter, he still wore it when he plowed to keep the bees off his bald head. The people thereabouts used to say they liked Guy Tremaine because he was the only minister they had ever known who worked. But when he wasn't working, Guy often performed funerals for the farm people he had served. He often whistled the special music in little Wesley Church on summer Sundays.

One of Guy's special kindnesses was the support he gave to a wet-behind-the-ears student-minister named Carver McGriff, who arrived one blazing Sunday in June of 1960, to be introduced as the new pastor. When it became apparent that this new pastor knew next to nothing about the life situations of his people, Guy stepped in and informed everyone that the new fellow just needed time. "Be patient. Love him, and he will learn to love you." One of the first visitors to the old parsonage in Waynetown was Guy with a load of corn and some fresh butter wrapped in lettuce leaves. Fairly unconcerned by the societal upheavals of the time, Guy simply did what his faith had taught him to do. He cared for others.

Ask a clergy person how he or she feels about having a former pastor in the congregation, and you're liable to hear some hemming and hawing. In truth, it depends on how supportive the former clergy proves to be. In this case, despite the usual assortment of gaffes and blunders I made as a new pastor, Guy was unfailingly supportive. He never spoke a word of criticism, and always offered loving support and confidence. If I ever amounted to anything, Guy Tremaine deserves some of the credit. Guy once wrote a book of poems. They were not great literature, but they were stirring evidence of a simple faith. He might very well have written his own epitaph with these lines:

> When stars peep out and the moon shines
> Over our countryside
> Our faith reaches up and touches God,
> And we are satisfied.

He and Merlie, or at least their mortal remains, now repose in the little cemetery behind Wesley Church which looks over Guy's old farm. The cemetery is within the sound of the music that comes from within the church. If one listens very carefully, and if one has ears with which to hear, at times the music seems to be accompanied by the sound of whistling.

~

Despite their confusion, the Methodist people never stopped caring for those in need. One event deserves recording which may very well characterize a hundred Indiana Methodist churches. While I was student-pastor of Waynetown-Wesley circuit, I attended Garrett Seminary Monday through Friday and served the church from Friday evening through Sunday. I burned a lot of midnight oil. People in Waynetown, and especially the many farm folks who worshiped at Wesley Church, were always up bright and early. One morning about eight o'clock, there came a knock on my parsonage door. I hurriedly dressed, cleared my throat, ran a brush through my hair, and opened the door to be confronted by three grinning men wearing dirty overalls. One extended a grimy hand of greeting, and all three enjoyed the realization that the preacher had slept late again.

"We need a cup of coffee," demanded one of my parishioners. They came in and began to explain. It seemed the three of them had learned of a widow living in Crawfordsville who had no heat in her little house. It was winter. These three men worked hard for their livings and had very little in the way of extra money. But learning of the old lady and her cold house, they borrowed a truck, drove to a coal yard, and proceeded to load that truck with all the coal it would hold. They drove to the lady's house and emptied the coal into her coal bin. After starting a roaring fire and assuring her they would return to see that it was safely banked, they headed off to my house for coffee. If anyone had doubted that Jesus was right when he said it was more blessed to give than to receive, they would have seen a glowing evidence of this truth on those three faces. Those men not only warmed a poor woman's home—they warmed a richly-blessed preacher's heart.

∼

The day came, though, when everything seemed to turn sour. The loss of moral certainty exacted a tragic price. The optimism which many felt as the new frontier of President John Kennedy beckoned us to ask not what our country could do for us, but what we could do for our country, died along with the man as an assassin's bullet struck him down in 1963. Crime, drugs, abortions, unwanted pregnancies, broken family relationships, betrayals of friends, alcoholism, and the resulting disillusionment began to turn some people back to the church, and turned others away from it. There was a widespread cynicism about religion in general.

Denominational loyalty had lost value. People wanted solutions that sounded quick and easy. Sects began to grow. Popular psychology was in. People began to make pilgrimages—not to some holy place, but to California to join any number of programs designed to lead people back to a healthy life, or at least to some new theory of a healthy life. Now the mainline churches were faced with a new dilemma. People were once more searching, but how could the church speak this new language?

Dr. Martin Luther King Jr. speaking at the 1960 Indiana Methodist School of the Prophets. Photo courtesy of Indiana Area Communications.

New Age philosophies were attracting millions of people. Divisions took place within larger congregations as pastors began to use what they considered valuable from the new insights. This had the effect of hardening the opposition from conservative members who still hoped to recapture the essence of the past. A balance would be found. But in the late seventies, that balance had not yet been reached by most churches. Robert Putnam, in *Bowling Alone,* observed, "A major impetus in this direction . . . was the thrust toward greater personal fulfillment and quest for the ideal self. . . . In this climate of expressive individualism, religion tends to become 'privatized,' or more anchored in the personal realm. . . ." David Brooks, in *Bobos in Paradise,* said, "Maybe people who go deeper and deeper into self are actually journeying into a void." Some, however, began to notice the soaring growth of very conservative churches preaching Biblical literalism. Perhaps, they thought, there is a hint for us Methodists in that.

Tragedies marked these years. President Kennedy was assassinated, beginning one of the nation's saddest eras. Bobby Kennedy, thought by many to be the logical successor to his brother, visited

Indiana. He was interviewed on a Church Federation–sponsored television show *Cross Exam* in Indianapolis on April 26, 1968, by a Methodist minister. He then went to California, where he stated that the only favorable attention he received from the media in Indianapolis was on a church television program. Then he too was assassinated. Then, that towering leader of the Christian faith, Martin Luther King Jr., went down from an assassin's bullet, and a nation grieved—and looked within.

Down in the South, America's great Civil Rights movement had begun on December 1, 1955, when one of this country's heroines, Rosa Parks, refused to sit in the back of the bus in Montgomery, Alabama. The suffering, injustice, violence, hatred, misunderstandings, and heroics of the years that followed are part of America's darkest past and her brightest history. It was a triumph not yet complete, to be sure, but a major victory over our devilish, mortal sin and naked prejudice. Just in the year of 1963, in eleven southern states there were 930 Civil Rights demonstrations in 115 different cities, and at least twenty thousand people were arrested—most black, but a great many white. Had those armies of justice worn uniforms, they would now be covered with medals, including hundreds of Purple Hearts. Not a few Indiana Methodists were there. David G. Owen, now serving as pastor of North Church in Indianapolis, was at that time an activist in Milwaukee. He took part in the march from Selma to Montgomery. So did Joe Emerson, former district superintendent and former pastor of churches in Columbus and Carmel. The people of Indiana began to realize that while our prejudice was not the militant sort of which we so easily accused the South, ours was often a more subtle kind, which in some ways could be more resistant to change. And, of course, standing at the front, larger than life, was the image of Martin Luther King Jr.

∼

One evening several fellow clergy were gathered together in one of our homes for a study group. One participant was Reverend George Rice, a graduate of one of Methodism's finest seminaries and pastor of University Methodist Church on the north side of

Indianapolis. He and his members were black. On this occasion, with an absence of emotion which bespoke a numbness from frequent injury, he shared with us that he had recently called on a family in a white Indianapolis neighborhood. Upon leaving just after dusk, he pulled into a driveway to turn around and saw a police car pull in behind him. Ordered to drive to the curb and stop, Rice was then ordered out of the car, frisked, and required to open the car's trunk. He identified himself as a Methodist minister. He was wearing a suit and tie. The police officer was polite enough, but he instructed this fine minister that in the future he should arrange not to be in a white neighborhood after dark. When Rice finished his story, the rest of sat stunned. We had heard such tales. But this didn't happen to people like us—like Reverend Rice—not in Indianapolis . . . did they? Of course they did. But not people "like us." Black people.

~

It was into this tumultuous, often tortured milieu that the churches of the country stepped forth with a prayerful hope to lead the people back out of darkness. To understand the dilemma which the preachers of the dawning sixties faced, it may be helpful to go back a bit. Let's return to the fifties for a moment and introduce one other aspect of the social upheaval of the era: generational alienation. Social historians may debate whether the movies of the fifties spawned a changing spirit in America, or whether they only mirrored the change. Maybe both were true. In any event, in 1953 Marlon Brando rode into town with a group of black-jacketed motorcyclists in the movie *The Wild One*. His gang's sole purpose was to disturb the tranquil setting of a small town of people who lived in peace. When a lady asked him what his cause might be, he replied, "Whad'ya got?" More profound was the tragic young man James Dean. Attractive, innocent, filled with rage at an ineffective father (on screen), vulnerable, and emotionally wounded, Dean personified a generation of youngsters who felt something indefinably wrong about their lives. *Rebel without a Cause*, released in 1955, featured this remarkable young fellow. In one scene, after a squabble with his father who gives him everything he needs except love, Dean takes part in a car race which ends at the edge of a cliff. His nemesis goes over. Dean stops in time, not completely sure why. And what an emotional experience for the millions who saw that movie—released just three days after James Dean died in a flaming car crash on a California highway. In the year following his death, he received more fan mail than any other film star. It has been said that his power lay in the fact that his vulnerability attracted young women, and his courage and sense of lostness won many adolescent boys who found, at last, someone who could face down the demons of their own adolescent lives.

We must leave it to the social historians to diagnose the complexities of the fifties and early sixties. This we know: suddenly triggered feelings of meaninglessness and hunger for community with their own peers caused a generation of young people to rally around rebellion without any real sense of purpose. Rock and roll would be their hymnology, Elvis Presley would be their Moses, and the Beatles would be their choir. Todd Gitlin, professor of sociology at the University of California, Berkeley, described the effect of the new music: "Being young means being able to feel rock. Whatever it is you're in, kid, you're not in it alone; you and your crowd are where it's at, spirited or truculent or misunderstood, and anyone who doesn't get it is, well, square." The bonding peace pipe was filled with marijuana—Mary Jane—grass. "More and more, to get access to youth culture, you had to get high," wrote Gitlin. "Without grass you were an outsider looking in."

In 1964, those youngsters, the first of the Baby Boomers, were arriving in college. Freshman enrollments that year were up 34 percent from the previous year. And over it all hovered the threat of atomic holocaust. In August of 1965, a nineteen-year-old kid named Barry McGuire wrote a song which swept the nation, rocketing to the tops of the charts despite the refusal to play it by many broadcasters. The title: "Eve of Destruction."

CHAPTER SEVEN

So here we are moving toward the exit of the twentieth century with a religious community largely adjusted to the status quo, standing as a tail light behind other community agencies rather than a headlight leading men to higher levels of justice.
—Martin Luther King Jr., from "Letter from Birmingham Jail"

Hearts Aflame: Civil Rights

A number of years ago, the Presbyterian Church conducted an intensive study of the denomination. Among their many findings was this unsurprising conclusion: Each local church is unique. That is something for us to keep in mind as we assess our own Methodist church life through the years at hand. We have to be careful not to lump churches together. Each local church retained its individuality, influenced by particular preachers and leading lay members. And yet, to simplify things a bit, there are several kinds of churches we will consider.

In the very early sixties, Martin Luther King Jr. spoke at Gobin Church, the campus church at DePauw in Greencastle. This created a new sense of the immediacy of the race issue, yet, in the opinion of several former district superintendents of the time, most people in rural churches believed that this was not their problem. The rural churches felt relatively untouched by the Civil Rights movement. People living in the countryside and in small Indiana towns usually had no contact with black people. They had some stereotyped perceptions and, as we all know, perception is reality. Reverend Richard Hamilton, while district superintendent of the Bloomington District, told of driving to a charge conference in a small town outside Bloomington, when he heard the shocking news of the death of Martin Luther King. His first order of business upon arriving was to announce the sad news. One member remarked, "It's about time." Bishop Sheldon Dueker recalls being with some laymen of his church that night and hearing one man, whom he described as "loyal and devoted," say, "He's been asking for it."

People had a lot to learn. The day would come when most Indiana Methodists would honor Dr. King and applaud the courageous efforts of those who sought equality for everyone. But in the early sixties, it was a new idea for many. The Civil Rights movement, commended by nearly every thoughtful Methodist today, was not nearly so popular in its early years. It takes time for people to change. The sin of most of us was not heartless intent to mistreat and dehumanize another race—although I suppose there were a few people like that. Rather, most of us were like the man Jesus talked about in Luke 16:19–31, the man sometimes referred to as Dives. His sin wasn't hatred of Lazarus the poor man. Rather, his sin was that he didn't even notice Lazarus. His sin was that he was so wrapped up in his own activities, so devoted to his own needs, that he didn't see another man's distress. So it was with many of us in those earlier days. Ominously, Jesus completed the story by reporting that the man whose sin was disregard for the suffering of another ended up in Hades.

Conservative Methodists, particularly those raised in small towns and rural environments, had little understanding of the suffering of black people. Virtually insulated from that entire dimension of American culture, and given the almost complete absence of black people from the entertainment media (the main source of role models at the time), the average Hoosier thought of blacks as people who had rhythm, who could jump high, and who lived somewhere else. As caricatured as that perception now appears, many people in the middle of the century had little to go on but Hattie McDaniel, Stepin Fetchit, and *Amos n' Andy.*

A. James Armstrong. Photo courtesy of Indiana Area Communications.

However, as the sixties arrived, that perception was about to receive a drastic revision.

Larger city churches had a different view of Civil Rights. It is impossible to generalize successfully, because opinions varied from a substantial minority who saw justice in the movement, to the larger middle majority who privately struggled with their own reservations, to the regrettably all too large minority who frankly hated what they saw happening. Clearly, the role of a minister in an urban church was not an easy one. He first had to settle in his own heart where he stood in the matter. Then he had to calculate how to address the issue most effectively without losing his constituency. Then he had to act, lest he later be found wanting in courage.

A leading layman in St. Luke's Church in Indianapolis tells of when he was president of his Methodist Youth Fellowship (MYF) in a small town near Indianapolis in 1958, as the Civil Rights movement was just beginning to come to the attention of most whites. One Sunday evening the invited speaker was a black minister from the city. Attendance at this MYF program was normally about one hundred young people. The night of the speech, attendance was very high. But the following Sunday, only about forty kids showed up, the others having been kept home by their parents. It was clear to this MYF president that any effort to introduce an awareness of the plight of black people in Indiana was destined to meet resistance from many otherwise good people.

Most of the action took place in churches located in downtown areas of the larger cities. In Indianapolis, Leroy Hodapp was the district superintendent of the Northeast District and a devoted advocate of human rights. Not a confrontational person and destined to become a bishop, Hodapp's strength lay in his willingness to stand behind any clergyperson who was willing to speak out and in a relentless refusal to remain passive in the face of injustice. We shall discuss some evidences of these qualities directly.

The pastor of Broadway Church, James Armstrong, was indisputably the premiere preacher not only in Indiana, but in the opinions of many, in the country. Because of his homiletical gifts, he was able to take controversial positions from his pulpit and retain a large membership. In truth, many a member visited other churches, but usually they returned to Broadway. Many of his people took the position that while they might disagree with their preacher, they honored the fact that he had the courage to say what he knew many people wouldn't like. As a result, Armstrong was able to keep the pressure on and, as one former member of Broadway recently observed, "Even though you disagreed with him, he made you feel like maybe you should take a good hard look at what you really believe." This is not, however, to overlook the fact that many clergy, in a variety of ways, stood up in courageous support of the Civil Rights movement. In the North Conference, the influence of Saul Alinsky, a highly confrontational community organizer, inspired many angry encounters, especially in those communities adjacent to Chicago.

∿

Luther Hicks was an impressive black Methodist minister and a most effective advocate on behalf of black young people. His style wasn't that of a traditional minister, which sometimes led to trouble. While at Riverside Church in Indianapolis, he managed to break some windows and make some people mad—his way of getting people's attention directed to the problems which troubled him. But he was also a courageous and devoted clergyman, ready and able to deal with people whose lifestyles he understood, even if many others did not. Two people in particular had faith in Hicks: Bishop Richard Raines and Leroy Hodapp. One day

Hodapp called Raines and talked him into assigning Hicks to an appointment which, though completely unorthodox, offered some real possibilities for a new inner-city ministry.

Opening a storefront headquarters by Shortridge High School, near Thirty-fourth Street and Meridian Street, and later at 1241 North New Jersey Street, Hicks began a group called "Dignity Unlimited." It was a program on behalf of black kids in trouble or those living in environments which might very well lead them into trouble. His objective was to find employment for the kids, who would then earn some money for themselves and at

Luther Hicks. Photo courtesy of DePauw University Archives and Special Collections.

the same time learn to support a worthy organization, like Dignity Unlimited, by giving to others. Supported by the bishop and by Hodapp, Hicks soon attracted the attention of the local authorities who viewed him with a great deal of suspicion. On one occasion, a group of black kids had congregated at the entrance to Shortridge High School to protest some issue which troubled them. One must remember that these were days when confrontational demonstrations were the means of getting an otherwise disinterested white populace to give a listening ear. On this occasion, Luther Hicks arrived at about the same time as a police car. He was quickly placed under arrest, though witnesses assured the police that Hicks had only tried to defuse the situation—and would likely have been successful had he been allowed to continue, since he knew many of the kids. It was by the intervention of Hodapp that Hicks was released. Not, however, without paying a fine.

On another occasion, a demonstration took place on
Monument Circle. Again, today's readers must understand that
when something was "going down," it was necessary that
anyone who presumed to fill a leadership role in the Civil Rights
movement attend whenever these things took place. Though
heated words were exchanged, the Methodist blacks in the
crowds had the private intention of entering in, becoming part of
the demonstration, then defusing anything actually violent.

Leroy Hodapp clearly recalls that afternoon. A group of
black kids, incensed that Alabama governor George Wallace
had been invited to speak, began yelling, shouting expletives,
and throwing things. Reverend Hicks, standing nearby, decided
to intervene in an effort to head off anything more serious. He
gathered the kids together and, after calming them, told them
to organize and to demonstrate in a legal way by requesting
first that Wallace not speak, and then, if necessary, by verbally
expressing their opposition. Unfortunately, the video cameras
located on buildings surrounding the crowd failed to record the
earlier part of the disruption. They only filmed Hicks seeming
to give orders to the kids. So the police arrested him for inciting
a riot.

To a great extent, it was thanks to people like Hicks that
Indianapolis was nearly the only major city in the country to
avoid any serious violence. The night following the assassination
of King, Hicks walked the streets of some of the most volatile
black neighborhoods, urging reason and patience. This was one
reason, apart from the fact that the great majority of black citizens were law abiding people, that there was little violent
action—despite the fact that there was a strong Black Panther unit
and despite estimates that the black population in the city was
nearly 20 percent.

In later years, with the vision which history affords, it can also
be said that the indigenous black leadership, people like Robert
DeFrantz who was head of Flanner House, Norman Lumpkin an
executive with the black newspaper the *Recorder* and radio
station WTLC, Reverend Hicks, and many black pastors of other
denominations, were law abiding citizens who fully understood

that the best way to bring about racial equality and peace was to avoid violence and to walk the way of King's non-violence.

I myself sat with Hodapp in the office of Police Chief Winston Churchill as an initially heated debate took place before calmer voices brought reason to the Monument Circle situation. It was fortunate that Mayor Richard Lugar was an active member of St. Luke's Church. Being a reasonable man as well as a devout Christian, he had a desire to see black people treated fairly. His administration earned sufficient respect from Civil Rights leaders of both colors to disarm the kind of violence so endemic at the time in America.

~

In 1964, the Indiana Area began to receive an infusion of moral courage in the form of several clergy from Mississippi. They had taken strong anti-racist stands among their people and, lacking the support of the southern church hierarchy, they chose to leave. Bishop Raines, honoring their courage, invited several of the men to come to Indiana. Among them were Reverends Gerald Trigg, Robert Hunt, Summer Walters, Hardy Nall, Bill Lampton, Paul Kern, and Charles Gipson. These men entered the South Indiana Conference. Trigg would later become senior pastor of First Church Colorado Springs; Hunt would be the founding pastor of Christ Church, Indianapolis, and a district superintendent; Walters and Nall would serve churches; Nall and Lampton later entered other vocations; and Kern became a district superintendent. Gipson continued to serve, currently at Epworth Church in Indianapolis. Into the North Indiana Conference went Charlie Bugg, T. W. Webb, Hubert Barlow, William Coker, and Roy Eaton. Barlow and Eaton both became district superintendents. Coker became a vice president at Asbury College. These men's names should long be remembered because of their courage in standing against the blatant prejudice which characterized Mississippi in the sixties.

Reverend Forrest Howell, superintendent of the Lebanon District, had an insight into the lives of southern pastors, especially

Forrest Howell.

those who were black, when, on behalf of Bishop Raines, he went down to Mississippi to interview Reverend Robert Smith. Ralph Steele, then superintendent of the Terre Haute District, recalls the story told to him by Howell. The two couples, the Howells and the Smiths (who were black), went out in the Howells' car. The Smiths began to slump down in the back seat, trying as much as possible to be out of sight from passersby. It began to dawn on all four of them that they were two whites and two blacks in a car with out-of-state plates. This was in the mid-sixties at the height of the Civil Rights unrest—a time when violence was routine among those who sought to bring changed attitudes. Though nothing happened that night, the truth was that they were probably in real danger. Howell was able to report firsthand the fear in which many people lived if they were in any way involved in racial issues in the South. He reported back that when one was in the South in the sixties, fear was real and justified.

The Smith family moved to Indiana, and Smith was appointed to a church by Bishop Raines. He eventually moved to another area, where he became a highly regarded district superintendent and, according to Steele, was viewed by some as a viable possibility for the episcopacy.

Reverend John Wolf, former superintendent of the South Bend District and pastor of First Church, Valparaiso, in the North Conference, has reminded us of the difficulties faced by those pastors. In an article in the *Hoosier United Methodist News* several years ago, he quoted Eaton in relating how twenty-eight Methodist pastors in Mississippi signed a statement of support for the General Conference position on open public education, law and order, and other highly controversial issues of the time. The pastors were immediately met with angry protests. The bishop refused to support the men, preferring instead to take a position of "don't rock the boat." Wolf wrote: "There were intimidations, salary cuts, threats to family, cross burnings, telephone harassment, gun shots through parsonage windows." Only after it had become clearly apparent that the bishop of the state would not support these men in their positions, and only after it was equally apparent that their effectiveness was severely damaged, did these men accept Bishop Raines's invitation to become Indiana pastors. As Wolf concluded in his report: "Thank God."

Reverend Phil Amerson, former pastor of First Church, Bloomington, tells that one influential Methodist during the hectic era of the Civil Rights movement was Herman Wells, then president of Indiana University. One day Wells took some black kids to lunch in a Bloomington restaurant which was known to turn blacks away. Of course, no one was going to turn away Bloomington's number one citizen, so they ate peacefully together. As they left, Wells sought out the manager and told him, "These kids are friends of mine, and I hope they will be well treated whenever they decide to eat here in the future." Wells was an active member of First Church.

∼

Subtle forces were at work. Each Methodist minister was faced with the dual task of working through his own feelings about race and facing the issue squarely within his own congregation. (Keep in mind that women were not yet fully ordained.) Often, courageous and visionary laypeople took the lead. John Mote was chair of the Christian social concerns committee at St. Luke's Church and was also vice president of Methodist Hospital, in charge of personnel. He took the venturesome step of employing "unemployable blacks" at the hospital. While the term sounds patronizing today, it was in general use to describe young people who had grown up without having learned a work ethic. Many of them operated on what Robert DeFrantz called "black time." DeFrantz explained this as an attitude which treated being due at work at eight o'clock as meaning, "I should be there between eight and nine o'clock . . . if I can." For a time, some of Mote's critics felt he was making a serious mistake, because people who had never held a responsible job were expected to do just that. But despite some predictable failures, Mote proved right and many an "unemployable" black person proved to be a highly reliable and valued worker at the hospital.

Methodists did not always agree on the issues. There was much ongoing controversy in most churches during these years. And there was quiet courage on the part of so many people, lay and clergy alike. People like Reverend Richard Hamilton who, while serving a far north side church in Indianapolis, St. Luke's, participated in a Civil Rights march in Washington and was present for Martin Luther King Jr.'s "I Have a Dream" speech. A television camera recorded Hamilton's presence, and he was met with disapproval upon his return. But it also speaks well for all concerned that Hamilton made no apology, and the congregation, while not in unanimous support of his actions—this was early in the Civil Rights movement—applauded his courage and supported his right to stand up for his convictions, popular or not.

At North Church in Indianapolis, a social action group approached the administrative board to request the use of office facilities. One female attorney on the board was strongly opposed and voiced her opposition. However, the board, by majority vote, agreed to allow the group to use the facility. The woman who opposed the action stated that while she disagreed, she believed in the democratic process, and since the group was coming anyway, she had some office equipment she would like to donate for their use. This was yet another example of the Methodist way of working through controversy.

Down in Lawrenceburg, in the early 1960s, there were two major industries which refused to employ black people, though many resided in the surrounding area. The local pastor approached one of the companies to inquire as to the reasons. The representative told the pastor that if he were to urge the employment of blacks, he would probably be fired. It also happened that the nearby community of Greendale had a swimming pool which, though technically for use by Greendale residents only, was actually used by nearby residents of both Lawrenceburg and another adjoining community, Aurora. However, when it was suggested that this should include black people, the board insisted once more on local people only.

Now two active members of the Lawrenceburg Methodist Church were Russ and Edna Wilson. Confirmed segregationists, they decided to attend a retreat led by Leroy Hodapp. The purpose of the retreat was to discuss the new conference relationships of the black churches which had, prior to that time, been part of the Central Jurisdiction. That all-black organization had been shuffled in with the white church. The gathering took place at Rivervale camp, and the Wilsons, not realizing the makeup of the group, had decided to attend. Upon their arrival, they were dismayed to discover that the majority of people in attendance were black. Nonetheless, they remained to take part in the discussions.

Reverend W. Robb Kell, later superintendent of the Evansville District, but pastor of Lawrenceburg Church at that time, loves to tell what happened next. Mr. and Mrs. Wilson returned home. Their experience of actually getting acquainted with the black people at Rivervale had changed them. One day, Mrs. Wilson and a friend took a black child to the Greendale swimming pool. In an act of quiet, unassuming heroism, Edna Wilson was risking the wrath of a community and ostracism by some of her friends by introducing a black person into an all-white swimming pool. In fact, there was no outcry. Edna Wilson probably knew her community better than some may have thought. The changes quietly accepted, the pool was henceforth open to blacks and whites alike. Not long after, local industries began to give jobs to black residents. Reverend Kell, in reporting this event stated, "The women of the United Methodist Women's Society deserve as much credit as anyone in the church for bringing about successful integration." The times, they were a'changin', but it was often because of the decent, kind-hearted people of towns like those who were willing to change so that the world could change.

~

There was disappointment up in the Northwest Conference which, in their 1966 Annual Conference, voted 213 to 123 for merger with the North Conference. The sessions closed in the belief that the following year would see a combined Annual Conference. However, a majority of members in the North Conference weren't ready yet, so the 1967 conferences met separately. Several former North Conference pastors said their resistance was based on the feeling that the Northwest Conference camping program was weak as compared to the North Conference, and of course there were other factors also. In any event, despite Bishop Raines's urging, and despite the fact that many North Conference pastors were reluctant to oppose the bishop, a strong lay opposition, perhaps encouraged behind the scenes by unhappy pastors, defeated the effort. However, with the 1968 merger of the EUBs and Methodists, it was inevitable that the Northwest and North Conferences would merge, and that's what finally happened.

It is interesting to note that although a third of a century has passed since the union of the North and Northwest Conferences, surviving clergy from those behind the scenes battles still believe the union was a mistake forced by Raines. Virgil Bjork, superintendent of the Fort Wayne District at the time, and a much admired conference leader who is now retired, recently stated that the merger did "irreparable harm." Young clergy today may wonder why this sentiment exists. The older generation felt that the merger caused damage to reputations and a lost sense of identity in relation to other pastors and churches, and this sentiment is by no means dead in the North. Bjork pointed out that conference leaders were spending so much energy getting acquainted across new and different lines that mission programs suffered, and there were no more new church-starts. Former Northwest Conference pastors have been heard to register the same complaints.

∼

In other news from the 1966 conference session, a special compliment was paid to Dr. William E. Kerstetter, president of DePauw University for his strong stand in allowing fraternal organizations to choose their members free of interference by national organizations and alumni. The conference also urged the United States government to pursue every possible means of bringing about peace in Vietnam, short of armed conflict.

The 1966 Northwest Conference minutes also contained an interesting observation by the chairman of the cabinet, Eugene R. Balsley, who foresaw the time ahead as "a period of church life [to be referred to] as the beginning of the second reformation." He foresaw the future as a time of profound spiritual revolution. History would reveal the truth of this observation, though perhaps not quite as Balsley had hoped. He closed his cabinet report with an interesting story about a Methodist church that caught on fire. It seems two members gathered to watch, and one said he hadn't seen the other near the church for years. The other man replied, "This is the first time I've seen the Methodist Church on fire." Balsley then expressed his hope that the Methodist Church would indeed catch on fire in the immediate future.

∼

Profound social forces were at work. Movies which had presented the black person as servant now began to change that

persona. In 1961, the movie *Raisin in the Sun* showed a black man
as a sensitive man of character. In 1966, *In the Heat of the Night*
featured a heroic black man, strong enough to rise above the forces
of bigotry while keeping his dignity and winning the respect of his
most ardent critic. That same year, *Guess Who's Coming to Dinner*
showed the discomfiture of a decent, prejudiced family when faced
with a black man who was clearly their peer. We saw the coming
clash within the black community through the character of the
black servant in the film, who had the greatest difficulty accepting
someone of her own race presenting himself as a peer to this
distinguished white family. Other black actors and action heroes
began to redefine the public perception of black males.

"The Times They Are a' Changin'" was a song, but also a
description of reality. Jackie Robinson's entrance into professional
sports, thanks to Branch Rickey, signaled another tidal wave of
social change. Initially, Robinson was greeted with derision and
embarrassing rejection—he wasn't even allowed to stay with the
rest of the team on road trips. The entire sports world applauded
the day Peewee Reese, seeing yet another grandstand full of
rednecks taunting Robinson, walked across the field and quietly
put his arm around his friend and teammate. And no mistake,
Robinson was destined to become one of the greats in baseball.
And so, the image of Black Person in the mind of White Person had
begun to undergo a transformation.

In Indianapolis, young black men like Ben Bell, Norman
Lumpkin, Luther Hicks, and a host of others walked the streets
standing tall, heads held high, making eye contact without
threat—but also without fear. Black women began to adopt the
clothing of the land they had begun to adopt in their hearts, until
the term *African-American* later became a proud appellation.
Someone else must record the emotional struggle precipitated by
all this change within the minds and hearts of black people of the
time. Despite a lot of emotional struggle, despite many heated
debates where white people gathered, despite many a Methodist
minister in big trouble in his church, and despite the fact that there
were inevitably a few recalcitrant people who would always hold

fast to their prejudice, the Civil Rights movement in Indiana was succeeding. In 1968, there was still a Central Jurisdiction, the black second-class citizenship Methodist organization created in 1939 by the reunion of the north and south Episcopal churches. By 1993, the Central Jurisdiction was no more, and my successor at St. Luke's was appointed by a black district superintendent, Reverend Harry Coleman, with the authority of a black bishop, Woodie W. White. Though we still had far to go, we had come a long, long, way.

~

The suburban churches of the sixties were divided in their concerns between a genuine desire to facilitate the changes in American society and the need to build and consolidate new churches. These new churches were often obliged to make large mortgage payments while being charged increasing apportion-ments as older churches either declined in membership or found themselves faced with aging congregations and falling income. It was popular among some social critics of the time, and this would include many Methodist ministers, to decry the suburban move-ment as "White Flight"—as though millions of white people were fleeing to lily-white suburbs to escape the black neighborhoods. Writing as a former pastor of two such churches, I find this an understandable but unfair criticism. This may possibly have been true of some people, but as the founding pastor of Asbury Methodist Church on the far east side of Indianapolis in 1962, a church which grew by a net membership of more than a hundred persons per year, I was close to a congregation of mainly low- to middle-income people whose occupations were white collar to blue collar. I don't recall ever hearing any bigoted statements to explain the decisions of those people to move to the suburbs. Their reasons were economic. Housing was easily affordable. There was little crime—though that would come later—and young people wanted to live where other young people could be found. Swimming pools, clubhouses, new schools, neatly trimmed lawns—these were the attractions. Houses were prefabricated, quickly constructed, and sold as fast as they were built in the early sixties.

It was still a heady time to be alive, and young people with little money but bright new dreams were stepping out to a new life. The Methodist Church with its church extension arm was ready to see that the Word of Jesus Christ was preached where the people were. Around the city of Indianapolis, the churches of Asbury, St. Paul's, Castleton (relocated), St. Luke's, Christ Church, White Harvest, and Church of the Savior were built. Small established churches like Old Bethel, Wesley, Speedway, Lawrence, and Forest Manor that were conveniently located began to grow. In Fort Wayne, St. Joseph, Aldersgate, Christ Church, Good Shepherd, and Waynedale churches were built. In Elkhart, Trinity Church relocated. In Lafayette, Christ Church was built in the suburbs. So it went as the structures of the cities changed.

Suburban people looked to their churches for stability in their neighborhoods. Pastors often felt overwhelmed. Weekday religious education, mothers' day out, preschools, Bible study groups in afternoons and evenings, building committees, fund-raising, multiple services as growing congregations outgrew sanctuaries— all these demanded the participation of pastors. Commitments to participate in district and conference activities, along with the work of preparing sermons, keeping a growing list of counseling appointments, meeting with families about baptisms, performing weddings, trying to stay up-to-date on the many religious periodi- cals, plus watching movies and reading books necessary to understand the changing times, all left the typical suburban pastor with very little time or energy for leadership in any sociological movement, no matter how worthy. This all introduced a new phrase which rather appealed to busy clergy: burnout. Sixty-hour workweeks had become the order of the day for clergy, and many a parsonage family began to suffer as a result. The role of most suburban clergy in the Civil Rights movement was that of inter- preter, helping members of their congregations absorb and understand the events of the day in light of Jesus' gospel of love and acceptance. Few occasions of public recognition for such serv- ices were recorded, but this work was the grassroots means of

St. Luke's, now the largest church in the state, began in 1953 as a small congregation in the northern suburbs of Indianapolis. Architect's rendering.

facilitating the changes which were taking place. It often called forth its own kind of moral heroism. Some suburban pastors did serve on various church-related agencies—Fletcher Place Church and Community Center in Indianapolis, for example, but most of the front line was manned by urban pastors and a few district superintendents.

Another form of ministry took place, like the time one suburban Methodist pastor, serving on the board of Fletcher Place, made inquiries at a local bank regarding a possible loan so a black family could relocate to a new home. The young bank official was very cooperative until he belatedly realized the family was black. He then slyly informed the pastor that they would no longer be able to consider the loan. But the kindly pastor turned out to be not so kindly when he implied to the young man that unless the loan was made, the newspapers would hear a verbatim account of the conversation. Chastened, the young fellow granted the loan and probably passed the word up the line that in banking, too, the times were a changin'. Bankers were having to grow just as preachers were having to grow.

∾

It must be kept in mind that black people were not the only ones suffering from mistreatment by monolithic systems bent on serving the best interests of the majority, with too little regard for the price in human suffering which could result from thoughtless planning. One summer day in 1965, the Reverend Ray Sells arrived on the Methodist scene in Indianapolis as pastor and director of Fletcher Place Church and Community Center, and he didn't take long to throw the first of his many hand grenades into the sometimes hidebound Methodist works. Bishop Richard Raines had assigned this brash young minister to one of the hot spots of mid-sixties action.

It is probable that Sells could only have served as he did with a bishop like Raines in support. But it is true as well that Bishop Raines needed people like Sells to stir the pot of civil action to the benefit of many of Indianapolis's poorest residents. President Lyndon Johnson had recently opened his war on poverty. Sells saw himself strategically placed to serve the best interests of inner-city Indianapolis's residents. His first job, however, was to win the rather impressive Fletcher Place governing board of suburban clergy and laypeople to his way of thinking. That way of thinking, though, was new to most of the members.

One day Sells presented the board with a motion to solicit federal assistance in establishing a preschool education program for community children. While the board was all for such programs, they were not in favor of government participation. After all, a women's group of volunteers was already performing such a service. Sells, however, believed that with funding, a professional staff could be built and the quality of education greatly improved. The Fletcher Place board argued, and then voted against the motion. But in the controversy which preceded the vote, Sells saw a determination to make Fletcher Place a force for community improvement. It would take time. Board members must be retrained and given a new view of the needs and possibilities. But essentially, though some board members were constantly upset with Sells and his relentless pressure to force change for the better, changes began to take place.

The day came when it was discovered that a new highway was planned to run through downtown Indianapolis. Dr. Sells remembers it this way: "Not only was it obvious that the path of the highway was following a route of least resistance from the poor and mostly elderly people, but it was also obvious they were making an economic decision. They were after the cheapest land they could buy for highway construction, and the poor were their target."

Apparently, government policy was to compensate home owners for the value of their homes based on prevailing values. This sounded fair. But homes in that depressed area, especially given the fact the word was around that these homes were soon to be torn down anyway, led to valuations so low that the poor and elderly had no hope of resettling. So an organization known as Homes Before Highways was formed with Ray Sells as co-chairman. The objective of the group was to try to force the Indiana legislature to compensate people with replacement values, a new formula which would more equitably compensate home owners being forced to move. In addition, the organization sought a guarantee that each home owner would receive sufficient moving expenses to make the move and a sufficient period of time in which to make arrangements.

This would not come about easily. On a cold winter night, demonstrators led by Sells and other local religious leaders gathered outside the governor's office to make their demands, only to learn that Governor Roger Branigan had departed for the day. Among the picketers that night was a man whom Sells remembers as "Old Joe," a tragic victim of economic blight who, along with his sad-faced wife, was attempting to do something to help himself and his neighbors. Sells kept Old Joe's tired face in his mind as he tried to remain determined in the exhausting fight.

When it seemed the cause might be lost, Sells approached Bishop Raines for help. Conservative by instinct, Bishop Raines was nonetheless ready to stand up for what he believed to be right and for one of his embattled ministers as well. After conferring with James Armstrong at Broadway and assuring himself of the importance of victory in this cause, Raines sent a telegram to the governor, urging him to support the proposed legislation. Branigan's initial reaction was anger that a man of such stature as Raines would involve himself in the nitty-gritty of partisan politics. Branigan called Raines to find out why he would interfere in such a public way. Raines stuck by his guns. Governor Branigan, realizing the clout of the Homes Before Highways coalition and realizing that such stalwart religious leaders as Raines, Armstrong, and Sells stood together in this cause, went to the state legislature in support of the desired legislation, which was duly passed. It became a landmark statement of rights for the inner-city people of Indianapolis living in threatened neighborhoods.

There is an interesting historical footnote to this story. The legislature was, in fact, due to end its annual deliberations. In accord with time-honored tradition, the clock was stopped prior to midnight, though the actual time was past midnight. If the legislation was to become law, it must be passed that night. However, most of the legislators had departed and the chairman, the lieutenant governor, had apparently adjourned to more convivial surroundings for a last libation with some friendly colleagues. People in the know, however, quickly located the lieutenant governor, who returned to the legislative chambers. Seeing a handful of members still present, the lieutenant governor promptly declared a quorum, the bill was passed, the governor would sign, and a victory of church over state had been won.

Fletcher Place would continue as a beacon of light in the center of Indianapolis. A health clinic was established which grew into the Southeast Health Center. Local residents were included on the board and given a voice in the center's operation. Seminary students began to spend time at Fletcher Place, which rapidly became a training ground for young laypeople and clergy who sought vocations in inner-city ministry. Looking back on those hectic years, Ray Sells, now a consultant in Nashville, Tennessee, wrote: "Fletcher Place helped shape a city from the opening days as the War on Poverty initiative was rolled out. We did it our way, drawing on the resources of the Methodist people and the gospel, using power and influence, and building a partnership that transformed lives and a community." Clearly, during the mid to late sixties and into the seventies, courageous Methodist leaders like Sells, arm in arm with devoted and courageous members of other denominations, were able to exercise sufficient influence to bring about changes which helped make Indianapolis, and thus Indiana, one of the finest places to live in America.

Reverend John P. Adams was pastor of a Methodist church in Hammond in 1963. He wrote:

> I left to participate in staff assignments throughout a summer filled with civil disorders, and began to see in Detroit, Newark, and Milwaukee what I had read about at the time of the Watts riot—broken windows, looted stores, and burned out buildings. At night the sky was alight with flames, and smoke hung heavily over large sections of the cities. Police and National Guard with military weapons dominated the streets. Helicopters chopped the air in tight surveillance as lights swept the streets and alleys during curfew hours. Gunfire was audible; tear gas smarted one's eyes. Like most white Americans, I simply did not understand what was happening.

So wrote one of the state's most courageous clergy. After sixteen years as a pastor, Adams left to become a staff member of the Methodist Board of Christian Social Concerns, first reporting in Washington, D.C. In the years that followed, he may have seen more action than any other Methodist minister.

Adams was destined to march in some of the most risk-filled marches in Milwaukee, led by the famous priest Father James Groppi. Adams participated in the action in Gary during the election of 1967, then went on to Jackson, Mississippi, where he spoke at Galloway Memorial Methodist Church, which four years earlier had refused admission to two Methodist bishops, one white, one black. That night he was a houseguest of a very heroic young couple, Bob and Kay Kochitzky who had hosted his very controversial appearance. As everyone was settling down to sleep, a bomb exploded in the front of the house, destroying the family's home and showering their five-year-old child's bed with broken glass. It was then that Adams said he realized, "The church cannot avoid violence in witnessing to a faith in Christ."

In 1973, having been at several more sites of violence and confrontation, Adams had displayed such qualities of courage coupled

John Phillip Adams, 1981.
Photo courtesy of Indiana
Area Communications.

with diplomacy that he was sought by authorities engaged in an armed standoff with Ogalala Sioux Indians on the Pine Ridge reservation in South Dakota. It had been the scene of a massacre in 1890. Now, the second episode of Wounded Knee was in process as authorities contemplated armed assault against an Indian enclave of lightly armed men. The issues are another story from ours, though involving justice and heroism. But John P. Adams interceded, and what might very well have been a deadly battle was avoided, though not without casualties.

Reverend Dean Stuckey, who is now pastor of First Church, West Lafayette, was the superintendent of the Fort Wayne District in the early 1980s. He recalls that Adams also took part in negotiations with the captors of American hostages in Iran during President Carter's administration.

Adams would continue to serve where justice was at risk, where people were in fear, and where violence and death were constant threats. The title of his book which detailed his harrowing experiences was *At the Heart of the Whirlwind*. Adams finally returned to the local pastorate at Woodmar Church in Hammond. Sadly, life is not always fair. On December 10, 1983, Reverend John P. Adams died of cancer.

Among the venturesome people who assisted in the Civil Rights actions in Milwaukee was Reverend David G. Owen, now senior pastor of North Church in Indianapolis. Owen served as chairman of the Inner Core Cadre of Ministers at a time when hundreds of people were marching in 1967. He served in that capacity until it was no longer politically correct, or, in other words, until white leadership was pretty much repudiated by the more militant blacks who insisted that only blacks need apply. Owen did go to Mississippi and take part in the Selma to Montgomery march.

~

God has a remarkable way of turning a curse into a blessing when people respond with faith. It is hard to imagine the Ku Klux Klan bringing a blessing, but that's exactly what happened in Fort Wayne several years ago. The Klan had obtained a license to conduct a parade on Sunday, September 9, 1979, at 1 P.M. A horrified Reverend Harold Leininger, pastor of Waynedale Methodist Church, was informed by a reporter that these people would be passing his church. He was then asked how he planned to react. Leininger quickly recovered and replied, "We will make an alternative response."

He got in touch with several other pastors of nearby churches. Carefully they made their plans. A prayer service was announced, and on the appointed Sunday, thirty-four Klan members arrived— surrounded by twice their number of local police, many of whom were black, but all of whom accepted that protecting the marchers was their duty. But those guys needed no protection. Their expectation that they would be the center of attention was usurped by a bunch of church people.

No doubt to their dismay, the Klan marchers learned that the five hundred seats in Waynedale Church were filled with Methodists, Baptists, Catholics, Jews, blacks, and whites; people of many persuasions but of one Spirit. All of them, though people of differing faiths, were united that afternoon in a service of prayer and love which, according to Leininger, filled the place with contagious celebration. Three television crews were present, and, impressed with this kindly act of peaceful opposition to the bigotry of the Klan, the media concentrated on what was happening inside the church.

Reverend Leininger opened the service with the statement, "Fort Wayne will not only be a 'city of churches' but a 'community of the Spirit.'" Rabbi Richard Safran read a psalm, the choir from Jerusalem Baptist Church filled the room with their ringing declaration, "I've been changed since the Lord has lifted me," and Robert Williams, director of the Fort Wayne Urban League declared, "This is a great moment of solidarity for Fort Wayne." There were others: superintendent (later bishop) Sheldon Dueker spoke, as did John Wolf, pastor of First Wayne Street Methodist Church. Then Roman Catholic Bishop William McManus of the Fort Wayne Diocese addressed the gathering, joyously announcing, "Soon we shall have more whites than blacks singing 'we shall overcome.'" Five hundred voices shook the rafters that fine day, singing their hearts out in rapturous fellowship.

People lingered, drawn together, many holding hands. Oh, it was an incredible day as the Klan faded and didn't return to Fort Wayne. The mayor, Richard Armstrong, later wrote in the local newspapers a glowing tribute to the clergy and people. He concluded with the declaration, "We have all become stronger, because of this crisis." Yes. God does this kind of thing when people of faith gather together in love.

≈

The Methodist Church has always felt kinship with other mainline denominations, and with Catholics and Jews. On one occasion, Leroy Hodapp invited a group of Methodist clergy to join in conversations with Jewish leaders at Indianapolis Hebrew Congregation (IHC) in Indianapolis. The meeting was primarily an effort to help Protestants like myself understand the Jewish ethnic consciousness. With the guidance of Rabbi Murray Saltzman, we spent a most productive evening. If we Protestants still didn't quite find anything in our own self-imaging to enable us to fully understand the Jewish consciousness, we certainly came away with fond feelings toward our Jewish neighbors. In following years, youth groups from IHC worshiped at a Methodist church once each year, and each year a seder dinner was sponsored by members of the Jewish congregation for outsiders. The dinner was always well-attended by Methodists eager to learn as well as to worship. On several occasions, Methodist pastors were invited to preach to the congregation of IHC.

It should also be noted that the day would come in 1992 when the General Conference, seeing the increase in the number of Hispanic Americans members and visitors, voted to prepare a plan for Hispanic ministries. In the following sessions of the Indiana Annual Conferences, this plan was announced, and preparations were made to carry out the plan in both North and South Conferences.

This challenge still confronts Indiana Methodism. A large and growing Hispanic population results from the fact that Hoosiers are basically kind, and people from Hispanic nations, aware of this, are arriving here in ever growing numbers. Estimates number Hispanics in Indiana at nearly seventy thousand in the year 2000. While many are Roman Catholic, many are not. Unfortunately,

Rev. Oscar Ramos sings with his daughter during a North Indiana Annual Conference session. Photo courtesy of Hoosier UM News.

*Oscar and Juanita Ramos
have co-pastored La Sagrada
Familia (The Holy Family)
UMC in Goshen, minis-
tering to the ever-growing
Hispanic population in
north central Indiana.*

one problem is that the majority either don't speak English or else
lack sufficient command of English to successfully function in the
economic community. Two of their fundamental needs are assistance in learning English and places to worship where they feel
welcome. Given the universal human tendency to seek out one's
own kind for worship, it seems wise that churches be organized to
meet this need among our new Hispanic friends. One such venture
has been undertaken by the members of First Church, Goshen,
where an outreach ministry called La Sagrada Familia (The Holy
Family) United Methodist Church is reaching a small number of
Spanish-speaking people. Pastors Oscar and Juanita Ramos are
leading them and, while the church only exists as a gathering, not
as a building, hopes are high for this project to prove a spearhead
for many further such efforts by other congregations. Oscar Ramos
points out that the tendency of newly arrived families to move on
can be disconcerting as one tries to bond a congregation. But God
and a determined congregation may yet perform this miracle.

Another Hispanic congregation, Vida Nueva (New Life)
Church was established in 1986 on the Indianapolis east side.
Pastored by Reverend David Peñalva, the church is reported to be
going strong. It recently sent a work team to Honduras. Also, two
Korean Methodist churches are actively serving the growing
Korean population. First Korean Church on the east side of

Indianapolis, founded in 1978, is pastored by Reverend Tae Joon Cho. Korean United Methodist Church in Bloomington, founded in 1987, serves a mainly campus congregation and is pastored by Reverend Byungchill Hahn.

∿

Close relationships were also sought with the Catholic Church. Certain restrictions in Catholicism prevented joint worship services, but other means were found to build a warm closeness. Many Methodist clergy joined with Catholic priests to perform interfaith weddings. On one occasion in 1967, Bill Hogsett, Methodist chaplain of Community Hospital, arranged for a group of Methodist clergy to meet with Fathers Roberts Borchertmeyer and Ed Sorgel at the Catholic CYO camp, Rancho Framasa, in Nashville, Indiana. In the course of a two-day discussion, which I participated in, we discovered strong mutual ground. Despite our obvious doctrinal differences, we were joined in mutual love and respect. We decided that we agreed a great deal more than we disagreed.

Years later, Borchertmeyer and Sorgel, along with the distinguished Monsignor Raymond Bosler, invited Hogsett and me to join them to watch the Notre Dame verses Southern Methodist football game at the Little Flower Catholic Church parish house. Memories differ as to the winner—Hogsett and I are fairly sure it was Southern Methodist. But as the years went by, it was generally agreed no one would look up the record, allowing each to be sure of victory that joyous day.

Tae Joon Cho. Photo courtesy of Hoosier UM News.

David Enrique Peñalva made news in Indianapolis in 2000 when he and members of his church, La Vida Nueva UMC, led a mission team to his native Honduras to help with the post–Hurricane Mitch relief effort there. It was a cooperative effort Rev. Peñalva had organized with the Indianapolis fire and police departments in an effort to foster tolerance and understanding of the city's burgeoning Hispanic population. Firemen and police worked alongside UM Volunteers in Mission to bring vaccines, basic health services, and other support to those displaced by the disaster there.

The Indianapolis Church Federation served as a bonding organization for the many local denominations in Indianapolis. Professor Alfred Edyvean, a Methodist minister and director of communications at Christian Theological Seminary, worked through the Federation to begin a current events television show, *Cross Exam*, on WTHR, Channel 13. The format for the thirty-minute show had a Methodist pastor serving as a moderator of discussions with local and national leaders in a variety of areas of national life. Reverend Richard Hamilton, then pastor of St. Luke's Church in Indianapolis, began as moderator. Local news people, either reporters from the local newspapers or news people from local television and radio stations served as interviewers. The show began in the early 1960s and soon won a prestigious news award under Hamilton's leadership. When Hamilton was named district superintendent of the Bloomington District in 1962, I replaced him at St. Luke's, and, apparently taking the easy way out, Edyvean asked me to assume the role of moderator of *Cross Exam* as well.

Cross Exam lasted six more years, with interviews of such national figures as Bobby Kennedy, 1968 presidential aspirant Eugene McCarthy, movie actress Laraine Day, race car driver Mario Andretti, several well-known athletes, as well as the head of Scotland Yard in London. Also among the interviewees were such Indiana leaders as Senator Birch Bayh, Mayor (later Senator) Richard Lugar, Congressman William Bray, the head of the Black Panthers, and a rich variety of others who influenced the course of events in the state of Indiana in the sixties and early seventies. Reverend Mac Hamon, who later became a district superintendent and the current pastor of Castleton Church, was then a student. He brought significant, energetic creativity to bear in arranging well-known guests. He knew no fear when it came to asking them to participate.

Local politics in the media ended the life of *Cross Exam*, so the church federation moved us across the street in 1973 to WRTV, Channel 6, where the same format was rebaptized *Aware*, which lasted two more years. During all those years, more than one guest expressed gratitude for an opportunity to be heard in an open and cordial setting. The show was not overtly religious beyond the church federation sponsorship and the presence of a Methodist minister. But the moderator was in a position to ask occasional questions from a religious perspective, so there was grief over the changing policies of television stations, who in general shied away from religious-based programming. Only with the advent of cable television many years later would churches again have a voice as widely heard.

CHAPTER EIGHT

*How will we tell
those dead soldiers
and those men dying now
That the war's been won?*

*Won at tables
by the old men of both sides,
giving this point—
taking that.*

*Erasing paragraphs
just as easily as they taught us
how to win lead medals
for erasing lives.*
—Rod McKuen

Years of Rage and Sadness: Vietnam

I n the late 1950s, in an area of southeast Asia all but unknown to most Americans, native warfare had broken out. Age old animosities, exacerbated by larger ideologies behind the scenes, unleashed a grim style of combat. The American military, imbued with the lessons learned in World War 2 and the Korean action, sent "experts" to help the South Vietnamese learn an up-to-date form of military action. However, the people of North Vietnam harbored resentment towards America. They had fought against the Japanese with us in the 1940s, and were angered by our response at the end of the war. They perceived us to be an arrogant nation, taking sole credit for the victory. This only deepened the determination of those people to invest everything they could to win.

Masters at the art of jungle warfare, like Brer Rabbit in the briar patch, the people of the North soon made it clear that the lessons of previous wars were no guide to warfare in Vietnam. Several years of tragic casualties and the surprising unpopularity of patriotism among a large segment of the young population of America eventually convinced a growing proportion of Americans that the war was not going to be won, that continued casualties were unacceptable, and that in the absence of a true moral basis for continued conflict, it was time to leave. Young men, most of whom would undoubtedly have stepped forth courageously in World War 2, used a variety of subterfuges to avoid serving. Ten thousand fled to Canada. Others found loopholes in the draft laws which permitted them to defer service. Adding to a rather arbitrary means of selecting men for service, differences of opinion boiled over into hatred and broken families. Meanwhile, young men who had dutifully gone to the war returned home expecting a hero's welcome, only to be received with varying degrees of rejection and sometimes vilification. Devastated by this reaction, the incidence of alcoholism, drug addiction, suicide, and crime among too many veterans was epidemic. True, the great majority of veterans quietly resumed their places in society, but many did so with a very understandable vein of bitterness in their disappointed hearts. The changed sentiments were symbolized by a remake of the 1960 patriotic war movie *The Halls of Montezuma*, which concluded with a gathering of Marines singing that rousing title song as they marched in victory. The 1987 reprise of the movie, set in the Vietnam War, *Full Metal Jacket,* concluded with the men singing the Mickey Mouse song.

≈

By 1965 the war in Vietnam had begun to escalate and inaugurate for America what Todd Gitlin, a former radical activist by his own definition and now a professor of sociology at the University of California, Berkeley, termed a period in our history akin to "a cyclone in a wind tunnel." In April of that year, 25,000 young people marched on Washington to protest the war—that was about the number of American troops in Vietnam. By the end of 1965, there were 184,000 troops, and by the end of 1967, there were nearly a half million American troops in

Vietnam. Gitlin described the years 1967 through 1970 as "the season of rage." Fifteen thousand of our men had been killed, the air force was flying two thousand sorties a week, and it is now estimated that by the end of 1967, 1.7 million acres of jungle had been defoliated. No one had any idea at all of the number of Vietnam civilian casualties. By that time, U.S. authorities in the field had begun to exaggerate enemy body counts to the point that one of America's greatest heroes, Colonel David Hackworth, who had been wounded in action eight times in three wars, resigned in disgust.

In Indiana, there was growing ambivalence. Youthful demonstrators weren't thought well of, especially as reports of car burnings, broken windows, disrupted cities, and the growing use of LSD had spread. There was the impression that many demonstrators were having a distorted kind of fun in place of the hard work of college, which did little to win support from conservative Hoosiers.

One sad development of these tragic times was the sudden unpopularity of the American flag and the whole idea of patriotism. An older generation had grown up revering the flag. It was instinctive for any thoughtful citizen to pause respectfully if the flag was displayed. If an American traveled to a foreign land, his or her heart would be warmed by the sight of the American flag. Now, young people, kids from fine homes, and college students were spitting on the flag, even burning flags. Clothing made with the flag, often inverted in disrespect, was worn by young people in a blatant act of disparagement. Fathers who had stormed the beaches of Iwo Jima, Normandy, Guadalcanal, and Anzio were angered at this disdain for the country for which some of their best friends had died. Generation was set against generation. For a time, the two simply could not understand each other. Critics of the time equated patriotism with chauvinism. The long-range effects are still visible—even into the third millennium, many people feel apologetic at any evidence of fervent patriotism.

This divided sentiment quickly invaded our churches. Members began asking why the American flag wasn't being displayed in the sanctuary alongside the Christian flag. Many ministers felt apologetic if an American flag appeared in their buildings, and many found themselves facing difficult moral decisions about the flag. At St. Luke's Church in Indianapolis, one member donated a beautiful American flag, and a group insisted it be displayed in the sanctuary. As pastor, I found myself faced with a traumatic and emotional choice. I'm of that older generation. As a teenager, I landed at Utah Beach in Normandy with an infantry company. But I also understood the sentiments of the young people who hated our involvement in Vietnam. While I rejected their disruptive behavior, I shared their opposition to America's commitments in Vietnam and understood the young people's frustration in trying to drive home to our country's leaders how wrong they believed them to be. To many young people, a public display of the flag in a church was tantamount to support of the Vietnam commitment. It was not an easy time to keep a congregation happy.

More than a few Indiana young people disappeared from home, only to be found weeks later in Haight-Asbury, or Greenwich Village, or downtown San Francisco. Television, supplemented by movies depicting jungle fighting in Vietnam, sowed seeds of doubt in a growing number of people. However, a World War 2 generation only just entering their early- to mid-forties, still held a view of patriotism which expected true American young men to step forward to serve as needed, and to do so proudly, without protest.

But returning Vietnam veterans reported a completely different feeling among battle-experienced young men. The government had made one terrible mistake in the process of bringing veterans back from the war. Unlike World War 2 and Korea, in which a man removed from battle waited weeks, even months before returning home, Vietnam veterans, especially those badly wounded, were flown immediately home without time for the emotional process of readapting to a civilized world. The result was emotional trauma of serious proportions. Given the easy accessibility of drugs and alcohol, it became apparent that something terrible was happening to our soldiers. They were fighting a war they didn't understand, led by generals who knew little about the kind of warfare in which they were engaged, and led by an officer corps which, though certainly numbering many heroes, was primarily interested in recognition and promotion. There were reports of generals awarding Silver Stars for gallantry in action to colonels who paid a brief visit to the fighting zones, only to have the favor returned by colonels who reported the heroism of generals who had come within earshot of battle. Colonel Hackworth at one time refused to award decorations to the men of his regiment because he felt the awards had been depreciated by overuse as a morale builder. Many veterans of earlier wars had begun to agree that this war did not deserve the lives of young men who had so much to live for. The U.S. authorities reported 570,000 cases of "draft offenders." Only 8,750 or 1.5 percent were ever convicted.

Hawks, those who supported the war, outnumbered the Doves, those who opposed the war, in Indiana for years. Then two things happened. In November of 1967, a crowd of youthful demonstrators gathered before the Pentagon. Armed troops faced them, carrying rifles at the ready. But the young people were there in peace. Some placed flowers in the barrels of the threatening rifles. They sang "Yellow Submarine," invited the soldiers to join their ranks, and called out, "We love you."

One GI stepped out of ranks and offered cigarettes to the nearby demonstrators. Young men bearing weapons took their fingers off the triggers. Photographs showed America's children, confronting one another, some with guns, some with flowers. People back in Indiana watched on television. Not everyone was yet convinced. But a growing number of sincere, patriotic Hoosiers began to think again about their support of a war they were told could never be won—a war opposed by hundreds of thousands of America's college-aged children. Their opposition to the war wasn't cowardice. It was sanity. They began to change.

For many of us, the final straw was the horrendous day in 1970 when a group of zealous students began an anti-war demonstration on the campus of Kent State University. Someone overreacted. The National Guard arrived, and somehow—no one really knows just why—a young fellow probably no older than the kids he was facing pulled a trigger. Other young men, whether prompted by fear or hatred or just plain nervousness, opened fire. Moments later, four innocent college students lay dead, and nine others lay wounded. America recoiled in horror. No matter what one might feel about a bunch of kids parading around on behalf of a cause in which they devoutly believed, no one—not a single person with the slightest bit of heart—could want to see any of them dead. If any event of the sixties turned the tide, it was probably Kent State.

Now staid business and professional people began to speak out against the war. Pastors found the courage to declare to their congregations the opposition they had felt in their hearts for some time. Wise political counselors began to tell President Johnson of their own misgivings about the war. In January of 1972, James Armstrong, pastor of Broadway Church in Indianapolis, led a seminar in Washington, D.C. He addressed several hundred Methodist clergy from across the country on handling controversy in the local church. Then, after one session on a cold, blustery January day, Armstrong invited those who were willing to join him in a demonstration in front of the capitol building. Armstrong had recently had surgery on his foot. Nonetheless, he limped ahead of us as we each accepted signs bearing the names of known prisoners of war. Standing there in a spitting winter rain, many of us wearing suits and ties, feeling foolish at this strange new experience, we begged whatever authorities might be listening to "bring the prisoners home." Our hearts were now with the flower children, the students, and the kids who had shown us the way. That didn't mean that we were happy with the militant Students for a Democratic Society, nor that we endorsed the drugs or the disruptive protests which lay ahead. But this we believed: the war was wrong, further casualties became atrocities, and the war must end. Such events began to happen across the country. President Lyndon Johnson was listening.

∾

Meanwhile, back in the suburbs, other matters preoccupied most pastors and church leaders. While it is impossible to understand the church and the nation of today without some understanding of the sixties and seventies, it does not follow that those controversial issues necessarily dominated the suburban churches. Concerned though suburbanites were with Civil Rights, the war on poverty, and the Vietnam War, and as important as suburban pastors considered these issues to be, the shoe pinched most tightly at the point of finances and church growth. The initial rapid growth of the late fifties and very early sixties had diminished, leaving many churches with hefty mortgages, but exuberant growth expectations on the part of many members of the hierarchy. Every preaching minister was faced with a perplexing moral dilemma. Many congregants were touchy about controversial issues. Outspoken pastors were already being removed from churches. In a mid-1960s sermon, Bishop Sheldon Dueker used an illustration about Medgar Evers, a Civil Rights leader who had been murdered. Dueker remembers, "Several families were so incensed by the fact that I used a black man as a favorable example in an illustration that they stopped coming to church." I recall having a guest preacher at Asbury Church who made a passing reference to President Kennedy in his sermon in 1962. When I returned and inquired of one older couple how they liked the visiting preacher, they grumbled that "all he talked about was politics." Almost every minister opposed the Vietnam War and supported the Civil Rights movement. All pastors struggled with the question of how to declare their conscience while, at the same time, retaining their congregations. It was a time of national turmoil to be sure. But it was also a time of inner turmoil for every Methodist minister.

Meetings were held with visiting "experts" sharing insights on how to grow a church. Not all such experts had very many correct answers. One man, however, did point an important direction for the future of Indiana Methodism. Dr. Richard Myers was a Methodist researcher commissioned by the Indianapolis Church Federation to determine just which factors do, indeed, result in membership growth. Using an early form of the computer in 1963, Myers examined hundreds of Protestant churches throughout the country to determine what characterized growing churches and which factors seemed to characterize failing churches. He determined that two factors made the difference. One, the number of small face-to-face groups in a church. Two, the number of program staff members.

Addressing a large gathering of Methodist pastors at Lawrence Methodist Church in 1964, Myers announced something else which impacted Methodism nationwide. He emphatically insisted that the membership of a local church was a largely meaningless statistic. It was average Sunday morning worship attendance which determined a church's real size. The percentage of attendance to membership became the reigning measure of a congregation's health—that and their record of payment of conference apportionments. Thus, a church of a thousand members might have an attendance of three hundred, while another church of a thousand members might have an attendance of six hundred. Ergo, the two churches were really far different in size. Since financial apportionments were based on the number of members, and since the number of members was no longer looked upon as a meaningful statistic, clergy began paring their membership rolls to reduce their apportionments. As denominational outreach and growing staff salaries were becoming more costly, apportionments had become a heavy if worthy financial burden. An example is Trinity Church in Elkhart. In 1969 the church showed a membership of 1,511 with Sunday morning attendance of 434. By 1999 the membership had dropped to 1,031, but attendance had actually risen to 596.

This also began to exact a toll on denominational size. It became clear that frequently a member of one church would move to a new location and in due time join another Methodist church. Often the paper work necessary to remove and add was not done, which resulted in probably thousands of duplications nationwide. Furthermore, many a Methodist had either stopped going to church, died, or joined another denomination. As a result, national membership figures were badly inflated. This led to a public perception which exaggerated any actual decline in the size

Dr. Carolyn E. Johnson's work in the Indiana Church and nationally is marked by a commitment to Christian Social Involvement. She was one of a select group to attend a special White House briefing on children and has been a church activist/leader for issues affecting the black family and children. She continues to be among the most prominent of our national lay leaders, having served at literally all levels of the Connection. In recent years she was vice president of the General Council on Ministries and held that same office for the General Board of Global Ministries. Immediate past national president of United Methodist Women, Dr. Johnson was the youngest woman ever elected to the post. She was also elected a delegate to the past four general conferences and continues to provide leadership for Black Methodists for Church Renewal (BMCR), among many other areas of service to the church and world community. Photo by United Methodist News Service.

of the Methodist Church, as knowing pastors "removed the dead-wood" from their rolls. Not immune to a spirit of competition, pastors had historically sought every legitimate means to show membership growth. Bishops often pointed fingers of guilt at churches which declined in size. Now, all of that had changed, and worship attendance was gaining acceptance as the true measure of a church's size. Many churches began tightening membership requirements and requiring attendance at church classes in preparation for membership. Those churches which still received members with no preparation began to show increasing disparity between membership and attendance, and the tightened requirements for membership began to strengthen the denomination, even if bottom line numbers declined.

Churches also began the small group movement. To what extent Myers is to be credited with this is hard to say, but he, along with other insightful researchers and pastors, had begun to make this a prime emphasis. Robert Raines, son of Indiana's bishop, wrote a widely read book *New Life in the Church*, which became a handbook for the developing of small groups. Books by other authors followed. It soon became apparent that meeting with a few other people who were serious about the Christian life, sharing, and searching was a powerful way to discover a deep and sustaining faith. It was also an effective means of dealing with controversial issues in a congregation. Shades of John Wesley. The church was rediscovering what Wesley had known from the beginning. Drastically modified, the class meeting was once more the means to a vital and growing church. The churches that followed this counsel began to grow once more. Myers also pointed out that small groups included not only adult search groups, but also church committees and commissions, and of course, Sunday school classes (which were, at about that time, renamed church school classes).

An example of Myers's recommendations can be seen at Asbury Church on the far northeast side of Indianapolis. Established in 1962 under the watchful eye of Forest Manor Church and Reverend Lawrence Cooper, along with Superintendent Kenneth Forbes, Asbury had begun to experience rapid growth through its first two years of life. But during the third year, attendance plateaued, and membership showed modest growth. Then after hearing a presentation by Myers, a group within the church remodeled the unused basement of a small building that was serving as their fellowship hall. With labor supplied by church members and with used lighting equipment provided by Forest Manor Church, five new classrooms were built. As predicted by Myers, Asbury's attendance grew by some 25 percent in the following year. Church school attendance grew, and with the addition of some adult groups in the evenings, Asbury once more experienced rapid growth. Myers also introduced another statistic, one which sounds crass in the reporting, but one which caught the attention of every pastor struggling to pay off a burdensome mortgage: each new small group, said Myers, would add six new pocketbooks.

There were those who criticized this emphasis on church growth. Many a dedicated servant of the inner city felt the people living in suburbia were ignoring the plight of the poor. People in the suburbs, on the other hand, contended that the only reason the church was able to serve the people in depressed areas was because of the money flow from those very suburban churches. In truth, there were people in suburban churches who either didn't give a hang for the poor, or they only did lip service to the idea of helping. But they were a small minority. The majority looked for ways to pitch in. Groups from those churches spent countless hours in volunteer service in economically distressed churches and community centers. Places like Fletcher Place and Central Avenue Church in Indianapolis were able to do what they did, in large part, because of these volunteers. Large groups of older women met at Methodist Hospital to wrap bandages. There was a rich variety of volunteer services, and many sacrificial financial gifts as well.

Another point is important. Granted, the focus in these years was on people living in poverty and people suffering from prejudice and racism. That was appropriate. But there was plenty of suffering to go around. People in the cities and towns and suburbs who appeared to live comfortably often had other problems. There were marriage problems, health problems, emotional problems, job problems, and family problems. And many people had serious financial problems, too. Someone once said that a boil on the end of your nose is a bigger catastrophe than a famine in China. Any minister who served in one of those supposedly successful churches can tell of the hours spent counseling and otherwise helping hurting people cope with their troubles. Sometimes people are so busy trying to act responsibly in the face of their own trials that they temporarily lack the energy to worry about others.

Each church had plenty to do right at home. Professor Robert Putnam of Harvard, in his studies of society's problems, referred to *Social Capital* as the combined energy available for creative and constructive living. The dust jacket to his book, *Bowling Alone*, states: "Communities with less Social Capital have lower educational performance and more teen pregnancy, child suicide, low birth weight, and prenatal mortality. Social Capital is also a prime predictor of crime rates and other measures of neighborhood quality of life, as it is of our health." And then this: "In quantitative terms, if you both smoke and belong to no groups, it's a close call as to which is the riskier behavior." In other words, his studies have confirmed that participation in groups is the prime source of this Social Capital.

Putnam also discovered that regular worshipers "are much more likely than other people, to attend club meetings, and to belong to sports groups; professional and academic societies; school service groups; youth groups; service clubs; hobby or garden clubs; literary, art, discussion, and study groups; school fraternities and sororities; farm organizations; political clubs; nationality groups. . . ." In other words, churches are the prime contributors to that Social Capital which builds strong, healthy communities. It was this, as much as ministries beyond their own borders, which occupied those churches. They were playing a major part in the creation of a quality of life which made this country a great place to live.

～

It may not be surprising to learn that during these eventful years, there was conflict between various clergy groups. Sometimes we seemed like Stephen Leacock's character who

"jumped on his horse and rode off in all directions." Based on
personality differences, differing life situations, and varying
political points of view, preachers squabbled. Some pastors
complained it was nearly impossible to get anything done at a
Methodist board or committee meeting because someone of each
stripe was a member. Suburban pastors complained that inner-
city people failed to understand that unless they supported the
expansion of the suburban church, there wouldn't be enough
money to carry out their plans for inner-city work. Urban pastors
complained that suburban pastors, busily living the easy life,
were not genuinely committed to the real work of ministry. Rural
pastors argued that the grassroots Methodist Church was
country and small town, and too little attention was being given
to those heartland churches. Members of the hierarchy—
superintendents, conference council on ministries staff, and certain
pastors on special appointments—felt the real mission of the
church in the sixties was to focus on the needs of racial integration,
ministry to the poor and homeless, and third-world concerns.
These members demanded ever growing budgets and made controversial statements which local pastors had to explain, while church
pastors complained that people in special appointments had
forgotten how tough it is to keep a congregation together in such
controversial times.

This was nothing new, however. Herbert Heller's history of the
Indiana Conference (as it was once known) covering the years 1826
until 1956 began with this observation: ". . . the author submits the
history of the Indiana Conference of the Methodist Church. This is
a story of ignorance, selfishness, narrowness, and petty politics. . . ."
But then he added this saving word: ". . . but much more it is a
picture of faith in Methodism as the means of achieving a Christian
way of life, a love of God and fellow man. . . ." And so this, too,
continued to describe the workings of the Methodist Church in
recent years.

The National Council of Churches had become a highly
controversial agency, suspected of Communism by a great many
members of the churches. While few if any clergy thought that,
many wished those folks in New York would at least quiet down

a bit so people could get on with the work of the day-to-day life of the church.

At many meetings, there was more heat than light. Talented laypeople often attended one or two meetings, decided the preachers would never agree on anything, and departed. This was the era of allowing everyone to have his or her say, no matter how long they required to do so. Meetings often ran late, and for a time those with the greatest capacity to endure lengthy monologues ruled the day. Richard Lancaster, pastor of Meridian Street Church, persuaded one of his highly successful business executive members to serve on a Methodist board devoted to urban ministries. After one meeting, the man informed Lancaster that the board had spent an entire evening trying to settle something that a businessman would have taken ten minutes to decide. The businessman thereupon resigned on the grounds that if they continued in the way he had experienced, nothing would ever be done. Methodist pastors, however, know that God works in strange and wondrous ways, and traditional business practices don't always work in church life. Belatedly, after many unnecessary and exhausting gatherings, those who serve Jesus finally draw together and do get a surprising number of worthwhile works completed. Maybe someone who has grown up in a very large family that squabbles frequently but ends up at a family dinner with laughter and hugs can best grasp the dynamics of clergy relationships. But during the sixties and seventies, this was certainly the way things often progressed.

Another favorite ground for hot debate was preaching styles. Ministers whose churches were growing were often accused of being "popular preachers," which was definitely not meant as a compliment. The opposite of this was "faithful preaching," by which one doggedly held before the congregation the expensive demands of Jesus' words. The German martyr-theologian Dietrich Bonhoeffer, whose writings were consumed by many preachers during this era, referred disdainfully to "cheap Grace," the offering of the benefits of Jesus' sacrifice without actually joining in that sacrifice. The amusing thing about preachers is that hardly any of us have ever heard each other preach on Sunday mornings

because we are in our own pulpits. Opinions about each other
tended to be formed more on the basis of hearsay from church
members or from discussions at meetings or over lunch.
Sometimes—because we are, after all, human—judgments were
based on envy. In truth, every preacher was preaching from the
heart, doing the best he or she could with the abilities that had
been developed and that God had given. Somehow, the church
with all its faults and frailties stood tall against the driving winds
of conflict, dissension, and uncertainty which beset America in the
sixties and early seventies.

$\sim$

Actions, though, always speak louder than words. Little did
Reverend Harold Leininger suspect the amazing adventure about
to unfold when his phone rang one June day in 1975. He heard
the voice of E. Ross Adair, former lay leader of the Fort Wayne
District and member of congress, who was at the time a foreign
ambassador. Adair had been in contact with the ambassador of
South Vietnam, Thoi Dat Lien. Relatives of Lien's wife had been
among the last people to escape from Saigon before its fall to the
North Vietnamese, and they were now interned at Fort Chaffee,
Arkansas. Adair then made a very daring request. He knew that
Leininger was pastor of First Church, Decatur. Was there any
possible way for the people of the Decatur church community to
extricate those refugees from Fort Chaffee and bring them to
Decatur?

People who know Leininger will not be surprised to know that
he quickly responded with an enthusiastic, "Yes!" He contacted
the pastors of three other congregations, St. Mark's Methodist, St.
Mary's Catholic, and Zion Missouri Synod Lutheran Church.
They in turn enlisted members of their congregations, and the decision was made to do everything possible to bring the four internee
families to Decatur. First, the congregations sought housing. Fifty
people of First Church found an old, dilapidated house. Then the
work began. They assembled furniture, bedding, and kitchen
appliances. They began the drudgery of restoring the house until it

Harold L. Leininger, 1975.

was not just a house, but a home. Contacts were made with physicians, dentists, and other professional people who agreed to help
when the refugees arrived. Food, clothing, and money were
collected. Everything was ready.

The hard part, however, was still ahead: how to get the
Vietnamese refugees out of Fort Chafee. Calls were made to the
White House, the State Department, and the office of Governor
Otis Bowen. Someone at Central Soya Corporation made
arrangements for Leininger, accompanied by Mrs. Lien and her
niece, to fly in a company plane to Fort Chaffee. They were
accompanied by a cameraman from a local television station.
Influence had been brought to bear successfully, and after
seventy days of internship, twenty-four Vietnamese refugees
were given permission to leave. Leininger later said, after
watching the joyous reunion which took place that day, "One of
the highest points in my ministry . . . was the thrill of being able
to fly down to Arkansas to give an advance welcome to our new
Decatur citizens." Governor Bowen had made an Indiana

National Guard plane available, the refugees were flown to Fort Wayne, and they were greeted by the Decatur Bellmont band playing the South Vietnamese national anthem. Then followed a performance from the First Church choir, singing songs of faith and greeting and a series of welcoming speeches by dignitaries of the town. One newcomer, a Mr. Trinh, wept at the sound of his nation's song.

In the months that followed, the Vu Lu Bang family served Vietnamese cuisine to visitors five nights a week to show their appreciation. At Christmas time, Thin Bang made sixty-four yule log cakes and delivered them to families on her bicycle. One man asked Leininger why the Americans had done all of this. He replied: "It is because of our Christian faith." Today, a quarter of a century later, Leininger states that those former refugees "are, today, ambassadors around the world sharing what God can do in a community of Christian love."

～

The mindset of Americans toward people in authority was irrevocably altered in August 1968, by events surrounding the Democratic National Convention in Chicago. In fact, attitudes toward legal authorities had been fraying for some time among the younger generation. The "don't trust anyone over thirty" philosophy which, in reality applied to only a relatively small minority of young people, was destined to redefine the meaning of authority in America. In many ways, the ultimate effect of this change would prove a benefit. In many other ways, the effects would undermine the very institutions which made America strong and free. The church would be one of those institutions. As Gitlin wrote, "For every face of authority, there was someone to slap it."

Those few dark and tragic days are embedded in the minds of many people in their fifties today. Mayor Richard Daley's police force and thousands of anti-war, anti-government protesters who had arrived to express their protests for the convention clashed repeatedly in numerous battles, which resulted in hundreds of injuries and millions of dollars of property damage. It is for others with appropriate qualifications to dissect and evaluate those events. It is public record, however, that the Chicago Police Department appeared to a college generation as little more than storm troopers, depriving thousands of young men and women— mostly law abiding people—of the right to protest. Ironically, many news people were injured or otherwise hassled, a fact which resulted in very bad press for the authorities. This unquestionably spilled over onto the candidates, and it is not unlikely that Hubert Humphrey's campaign was badly damaged as a result. He lost the election to Richard Nixon.

It is probable that the average Hoosier applauded the early reports of police enforcement of law and order. That very phrase, "law and order," was becoming a catch phrase for an orderly society. It was only later that the excesses of the enforcement process in Chicago were known, raising alarms and second thoughts on the part of many of us. America was still in the hands of a people who had been raised to respect authority, whether parents, teachers, ministers, police, government officials, leaders in education, the military, or the people who ran the industries which provided livelihoods for our citizens. Now a new attitude had begun to infect the young. Why trust someone simply because that person has managed to achieve authority? If the police in Chicago could be as corrupt as many believed, was it not good sense to keep an eye on them everywhere? Look at what they had done in Mississippi, Alabama, and Arkansas. And if we are keeping an eye on the police, why not on the rest as well?

It was in hotbeds of activism that these sentiments were most vividly and emphatically evident—Berkeley, Harvard, Stanford, San Francisco State, Columbia, Cornell—but a diluted version of this new suspicion of authority was seeping into all the colleges, including the universities of Indiana. In late 1968 researcher Daniel Yankelovich reported a poll showing that 42 percent of college students said they were unconcerned with college's practical benefits. In the two years of 1968–69, there were well over a hundred campus bombings and incidents of arson nationwide, usually aimed at ROTC buildings and other campus buildings. In the spring of 1969 three hundred colleges and universities saw sizable demonstrations. Following the shootings at Kent State, seventy-five campuses nationwide remained closed for the rest of the school year.

This new attitude had a profound effect on churches nation-wide. Methodist seminaries fed this new sentiment into the churches. The idea that a student attended a college or seminary in order to learn from a group of educators who knew things the students did not know was rapidly eroding, as many members of a generation of young people began to suspect—usually incorrectly—that they knew things the faculty did not know. It was heady stuff for those who assumed the mantle of youthful leadership. At Garrett-Evangelical Theological Seminary in Evanston, Illinois, which sent a steady stream of newly trained clergy into Indiana, a group of militant students one day interrupted the venerable Edward Blair's class in New Testament and informed him that what he was teaching was irrelevant to the new world. Dr. Blair is said to have strode to his office, packed up his briefcase, climbed in his car, and headed for home, his resignation letter already being composed in his mind. Fortunately, this kind and brilliant man was persuaded to reconsider. But the ground had shaken. Nothing would be the same.

One day a group of students, led by a young man from a prominent Indiana Methodist family, barged into a meeting of the governing board of Garrett carrying a casket, which had been painted with the words "Body of Knowledge." The message was clear. Education as learning was, in the minds of these young people, a dead issue. It was their perception that a whole new world was bursting into life, that the ancient truths no longer applied. New days would teach new ways.

Similar intrusions were happening throughout the educational system of the church. Seminary officials were in too many cases intimidated into granting outrageous demands by imma-ture, though sincere, young people who had not yet learned the lessons in life which would qualify them to decide which "truths" are really true. Preaching courses were now optional.

Students would now learn how to manipulate community structures. Never mind that nearly all would soon be sent out to some
small, rural church to tell a farm or small community congregation about the love of Jesus. Let them develop zeal for ministry
to third-world nations, and let them learn how to work with
political systems for the betterment of the community—a
community which often had gotten along quite well for many
years prior to the arrival of the brilliant new expert. The problem
was not that these issues were unimportant, because, of course,
they were. The problem was that many new clergy were simply
not adequately prepared for the beginning-level church situations
into which they were thrust.

Many clergy, trained to be ministers of the gospel, were
assuming the roles of sociologists or community activists. This
role ambivalence would trouble many in the church for some
time. Among those troubled would be pastors themselves as they
genuinely sought to carry out the ministries they felt led to do.
Often frustrated with what they viewed as intractable conservatism by their members and by older clergy, a trickle of
departures from ministry would result. Others would move after
short pastorates. But of course, many learned the work of loving
ministry and discovered that after a pastor has earned the love
and respect of a congregation, they can then present any unpopular, controversial beliefs, and the congregation will honor those
differing points of view—often changing their own opinions in the
process.

One of the charming structures on the Garrett seminary
campus was a small medieval style chapel. Its interior was dark,
quiet, and authentic. Generations of students studying the theolo-
gies of Luther and Calvin and a dozen other fathers of the modern
church found solace in that quiet place. Students struggling with
a faith issue or small groups wishing to worship together looked
upon Howes Chapel as a place of sanctuary from the pressures of
a difficult education while often serving as student-pastors as
well. It was a splendid place to pray. But one day a representative
of this new view of creation led in a group of carpenters who
gutted the interior of the chapel and replaced it with light blond

oak furnishings, giving it the character and the atmosphere of a campus club. This pretty much typified prevailing attitudes for quite some time. The prior generation who had attended while Dwight Loder was president devoutly wished for his return despite his relative unpopularity due to a very iron-handed administration.

These are only symbolic examples of a growing unrest and redefinition going on throughout American society and throughout the Methodist Church at the time. Clearly, the trajectory of these changes as we entered the seventies would have profound implications for the role of bishop, superintendent, or pastor. The entire appointive system would, as soon as a generation of old heads had quietly stepped aside to write their memoirs, be radically changed.

The Era of Permissiveness: The Seventies

During this period, many young people turned from the church. Harvard professor of public policy, Robert Putnam, in his book, *Bowling Alone,* examined the breakdown in health and emotional stability of people living without small group relationships. He reported results of surveys which revealed:

> Large numbers of young, well educated, middle-class youth . . . defected from the churches in the late sixties and the seventies . . . Some joined new religious movements, others sought personal enlightenment through various spiritual therapies and disciplines, but most simply "dropped out" of organized religion altogether.

It was in 1968 that the Methodist Church united with the Evangelical United Brethren Church, thereby cementing a long-lived cordial relationship and also inheriting a new bishop at a crucial time in the life of the church. By and large, things went well since there were few differences to be settled. Indiana Central University, soon to be renamed the University of Indianapolis, came into the United Methodist fold, as did many fine churches like the campus church, University Heights. Along came some splendid clergy, men like Gene Crawford who would become a superintendent of the West Indianapolis District. Crawford soon won the admiration of his new colleagues by coupling a devout and pious spirituality with a generous understanding of the foibles of his pastors. Many other fine pastors became part of what had been the Methodist Church and was now the United Methodist Church. Entering upon the scene at a time of frequent controversy was the bishop of the EUB Church, who now became the bishop of the Indiana area of the United Methodist Church, Reuben Mueller.

The union was not without its problems in the early process. Some EUB members were opposed, as was true of a small number of Methodists. But this was the era of ecumenism, a time when many denominations were looking at unions. Finally on April 23, 1968, former EUB Bishop Reuben H. Mueller and former Methodist Bishop Lloyd C. Wicke shook hands and formally sealed the union of 10,289,000 Methodists with 739,000 Evangelical United Bretherens into the United Methodist Church. Dr. Ralph Steele, superintendent of the Terre Haute District, chaired the Indiana area delegation.

Methodism now had three universities in Indiana. Indiana Central College was founded in 1902 by United Brethren Church officials who entered into a real estate deal with William Elder in which the school received eight acres of ground in return for assisting in the sale of home lots in an area now known as University Heights. The school now occupies sixty-five acres and was cited in an issue of *U.S. News and World Report* in the year 2000 as one of the top universities in the Midwest. Under President Lynd Esch in the 1960s, Indiana Central pioneered night school degree work, enabling working people to continue their work while earning degrees. In 1986 under the presidency of Reverend Gene Sease, the name of the institution was changed to the

Gene Crawford.

University of Indianapolis. Currently under the presidency of Jerry Israel, the school has an enrollment of over four thousand students and is a widely recognized university of which, along with the University of Evansville and DePauw University, the Methodists of Indiana are justifiably quite proud.

Enough years have passed that we can relate an incident involving Reverend Gene Crawford, one which cemented his image in the minds of many former Methodists and helped clarify in their minds what those former EUB guys would be like. One evening at South Annual Conference, shortly after Crawford had become a district superintendent, several of us were gathered in the room of one pastor who was—there is no other way to put the matter—roaring drunk. An otherwise brilliant preacher and pastor, this man had not yet won his battle with the bottle. Someone saw Superintendent Crawford approaching and hurriedly tried to quiet our sad friend. When there was a knock on the door, we all remained quiet, hoping our friend could sober up and avoid being caught, especially since he was counting on a new appointment. No luck. He stumbled to the door, pulled it open, and thus entered a suddenly shocked Gene Crawford. Assuming that this man from the EUB Church would prove to be very conservative and perhaps judgmental, we also assumed our friend would be in dire trouble.

Gene Crawford was a saint that evening. He became deeply concerned. Showing great compassion, he urged us to see to the man's care. In the weeks and months that followed, no man could have been more supportive or more understanding than Crawford. He did everything he could to help the man deal with his problem. Far from critical judgmentalism, that man received the gentle kindness which led him to seek help for his problem, and his ministry was not destroyed. For some of us from the Methodist system, this was not only a discovery about one man. It was a confirmation of the quality of our new sisters and brothers from the Evangelical United Brethren Church.

≈

Bishop Reuben Mueller was a fine old gentleman. Although he was older than Raines, who was required to retire, the differing rule of the EUBs regarding age was grandfathered in, and Mueller was allowed to remain. By the time he assumed the United Methodist episcopacy, his health had placed serious limitations on his capacity to spend time with the drastically expanded area of his responsibility. The new colleagues joining the clergy from the EUB Church spoke with reverence of Mueller. The clergy of the original Methodist Church, used to the firm and demanding administration of Bishop Raines, took time to learn how to work with Mueller. In truth, Bishop Mueller quickly earned the respect of the clergy but never was able to assert the leadership to which they were accustomed. He was past retirement age. Health problems plagued him. Most clergy responded with kindly understanding and the Indiana area continued to function efficiently, thanks to strong cabinets and especially thanks to the leadership of Reverend Kenneth Forbes, who became Mueller's executive assistant in December of 1969.

Ken Forbes had long been an influential member of the Methodist Church. District superintendent of the Indianapolis

Bishop Reuben Mueller.

District from 1962 until his appointment to Irvington Church in Indianapolis in 1965, Forbes was a feisty leader who had an unshakable sense of direction for himself and for the conference. Ken Forbes did not take easily to disagreement from other pastors. And yet, deep down, he was able to respect those who openly disagreed with him—provided they had already earned his respect as pastors. Always ready to do battle on the conference floor, anyone who decided to oppose Forbes in any of his programs had better be ready to do his or her homework before taking Forbes on. Forbes did not easily forget those who opposed him. Nonetheless, he was dedicated to the mission of the church and spent himself tirelessly for that purpose. People close to him saw a kind side, like the time Asbury Church was struggling to keep a volunteer youth pastor who was trying to get through school, and Forbes, district superintendent at the time, often slipped a healthy check into the pastor's hand and suggested it be given to the youth pastor as a bit of help.

Forbes wasn't particularly happy in a large congregation such as Irvington Methodist Church, which he served from 1965 to 1969.

Bishop Reuben Mueller (left), representing the Methodists and Bishop Lloyd Wicke, representing the Evangelical United Brethren, shake hands during the ceremony in which the two denominations merged in 1968 in Dallas.

Motivating staff members to the same level of tireless effort which came so naturally to him was more than he could abide. He once said he would never again serve a large congregation. Nor did he find that necessary, as his excellent administrative talents caught the attention of Bishop Mueller, and Forbes found his niche as executive assistant to the bishop. He served in this capacity until his retirement in 1986 when he and his wife, Jane, retired to the Franklin Home, where, at this writing, J. Kenneth Forbes is still making a difference. He is one of those clergy who felt called to keep the organized church a strong institution, and he never seemed troubled by doubt about the means to this end. Forbes and Mueller made a good combination as America and the Methodist Church faced new challenges going into the 1970s.

Credit must also go to the cabinets of both conferences. Most had been chosen by Raines, and they were strong except for a couple of exceptions. (I include that observation, not because I could name an exception, but because the surviving members of those cabinets will think I know more than I do.)

Typical of the strong superintendents is Charles Ballard. "Charlie" was popular because he was honest, fair, and direct. In truth, his strong suit was pastoring but he spent a dozen years as a superintendent, first briefly in Columbus, then in Indianapolis. He used to claim that he had a sign over his door which read simply "damn." He didn't, actually, but that was part of his colorful reputation. In fact, the sign read "I'm not worth a damn in the morning until I have my coffee." I knew I was going to like Ballard when he pulled up next to me on Pennsylvania Street as I was driving my new, stripped down Chevrolet. Charlie rolled his window down, grinned at me, and observed, "It sure do pay to serve Jesus." Every pastor I knew who served under Ballard thought the world of him. He was cut from the same piece of cloth as Ross Marrs. They may not always have won prizes for diplomacy, but you always knew where you stood with them. It was men like these who carried the area through a time of restless change.

∽

The one dilemma every clergy person faces is this decision: to what extent must I stand apart from my surrounding culture in order to pronounce the judgment of the Bible on the sins and excesses of that culture, and to what extent must I immerse myself in that culture in order to correctly understand it, lest I be guilty of making demands and rendering judgments which simply do not ring true to a knowledgeable listener? Many a congregation has endured the wet-behind-the-ears preacher whose pronouncements land with jarring irritation on people who are not guilty. I listened to one young preacher in Chicago berate his congregation for twenty minutes for not attending church. The poor man did not seem to realize that the only people who could hear his indictment were those who were *in* church. Not to mention that tirade sermons almost guarantee poor attendance.

But likewise, many a congregation has been exempt from the full demand of the gospel by a good-guy clergy person who prefers not to upset people with criticisms of their lifestyles, however short of Jesus' Word they might be. In truth, nearly every clergyperson educated in the mid–twentieth century can quote ethicist and theologian Reinhold Niebuhr's famous observation, "As individuals, men believe that they ought to love and serve each other and establish justice between each other. As racial, economic, and national groups, they take for themselves whatever their power can command." Clearly, if there is truth to this sobering judgment, all of us must continually be reminded of the acquisitive impulse which resides somewhere in every human heart.

Understanding the culture that washes about us is essential for anyone who presumes to preach the Word of God, be that person clergy or lay. Understanding the culture of the new millennium requires some understanding of the ten years of the 1970s. Those years were the culmination of the sixties and set the stage for the era in which we now live. David Frum in his book *How We Got Here: The '70s—The Decade that Brought You Modern Life—For Better or Worse* declares that events in the sixties and seventies changed us from a silent, suffering people with a strong Puritan heritage to one that became self-seeking, valuing personal identity above all else. He contends that, despite some changes, our lives today are rooted in the social changes of the seventies.

Without belaboring the point, let's consider a few of the changes which were brought to us by that remarkable decade. Frum describes those years as "a time of unease and despair, punctuated by disaster." In short order, Israeli athletes were murdered at the Olympic games, the desert emirates reduced the flow of America's oil which produced runaway inflation, and America suffered a humiliating military defeat in Indochina, even though we declared a victory. Criminals took control of America's streets, marriages collapsed, drugs became available on college campuses and in high-school parking lots, a vice president was indicted, a president was forced from office, our diplomats were taken hostage, and our own government was baffled by the dilemma thus presented.

As usual, the movies described our culture. *Dirty Harry* introduced the cop who ignores the rules and deals out justice, vigilante style. The James Bond movies ushered in the hero whom everyone likes—urbane, handsome, and as far as the ladies are concerned, predatory. Bond always won, but by his own rules. In the movies, the government became the bad guy. In 1972, *The Osterman Weekend* depicted a middle-aged businessman who is told by the CIA that his friend is a Soviet agent, only to discover that the CIA agent who is supposedly protecting him is, in fact, out to get him. In the 1975 movie *Three Days of the Condor*, starring Robert Redford, the government intelligence service is trying to kill the hero because he has learned too much about their inner workings. The 1972 movie *The Parallax View* has the CIA misleading a man into thinking his friend is a Soviet agent, only to discover it is the CIA agent who is wanting him dead. In the movies of the era, the government is either dishonest or stupid. The hero eventually becomes the rogue cop, the suspicious outsider, or the crook turned good guy.

Conventional values became stuffy—an embarrassment for many people. Rules were for naive losers. In March 1971, someone broke into an FBI office in Media, Pennsylvania, and stole hundreds of secret records which revealed the misdoings of the FBI in creating thousands of files on innocent but politically suspect citizens. Phone taps had been illegally placed on hundreds of homes including that of Indiana Senator Birch Bayh. J. Edgar Hoover was revealed to be a man of far less admirable character than the world had supposed. Meanwhile, former President Kennedy was implicated in murder plots against third-world leaders. In 1971 the Pentagon Papers were released detailing Defense Secretary Robert McNamara's fearful but ongoing conviction that the war in Vietnam could not be won, and that the Kennedy administration had advocated the war. President Johnson, realizing how many unnecessary deaths had occurred in Asia, refused to run for reelection. Then followed Watergate, the indictment of Vice President Agnew, and Nixon's resignation in disgrace. And so the loss of integrity began to infect America.

In 1973 the young fellow who won an American classic, the Soap Box Derby, was stripped of his title and scholarship when it was learned he had cheated. In 1976 the bastion of honor and fidelity, West Point, was torn by a cheating scandal in which ninety-four cadets were expelled and forty-four quietly resigned. Later, a knowing student reported that more than four hundred students had cheated. This in the institution which prides itself on the fact that a cadet has sworn by his sacred honor neither to cheat nor to tolerate cheating by another. And the significant footnote to it all: the secretary of the army, apparently accepting that this was a new day, ordered that the expelled students be allowed to reapply for admission. We would see the depreciation of marriage to the point that for a large percentage of Americans marriage has become what one recent editorial writer called "a mere anachronism." And of course we learned about one William Calley who ordered his men to slaughter five hundred residents of a village in My Lai, Vietnam. Perhaps our hearts finally broke when we saw a little girl running naked toward the camera, shrieking her pain, her body fried by napalm.

In 1972, the United Methodist Church in its General Conference adopted a new doctrinal statement entitled "Our Theological Task," which recognized the new pluralism in

America. Taking account of the role of reason in theology, the statement opened the way for new enlightened interpretations of the gospel. A welcome step forward in Christian understanding for some, for others this statement was only another evidence of the waning power of the gospel's demand for what John Wesley called Scriptural holiness. The difference of opinion which began here would culminate in a threatened schism in the years to follow. Conservative Christians viewed the state of the church like an island being washed away by the sea—the cultural sea with crashing waves of moral and religious compromise.

Back home again in Indiana, the effect of this changing world was—change. Seminaries like Garrett, Wesley, United, and Christian Theological were turning out well-educated clergy, but clergy with values quite different from those of the older generation. Not necessarily better or worse—different. Members of this new generation were forthright in their personal concerns for such issues as salary, work hours, freedom to pursue avocations, and of great importance, the role of the spouse in congregational life. Though it may be disputed by some, the view of most Methodists was that the new clergy generation were far more practical, career oriented, and more openly concerned for advancement and recognition than was true of earlier generations. This probably was a manifestation of changing times and the resultant changing values. This was the generation that had led the charge against reigning authority. Not that the new clergy were disrespectful; but, neither were they intimidated. A new outspokenness would characterize this clergy generation.

One interesting change in attitudes was noticed by Reverend Steven Burris, director of the council on ministries of the North Indiana Conference. After serving for several years as a pastor, Burris left the active ministry for a lay vocation, doing so from 1968 until 1985, when he returned to the Woodburn-Maples charge. He says now that he observed upon his return that whereas the prevailing sentiment among pastors had been that of having been called by God to the ministry, most newer clergy saw their vocation as a professional choice. Not all felt this way, but Burris saw this as a characteristic of the newer generation. This may help explain the higher expectations of younger clergy in regards to salaries and other perks of the profession.

It was also during the 1970s that the leaders of the church began to become concerned about the relatively poor housing in which many clergy were required to live. The parsonage in which my family lived in our student charge had rats, one of which chased my daughter across a hallway and into a bathroom. At night we could hear little animals scurry across the attic floor. On a cold day, the temperature was never above the low sixties in the house. It was just a typical small church parsonage. But this would soon change. The old rule—the pastor shouldn't live in finer quarters than those of the less prosperous of his members—gave way to the realization that one good way to retain a good pastor for a longtime was to be sure he or she and his or her family were reasonably comfortable in their home life. So many churches began to buy or build better housing.

Most ministers eventually discover that the greatest rewards for ministry are not always material. Kate Lehman Walker, now superintendent of the Lafayette District (and North Conference candidate for the episcopacy in 2000, along with Reverends Thomas Rough and Philip Granger), learned this while serving a small church as a student at Perkins Seminary. Her face still lights up when she mentions the name of T. D. He probably had a real name to go with those initials, but everyone out on the road and in the rail yards where he spent most of his wandering life had known the man for many years as just T. D. By the time Walker knew him, he was seventy-two years old—and very ill.

The call came one day that T. D. wanted to be baptized. The lay leader of her church insisted on going with Walker to see the old man. They arrived at his home. T. D. asked to be baptized on the spot, but Walker asked that he have it done in church the following Sunday. He agreed. Then he reluctantly confided that he had recently received results of X rays which revealed a

During the 1988 North Central Jurisdiction conference at Northern Illinois University, five bishops from Indiana pose for this rare photo: (From left) Bishops Edwin Garrison, Ralph Alton, Leroy Hodapp, Sheldon Dueker, and David Lawson. Photo courtesy of Indiana Area Communications.

shadow on his lung. He knew what this meant. And now, after a lifetime of aimless existence, he realized he wanted to know the power of God's saving presence. He had decided he was ready to accept Jesus Christ as his Savior. He explained that he had withheld the information about his illness so that no one would think he wanted baptism only for that reason. To which the lay leader said, "T. D., don't let what people think keep you from having eternal life."

The following Sunday, Walker baptized T. D. A few weeks later he died. But he died with the peaceful knowledge that he was promised safe passage. And Kate Lehman Walker often tells people that the gift of having shared in a man's entry into the Christian life, and having known him through the course of his Christian experience, was a precious gift she will always cherish.

~

In 1972 Ralph T. Alton arrived from Appleton, Wisconsin, as bishop of the Indiana area. He well represented a subtle change in the bishop's role in the Methodist Church. Lacking the commanding presence of a Raines, Alton personified the Father-in-the-Faith role originally envisioned for a bishop. A good description of Alton appeared in the 1975 North Conference minutes:

> Clergy and laity alike express appreciation of:
>
> Bishop Alton for his strong and patient leadership in the councils of the church at large, our denomination, and our area, but in particular, we are grateful in Indiana for its guidance and support in the cabinet, and his skillful and fair direction of the Annual Conferences.
>
> Bishop Alton for a Christian quality of life that sets a style of conduct that challenges the best in those of us who work closely with him.
>
> Bishop and Mrs. Alton for their understanding and their continuing ministry of concern to pastor's families and congregations.

Alton was perceived by the rank and file of the church to be a good man, unpretentious, permissive up to a point, sensitive to the feelings of the clergy, and in every way a model of probity and integrity. Yet he was also a man with the firm sense of direction for the area that was needed at a crucial time in America's history. It should also be reported that prior to his assignment to the Indiana area, Alton was bishop of Wisconsin. One day he was asked to take part in a Civil Rights march. Reverend John P. Adams frankly indicated that to do this would be unpopular and, quite possibly, even dangerous. Bishop Alton marched.

Honesty requires a notation that to some who served in Alton's cabinets, he was seen as occasionally dictatorial. In truth, a bishop's life can't be easy. There are few positions more completely powerful in America than that of a Methodist bishop. He or she has the power to move people as may seem wise, and there is no appeal from an episcopal decision. Including children, there are probably more than four thousand people in Indiana at any given time whose futures are determined by the decision of a bishop. There are something close to thirteen hundred churches, each of which is subject to the decisions or, as some detractors would insist, the whims of a bishop. Since all bishops are human, there will be errors and there will be times when injustices occur. Perhaps John Wesley's early warning that a bishop must take care never to use that office for personal aggrandizement should be recalled from time to time. In general, Indiana has been fortunate. Our bishops have nearly always been people of exceptional character.

CHAPTER TEN

*Fill your minds with those
things that are good and that
deserve praise: things that are
true, noble, right, pure, lovely,
and honorable.*
—St. Paul
Philemon 4:8

Changing Values

For years Indiana Conference boards of ministry discouraged ministerial candidates from attending Asbury Seminary in Wilmore, Kentucky, saying it was too conservative, and more than a few candidates were told they might not be ordained if they remained there. Now and then, however, a graduate was successful in getting ordained, and as he or she demonstrated gifts for ministry, the prohibition was relaxed. Thus, in recent years, Asbury has begun to send well-educated clergy to Indiana. Its graduates are generally more conservative than graduates of United Methodist seminaries and more inclined to adhere to traditional views of theology and ministry. A friendly difference of opinion has marked many a clergy gathering. This has often proved a blessing as each group caused the other to rethink their beliefs. United Methodist graduates were focused on mission, outreach, and church building, while Asbury graduates focused on evangelism, theological fidelity to the Wesleyan tradition, and a sense of what some of them perceived as the church's general misdirection. This doesn't mean each was uninterested in the other's issues, but the emphases were clearly there. Most of these differences were practiced in love. Good friends and lunch buddies could still debate, sometimes heatedly, yet still walk away as friends. But the effect on the Methodist Church was real nonetheless. While the General Conference in Cleveland a quarter century later would end amicably, delegates would go there using words like *schism*, *split*, and *separate denomination*, and would come away wondering what would happen four years later. But I'm getting ahead of our story.

~

The upshot of all this change was, first of all, a changing mindset on the part of congregations. Much was written about the decline of all churches including the Methodist Church. In part, this may have resulted from an inability by some of us pastors to accurately understand where our people were "coming from." Bombarded as they were by television, movies, and books—all of which paraded the new values, it was inescapable that a new permissiveness would pervade the church scene. It would soon be announced that 43 percent of all new marriages would end in divorce. Men and women began living together out of wedlock. Some did so in a genuine effort to determine compatibility. Others did so to escape commitment. For still others, it was simply a way to avoid any responsibility. As a pastor, I performed more than a thousand marriages, and I would estimate that during the seventies and eighties, at least half of the couples whom I married were living together prior to marriage. Fellow pastors reported essentially the same experience. One couple came to me for marriage from the Catholic Church. I inquired why they did not get married in their own church. The eager young groom-to-be earnestly replied that if they did so, they couldn't get divorced later if they chose. To make all of this easier for happy couples wishing to avoid the inconvenience of commitment, the Supreme Court of the United States, by a seven to two decision, ruled on January 22, 1973, that the option of choosing an abortion in the first trimester of pregnancy was a fundamental constitutional right. By the early nineties, thirty million abortions had been performed legally. Meanwhile, the American Civil Liberties Union took care to see that religion was kept out of the American common life.

Cheating was accepted. David Frum reported one survey of high school students which revealed that those admitting to cheating in school jumped from 34 percent in 1969 to 60 percent in 1979. A 1979 Carnegie Foundation report lamented a "general decline in integrity on campus." An editor of *Time* magazine wrote in a 1972 memoir: "It has occurred to me that I've lived all my life for other people, not for their sake, like a saint, but on their say so. Be nice to your mother. Don't slap your wife. Responsible fatherhood. Succeed at the job. Pick up your socks. Don't offend anyone. Don't make waves. Conform. I'm tired of all that." This gentleman then did something which would become a trend in the seventies: He quit. Moved to Pago Pago.

Paul Johnson in *A History of the American People* proposed this analysis:

> [The decline of the church] was an important factor in what, to many analysts of American society, was the decisive single development in America during the second half of the twentieth century: the decline of the family and of family life, and the growth in illegitimacy. . . . The enormous number of children born outside the family structure altogether, or raised in one parent families, appeared to be statistically linked to most of the modern evils of American life. Poor educational performance and illiteracy or semi-literacy, children out on the streets from an early age, juvenile delinquency, unemployment, adult crime, and above all, poverty. The break down or even total absence of the marriage/family system, and the growth of illegitimacy, was right at the heart of the emergence of an underclass, especially the black underclass.

Note that the author attributes this breakdown to the decline of the church in America.

For a time, the clergy were nonplussed. Caretakers by nature, we saw the unhappiness of a growing number of people, and much of our preaching was designed to comfort the afflicted. As I have reviewed my own preaching through the years, I realize how seldom I held forth the unequivocal demands of the gospel to lead a holy life. Like so many of my colleagues, I forgot about sin for awhile. It was reigning in my society and I was failing at times to realize that the Bible's antidote is the call to repent and be saved. The church was still in the grips of situation ethics. Even as moral values were falling aside, a generation of young people were finding not a breath of fresh air, not joyous freedom, not the fulfillment of life which they sought—they were finding rootlessness of spirit. Drugs were available in every high-school parking lot in suburbia and on many street corners in the downtown. I once sat on the porch at the home of a man later sent to Federal prison for drug dealing, who told me that the easiest place to buy drugs in Indianapolis was in the parking lot of North Central High School.

Young girls were getting pregnant. They were called teeny-boppers—children who did not have the remotest concept of the damage to their own lives when conception took place. Nor the damage to their own spirits at the devaluing of something intended to be sacred. Births out of wedlock, formerly a rare family secret, now were widespread. By the year 1998, 1,293,567 babies—one third of all newborns—would be born out of wedlock. Middle-aged men, seeing all the temptations of the flesh and no longer feeling so bound by the values of honor and faithfulness, were leaving home and family in discouraging numbers.

Pastoral counseling came into vogue. Though always a responsibility of pastors, a growing number of people were opening private practices. As people in public life began to display their emotional hang-ups as badges of courage, the person on the street began to realize there is nothing wrong with getting help when one is disturbed. Frequently church pastors received notification that yet another graduate of a seminary had opened private counseling services. Clergy schedules began to fill up with counselees—mostly women, and most of them making efforts to save troubled marriages. The Raines Counseling Center in Indianapolis under the leadership of Dr. Edward Alley was adding counselors and was constantly busy. The counseling center at Methodist Hospital under the leadership of Dr. Ken Reed was likewise swamped.

Another effect of all this was on weddings. It was about the 1980s that clergy were besieged with demands from brides-to-be for a variety of departures from church tradition. Weddings in gardens. Weddings on the beach. Weddings in the park. Weddings in the backyard. Weddings in a variety of venues far from any church. Brides who still preferred the church began to write their own vows. That gentle departure from tradition was quite popular for several years. Every minister learned to introduce the services by sweetly announcing that "Michael and Eileen have lovingly worked together to prepare the vows which they will now exchange," which, translated, meant "Folks, don't blame me for the sentiments you are about to hear." Theme songs from popular movies began to replace Mendelssohn and Bach. "We've Only Just Begun" by the Carpenters left all the traditional numbers in the dust. Not a few churches began using guitar accompaniment to choir numbers in worship. One wedding at St. Luke's had a dog as best man. Only by virtue of a mercifully strong headwind was I excused from performing a wedding in a hot air balloon. The family still says that incident convinced them of the power of prayer (my prayer).

Still another sign of the times was a change in dress styles. God forbid a college-aged person would actually dress up to go to church or a wedding—or even a funeral. Jeans, sandals, shorts, T-shirts—those were the styles. Preachers soon became used to this, the next older generation began to emulate this style, and now the majority of those attending a Methodist church are casually dressed.

The trajectory of this transformation would issue in informal worship and preachers casually strolling back and forth across the chancel during sermons—an especially irritating custom unless the preacher stands still. This casual attitude probably opened the way for the many experimental forms of "contemporary worship" common today.

Study groups were formed. Some were Bible-based, but many were groups studying recent psychologically-based books. These groups often provided the opportunity to work through problems, which held similar benefits to one-on-one counseling. Singles groups began to minister to the growing number of people, mostly women, who were either divorced, unsuccessful in finding mates, or who preferred the single life. St. Luke's Church in Indianapolis formed a singles group which soon had more than three hundred people in attendance on Wednesday evenings. In one year in the early eighties, that group served more than two thousand individuals (and in a few years, the group led to over a hundred marriages).

Social action sermons were a major emphasis among clergy. The master of this style was James Armstrong at Broadway Church in Indianapolis. This was not a popular theme among parishioners, who felt themselves captive audiences. Nonetheless, most church members remained faithful to the church and one often heard the refrain: "I disagree with him, but I respect him for having the courage to say what he believes." Also, "he" was just beginning to be replaced by "she." The practice of having women in ministry—a brand new idea for most Methodists—was just beginning to become common throughout the church. People who didn't like controversy and who sought a place to go soon discovered that what was true of Methodist preaching was essentially true of preaching in other mainline denominations as well.

A growing number of clergy during the seventies began to subscribe to the theory that while social issues were the proper concern of the clergy, the pulpit was not the proper place to deal with them. Small groups, symposiums, after-worship adult classes, and programs featuring informative speakers were far more acceptable and, in the opinions of many, far more effective. This, however, brought about a split among clergy between the two points of view: one side accusing the other of a lack of courage, the other side accusing the first of having the clearly mistaken idea that they were prophets. One result was a lot of moving around between churches as Methodists who preferred one of the two approaches sought churches with pastors who were like-minded. Either way, people could run but they couldn't hide. Race, the Vietnam War, the war on poverty, and sexist language were issues to be faced—and solved. There was a lot more smoke than fire for

a time. Many of the solutions to the country's problems put forth
from pulpit and elsewhere were simplistic and, as history would
show, wrong.

But two things may be said with certainty: one, the great
majority of church leaders were unafraid to face the issues, and
two, the church began many efforts and programs which helped a
great many needy people. The racial situation in Indiana was
dramatically improved thanks to many clergy and lay leaders—of
all denominations, but certainly of the Methodist Church. Virgil
Bjork, who served as superintendent of the Fort Wayne District
recalls that it was the Methodist Church that took the lead in
creating dialogue between black leaders and realtors in regard to
open housing in that city.

~

Down in Evansville, a creative new venture known as Patchwork
Central was conceived and birthed by three clergy couples. In 1976,
Phil and Elaine Amerson, along with John and Ruth Doyle and a
couple from the Tennessee Conference, Calvin and Nelia Kimbrough,
conceived the idea of a neighborhood organization in an inner-city
situation to help discover how people living there could create their
own self-help ministries. As Dr. Phil Amerson phrased it, "We wanted
to see what pieces could be found for community organization," thus
the pieces, like those in a patchwork quilt. Described by Amerson as
"a crazy program" at the outset, Patchwork Central opened for business on the near east side of Evansville in June of 1977. Due to the
courage of six risk-takers, the organization was destined to become a
pattern for others nationwide.

By the end of the century, Patchwork Central would have a
bakery (where Amerson had worked during the early years), a food
program, a health clinic, and an after school program for kids
whose parents work. Among the many other innovations, there is
an economic self-help program which actually assists in the
financing of independent businesses, anything from a barbecue
stand, to a hair care shop, to a retail store. By working through a
local bank and by assisting in the paperwork and the actual

finances, Patchwork Central has enabled over one hundred such loans. Clearly, the contribution to the community, not only economically, but psychologically and spiritually, has been incalculable. The Kimbroughs, under appointment from the Tennessee Conference, still oversee this work.

In a recent interview, Dr. Amerson paid tribute to David Lawson, later a bishop, but then the conference council director, and to Lloyd Wright, district superintendent of the Evansville District, for their encouragement. Amerson further noted that one of the strengths of the leaders of the Indiana area at the time was their willingness to enable new programs which broke the mold and were innovative departures for a changing nation and a changing church.

∾

Trinity United Methodist Church in Muncie was a mainly black church. Their pastor Reverend J. C. Williams was deeply concerned about the failure, as he saw it, of the North

Rev. J. C. Williams
preaching, 1997.

Conference to include his members as worthy equals. "African Americans . . . were not being heard or adequately respected as people. This was reflected whenever and wherever we were involved with Caucasians in mutual endeavors," he contended. In response to this concern, a group of people, black and white, lay and clergy, male and female, began a program in 1977 at Epworth Forest Camp near North Webster. It would be called Camp Inclusion. Williams prepared a book listing the "seven greatest sins" as proposed by the Indian mystic, Mahatma Gandhi. The works of Martin Luther King Jr. were also referred to, as young white people came to learn about the culture of their African-American friends and about their alternative worship celebrating Kwanzaa. One girl, Liz Gatarana, who attended may have spoken for most of the participants from that three-year program when she said that she loved Reverend Williams and, "It was just an incredible experience."

~

Preaching for most clergy tended to emphasize basic biblical themes with a frequent emphasis on psychological insights. As people began to realize that the traditional family was in jeopardy, clergy began to preach sermons on love, reconciliation, forgiveness, and faithfulness. Rather than denouncing wayward spouses and disrespectful children—both increasingly evident in middle-class life—the emphasis was on making love work. In the late seventies, Scott Peck's runaway best seller, *The Road Less Traveled*, found itself in many a sermon. Peck himself gave a series of lectures at Indianapolis's St. Luke's Church and addressed a large gathering.

~

Methodist camps were popular among young church members, especially in the earlier years, before young people faced so many options for their summer activities. Many an active church leader, lay or ordained, first found a strong faith in

Epworth Forest on Lake Webster, May 1995, during the Youth Council's first International Fest. Photo courtesy of Hoosier United Methodist News.

the ministries of those camps. Rivervale in the South Conference, for instance, was the scene of many happy memories and not a few romances. William Kearney remembered very well the time he attended Rivervale with Reverend Robert Myers of Manilla. He happened to meet a lovely young lady named Pauline Gulley while attending the chapel service. In 1938 they were married— and lived a happy fifty-three years together. Maybe Sheila Beaver Richards did as well as any former camper with these words which capture the feeling of the place from the 1950s: "I can see in my mind's eye, like it was yesterday, the evening tabernacle service. I can hear the music. I can still smell the smells, the sort-of moldy showers, the leather in the craft shop, the newly mowed grass. I can still feel the dew." It was there, she said, that she made her first real commitment to Christ. She also probably spoke for many campers when she said, "In all honesty, most of us went to camp to have fun and meet boys." And like so many, she found Christ, too.

This vintage postcard of Epworth Forest Campground, Lake Webster, Ind., is dated ca. 1930. The cars lined up along the driveway to the old hotel attest to the spot's popularity at that time.

Horseplay was, of course, an important part of the ritual at camp. In about 1967 Reverend Bob Pollock was the dean. Every morning, he would ring the bell in front of the dean's cottage to awaken some sleepyheads who had not all made it to sleep quite as early as the rules would have recommended. I happened to have been a counselor that year and, having difficulty sleeping on a rather squeaky metal cot, I awakened one night at about three in the morning, just in time to hear some not-quite-successfully repressed giggling outside. As I watched through the window, I saw several boys skulking in the moonlight, disengaging the camp bell from its stand. They managed to carry the heavy bell some distance in the darkness across the grounds to the top of the hill beside the camp. With a one-two-three heave, they lofted the bell some distance down the hill and into some heavy bushes, where it could never be found until such time as those boys decided to disclose its location. Or so they assumed.

I remained concealed until the boys were safely back in their cabin. Then I awakened Pollock, and the two of us quietly slipped across the grounds and retrieved the bell. That morning the bell rang as usual. A stream of confused campers, the word obviously having been passed that the bell would not ring, strolled by on their way to breakfast. We all kept straight faces, and in all probability, none of those boys ever figured out how that bell found its way back to its stand. They would be in their fifties today, and perhaps they will now be glad to learn how their nefarious plan was uncovered.

On another occasion, one unnamed reverend, unable to sleep, decided to slip through the woods to another cabin which was not in use that week. It was well past midnight, so he put on a pair of shoes, wrapped himself in a sheet, and ran through the woods to the cabin on the other side of the camp grounds. There he found a quiet room and fell asleep. The next morning as he was passing through the food line for breakfast, he noticed the lady who did the cooking with a shocked expression on her face. As he was passing by, he heard her earnest report to another minister: "I know no one's going to believe me, but I really saw it. It was figure all dressed in white. I'm sure it was a ghost. It moved through the trees without a sound." The guilty pastor chose to remain silent.

The Otterbein Center at Rivervale Campground, around 1971.

Oakwood Inn. Oakwood Park, a much beloved church camp on the shore of Lake Wawasee was founded in 1893 by the EUB church. It was reincarnated in recent years as an ecumenical retreat and conference center. The $8 million inn was underwritten by a gift from Howard and Myra Brembeck, Goshen, who had first met at one of the old Oakwood youth camps.

Back in 1940, the cost of a week at Rivervale was a dollar and a half for registration plus five dollars for a week's meals. If a kid really wanted to go to Rivervale, and if he or she couldn't afford it, someone was always around to see that no one missed out. It was a splendid week in a young person's life as everyone, following a very busy day, sat around the campfire and sang the song:

> Here heaven and earth surely meet
> Rivervale, our Rivervale.
> We linger at the mercy seat,
> Rivervale, our Rivervale.
> And as the closing hour draws near
> On every hand these words we hear
> We're coming back another year,
> Rivervale, our Rivervale.

Up along the shores of Lake Wawasee, the EUBs had a camp named Oakwood Park which played the same role in the lives of their young. One former camper said it well: "Whether you remember Oakwood because of the dinner bell or the altar call; a baseball championship or a special friendship; what you learned, whom you met, or what you felt; it happened to you that summer, in that special place, and that keeps Oakwood Park firmly situated in a special place in your heart."

Oakwood Park's history is long. Helen Rumpf, a member of Christ Church in Wabash remembered the separation from her husband in World War 2, and how the memories they shared from camp and the faith they shared which was nurtured there, enabled them to endure those troubled years. Rose Wolf, who later moved to Bozeman, Montana, told of the summer she had three teenaged grandchildren living in her home, and one of the boys had a tendency to get into trouble. So off to Oakwood Park he went, where he decided he wanted to stay longer. He told his grandmother that he had learned that Jesus was his friend. Years have passed, but that boy, now a man, lives by that faith.

Marjory Wellborn Wissler fondly remembers standing in the moonlight on the hill behind the cabins, with a fine young man, as they pledged themselves to each other—and to Christ. That was in the summer of 1932. The day came when the two of them, Marjory and O. D. Wissler, headed off to Evangelical Theological Seminary together. Many a camper, having long since become an adult, can still sing the words:

Oh, beautiful for silver waves,
For whitecaps rolling high,
Thy sandy beach for tender feet
The boats thy waters ply,
Oh, Wawasee, Lake Wawasee,
We love thy sandy shore,
We come for good to old Oakwood,
To gather sacred store.

In 1992, the process was officially begun to gradually divest the North Indiana Conference of the camp property. A foundation was created by conference action. Known as the United Methodist Foundation for Adult Christian Ministries, the group will maintain a cooperative relationship with the conference. The years that have passed have not always been kind in their treatment of old buildings. There is always sadness when something treasured must be given up. Times change. But many a Methodist heart still warms at memories from the past at Oakwood Park camp. Today the rustic cabins are gone. Oakwood Park, though, will go on making its "sacred store" available to more and more searching people. Now an ecumenical retreat and conference center, the camp makes available retreats, elder hostels, health and wellness events, a new labyrinth walk, and a host of other means by which Christian community is fostered and individuals seeking a closer walk with their Lord can find him there.

～

Up near North Webster in 1924, the Methodist Church began a grand new venture, a camp to be known as Epworth Forest. Reverend John and Joyce Elliott have recently recorded the history of the past twenty-five years at this North Conference camp in their book *A Forest Aflame,* which shares numerous heartwarming stories of the ways in which the Holy Spirit has touched the lives of so many camp residents through the years. The Elliotts have reminded us that that Spirit has a wonderful way of working through people like us. Reverend Riley Case, a North Conference pastor and noted historian, calls Epworth Forest "a holy place."

Some years ago, a cottage resident of Epworth Forest named Bill Beuoy became acquainted with a new neighbor, a man who was recovering from alcoholism. For several years, the two men shared an acquaintance which was kept at some distance by the neighbor's penchant for swearing. One day the man's wife died, and he resumed his heavy drinking. Before long, he ended up in jail. When he was released, he returned to his cottage and invited Beuoy over, asking if he would be interested in purchasing some of the man's furniture. Beuoy demurred, and the man then admitted that he was without money and needed to sell his possessions. Beuoy, however, offered the man an alternative. Beuoy spent much of his time in the summers putting in and taking out piers for the boating residents. He offered to employ the man if he was willing to work. The man initially showed no interest in working. But some time later during morning prayers, Beuoy felt a summons to go back and try to help the poor neighbor. This time he enlisted the man's assistance with two provisos: the man must not swear and he must not drink.

In the days that followed, the man, apparently after some intense inner struggles, managed to comply with the rules and began to work alongside his acquaintance, who was fast becoming his friend. Then one day, after Beuoy had mentioned how much his church life meant to him, this new friend asked if there was something he could do for the church. Beuoy remarked that the church always needed cookies. The man was excited. He loved to make cookies. And so he did. He began to attend the church, then became an active member. There was more. He became the church's lay leader and their delegate to Annual Conference. From that time onward, he became known as "the Cookie Man." And God, working through a fine Christian man, had once again shown that redemption can take place through the church.

Retired bishop Sheldon Dueker said, "Epworth Forest is a living shrine." The Elliotts wrote, "Epworth Forest is more than a wooded campground. It is, and has been since its beginning, *A Forest Aflame* with the Holy Spirit." Dueker gave yet another example of the wonderful ways in which camp life can open people up to change and renewal in the story he told of a young boy who attended one year and who quickly proved undesirable to the rest of the kids. Apparently they disliked the kid because of his strange personality. Life was obviously unhappy for the boy, who seemed unable to do anything about his strange ways. But one evening, as various kids were sharing some of their deepest feelings, the boy said he had suffered a brain injury as a small child, and it had affected the way he talked and acted. He shared how he realized people thought him strange, how he never felt acceptance, and how his life was one of sad loneliness. The other kids, now understanding, immediately surrounded him with their love and assured him that henceforth he would be one of their family of friends.

Reverend Marcus Blaising, a former leader in the North Conference and one time executive assistant to the bishop, becomes pensive when he discusses Epworth Forest. "It was the nerve center of the conference," he recalls, especially during the years preceding the merger of 1968. Its strong emphasis on ministry to youth led to numerous commitments to Christian vocations. Every district superintendent made an effort to spend time with kids from his or her district. Blaising, a one-time district superintendent, stated, "You almost had to be on your deathbed not to be there." Six to eight thousand young people attended Epworth Forest in a summer, and the later leadership of the church was wonderfully benefited by those early years.

In more recent years Epworth Forest, like all church camps, has undergone change. The merger of the EUB and Methodist Churches in 1968 brought about some changes which signaled "a watershed into a whole new era of life for Methodist institutions everywhere." The story is best told by the Elliotts' book, which discusses the ministry to the deaf, the Re-Yo-Ad program (Retarded Young Adults), the outreach to Africa, the adventure camp, Camp Inclusion, and so many other programs which keep Epworth aflame with the actions of the Holy Spirit.

Reverend Bill Kaster had a memory of the day a few years ago at Epworth when he was out for a walk and encountered a kind African-American gentleman with whom he was soon in friendly conversation. The man inquired about Kaster's work and his church and showed genuine interest in him as a person. Toward the end of the conversation, Kaster admitted that he didn't know the man and thus asked his name. The man smiled and introduced himself as "Woodie White, your new bishop."

Times bring change, of course, and the day when nearly every North Conference pastor expected to spend a week with his high school kids at Epworth is gone—though still treasured in vivid memories by those surviving pastors of yesteryear. And many a middle-aged church leader still remembers being there as a teenager and finding something precious, something life changing.

Dr. Riley Case quoted one friend who recently said that when he heads for Epworth and gets within a couple miles of the place, he already begins to feel a sense of peace. But the Elliotts, after reminding us of the many ways in which the Spirit is enabled to work at Epworth Forest, concluded their story with this prediction: "If we are obedient in these ways, Epworth Forest will continue to be *A Forest Aflame*."

~

Dear to the heart of older Northwest Conference Methodists was Battle Ground Camp. Its history ebbed and flowed. Founded in the form of a school called Battle Ground Collegiate Institute on December 16, 1857, on the original eight acres of the camp, the name was appropriate because it was located at the site of a battle with Indian tribes of the Upper Wabash which took place on November 11, 1811. The battle was referred to by one historian as "the curtain raiser" to the War of 1812. The location was also associated with the Battle of Tippecanoe. The hero of that war, General William Henry Harrison, was elected to the presidency of the United States by a patriotic and grateful nation. From time to time additional grounds were added to what is now a large encampment.

The early life of Battle Ground was conservatively religious. The Cane Ridge revival in Bourbon County, Kentucky, back in 1801 had sent a wave of religious fervor throughout the Indiana Territory, and this seems to have carried many early Methodists through a happy life of faith. So much so that camp meetings and revivals were an essential part of Methodist worship life in the mid-nineteenth century. Battle Ground later became a favorite place for those events. A Camp Meeting Association was formed in 1875 with Mark Jones as president. The first camp meeting had been held the previous year and the spiritual life of the camp was off and running. The theology was that of scriptural holiness.

A thorough review of the history of Battle Ground would include a look at many differences of opinion, not a few divisions and disagreements, a rocky course of events frequently due to financial restraints which constantly plagued the camp, and the leaders of the old Northwest Conference, who faithfully tried to keep the camp alive. One history of the camp written several years ago observed, "The ownership and management of the Battle Ground property have gone through several changes as the program has varied with the years and finances have fluctuated up and down." Having reviewed that history, I would call that an understatement. Nevertheless, the Holy Spirit is never to be outdone, and the camp continued to thrive as it blessed the lives of countless visitors.

One gets a sense of the ambience of the early setting from this description: "The town was in 1867 described as 'a fine little village without a doggery, a saloon, or a gaming table.'" As the years passed, Battle Ground was the scene of many happy family gatherings, many rousing worship experiences, and many pleasant summer outings. Cottages were built, many privately owned, schools of one sort or another were centered there, and, all in all, much of the culture of the Northwest Conference was sentimentally entwined with Battle Ground. The available history of the camp, while complete in details, lacks the stories of faith which could have made it come alive. Nonetheless, we can be assured that many devout Methodists and guests found a deepening of faith in those great times past, and many searching sinners found new life in Jesus Christ through the ministries of Battle Ground Camp. If their names and stories are unknown to us, they are known and treasured by the One who touched their lives in that place. The camp was closed by the North Conference in 1971.

～

An innovation in camping for young Methodists was conceived in 1971 by two men, Eugene McCormick from Liberty and Lyle Rasmussen the pastor of Mount Olive Church in Indianapolis. The two had taken a trip on a bus from Taylor University called "the Possum." It was a bus which could transport a group of young people on camping trips, but with facilities

David L. White Jr. has served prominently at every level of the Church, and was elected a member of the last six General Conference delegations. He was Assistant General Secretary of Ethnic Ministries, Laity in Ministry of the General Board of Discipleship. Dr. White served as chairperson of North Central Jurisdiction BMCR and hosted a forum during which candidates for the episcopacy were introduced.

which enabled people to sleep and to talk together. The director of the program was Bob Davenport, a former all-American football player, who encouraged McCormick and Rasmussen to begin a similar program for the Methodist Church. Charmed with the concept, they enlisted "Chuck" Armstrong, then pastor of St. Paul's Church in Bloomington. They obtained a bus in 1972 and began a program of camping on what they called a "rolling retreat." A name contest was held and the bus was named "God's Nightcrawler." With the assistance of some members of Liberty Church, it was equipped with beds which were movable, allowing the passengers to sit up during the day and to sleep on late-night rides. Combining fun and worship, hundreds of kids have found a healthy fellowship experience on "God's Nightcrawler." Through the years, the busses have been replaced and have changed from that first $37,000 bus to today's $300,000, air-conditioned, diesel, moving dormitory, replete with restroom facilities and an audio system. The program has grown, and today the bus, when not in use, resides in Princeton under the oversight of Kent Toole. Anyone who attends Annual Conference in Bloomington is accustomed to seeing the Nightcrawler parked in front of the auditorium.

~

By the late 1960s, the black Methodists were joining the whole church by virtue of the long delayed dissolution of the all black Central Jurisdiction on August 19, 1967. While this was an important step in the right direction, there was a downside. There was concern by the black members about the role they would henceforth play in the whole church. Would they be included in the power structure? Would they be enabled to participate in decision making and policy determination? Being a minority, they realized some protection from de facto continued second class citizenship was necessary. Accordingly, a group of black leaders was convened in Detroit at East Grand Methodist Church on February 6, 1968, with the question before them: "How do we ensure that there will be a permanent place for blacks in the new United Methodist Church?" Empowerment was the issue. The concept of black power was an important ingredient in the black psyche by this time. No more back of the bus. Out of this gathering came Black Methodists for Church Renewal (BMCR).

A very creative statement issued from the early meetings was called the *Black Paper*. This statement was in frank opposition to racism in American society, but with equal frankness, it confessed the earlier failings of black Methodists and defined new directions. It went on to state a new identity for black Methodists. The effect was almost immediate. The 1968 General Conference created a new Commission on Religion and Race. Reverend Woodie W. White, destined to become bishop of the Indiana area, was elected general secretary. Other actions followed. A new hymnal was prepared using music which expressed the black style. *The Songs of Zion* was born. Other black members began to be elected to positions of influence, people like Reverend Mel Talbert as general secretary of the General Board of Discipleship. These numbers were due to increase.

By 1976 Reverends George Rice, David L. White, and Lawrence Johnson led in the establishment of the South Indiana Caucus of BMCR. All racially black churches in the South Conference were included. By 1977 they were officially recognized as a caucus amenable to the Annual Conference. It wasn't long before the influence of this group was evident throughout the conference. Granted, there would always be work to do, battles to win, and prejudices to overcome. Fulfillment of John Wesley's hope for Christian perfection and sanctification was still far ahead. But the process had begun. And people were beginning to find that when those who are different from each other get to know each other, love frequently results. A distinguished list of leaders brought the caucus through the growing years of black church inclusion, such as: Reverend Martin McCain, Gwendolyn Mason, Reverend Jerry Hyde, Reverend Ivan O. Jenkins, Reverend Ida Easley, Margaret Mayo, Reverend Michael Anderson, Delores Casey, Reverend Sharon White, James (Jim) Lewis, Dr. Carolyn E. Johnson, and so many others who deserve to be named. So, as the new millennium now begins, this great work proceeds until the distant day when a group like BMCR is no longer needed.

≈

In the North Conference, the concern about racial representation, while no doubt pressing in the minds of many people, did not result in a BMCR caucus as in the South Conference until August 7, 1995. Then a group of black leaders including Carnell Scott, who is currently vice chair of the executive committee of the North Central Jurisdictional Committee on Religion and Race, gathered together to officially establish a caucus of BMCR. Encouraged by Bishop White, Scott, along with Reverend Shepherd Harkness, Roy Hamilton, Frederick Davidson, Esther Ross, Edna Scott, Suella Mayfield, and Burnetta Williams, to name at least some of the participants, formed the North Indiana Conference Caucus of Black Methodists for Church Renewal. Scott indicates that this move did not mean dissatisfaction with the current situation but, rather, it resulted from the very practical realization that it just made good sense to have some form of a watchdog committee in place.

In 1997 at the annual meeting of the jurisdiction and national BMCR in Merrillville, Bishop White spoke at a banquet and gave a speech which impressed Scott as a galvanizing call to action. One of his friends, a longtime Methodist, remarked that Bishop White's presentation was the most inspiring speech he had ever heard. At present, if one is to judge by Scott's good-spirited description of these events, while there are some black pastors who are not wholeheartedly supportive of BMCR, there is a general good feeling about the current state of affairs within the black church in North Indiana. Obviously, there will always be progress to be made and problems to be solved. But now the organization is in place to work toward those ends. Perhaps the most significant indication of the progress made by the Methodist Church in regard to racial attitudes is the fact that in the year 2000, of the thirteen new bishops elected in the five jurisdictions, seven were African Americans. Regarding this, Bishop Woodie White wrote: "Such a history making occurrence does not mean racism has finally been eliminated in the United Methodist Church. It has not, and the seven new bishops will discover that in surprising and in personal ways." Still, someone standing outside the process must surely be impressed that the overwhelmingly white denomination chose minority persons to lead them in seven of thirteen areas.

∾

One dramatic change in American life during the seventies resulted in equally dramatic changes in the lives of all churches. The Arab oil embargo in 1973 ignited runaway inflation. People began to realize that almost every product we take for granted uses oil products in one way or another. Prices rose. By the mid-seventies, inflation was nearing 20 percent annually. People began to realize that a television set which costs $300 today would cost $315 next week and $360 a year from now. What to do? Buy now and save money—this philosophy rampaged through the American psyche, setting loose a red hot economy. The Great Depression-minded older generation, who still taught that you buy something when you have the money, gave way to the credit card, the careless rush to debt, and the "live now because you have no idea how bad it's going to get tomorrow" school of living.

One young couple with two small children arrived at Asbury Church in Indianapolis and quickly became active in church life. The young woman taught Sunday school, and the man volunteered in church activities. They moved into a new home and when the pastor paid them a visit, they proudly showed off their new stereo music system and their new television set. They were the ideal young American family. Attractive, bright, optimistic, devoted to their church and, as it turned out, broke. A later visit from the pastor, who hadn't seen this charming family for a few weeks, revealed that they had left in the dark of night, leaving all their new toys behind—along with an unpaid mortgage. The pastor later heard they had settled somewhere out west. Two more victims of the race to prosperity in the seventies. The word to describe the new phenomenon was *consumerism*. John Wesley's well-known injunction that a Christian should earn all he can, save all he can, and give all he can was still on first base.

For many people, there was a definite upside to this inflation. It had the effect of reducing existing indebtedness. Of course it had the opposite effect on personal savings accounts, rendering them of less and less value, so that it was better to spend than to save. The prevailing ethic of fiscal conservatism so central to most middle-class Americans was now replaced by a totally new way of understanding economic wisdom. This change would have profound influences on the years to follow.

A mortgage which looked enormous in 1970 looked small in 1980. In terms relative to the average person's income, the mortgage was in effect cut in less than half. Church leaders who saw this reality quickly began planning new church buildings. With prices rising, the quicker a church could build, the lower the cost in the long run. Builders began adding future inflation into building costs. Building committees, weighing the pros and cons, began to hurry. It was a time of frantic church expansion. But operating budgets were rising as well. Not everyone's income kept pace, and pastors discovered that fund raising was becoming an increasingly important part of their job descriptions. Grumbling was heard in many congregations in which "all the preacher talks about is money." Also, preachers, traditionally expected to accept whatever salaries they might be offered without protest, began realizing they must fight for raises. Thoughtful laypeople began raising clergy salaries and increasing various expense allowances. While churches reaped the financial benefits of church-owned parsonages, pastors saw the hope of owning a home in retirement fading. Pastors of large churches began buying their own homes with their congregation's assistance, which gave the pastor second thoughts about moving to a different church. Cabinets were less inclined to ask a person who owned a home to move. With his or her family now well settled with a sense of ownership, a pastor often preferred to remain. As a result, longer pastorates in larger churches became the norm. The old days when a five-year pastorate was considered long were on the way out. Warren Saunders, the pastor of Carmel Church, retired in 1982 after eighteen years in that pastorate. Richard Lancaster retired from Meridian Street in 1988 after a twenty-six year pastorate. I retired from St. Luke's in 1993 after twenty-six years there. Richard Hamilton retired from North Church in Indianapolis in 1997 after a twenty-three year pastorate. We all owned our own homes. If people really do turn over in their graves, Francis Asbury must be exhausted.

~

Out in back of St. Luke's Church in Indianapolis was a picnic table. One Saturday afternoon, a car pulled into the parking lot and a young couple got out, sat at the picnic table, and bowed their heads. The young man was a student-pastor of a non-Methodist church and was struggling with a call to full-time ministry. He had about decided not to follow that call, but his wife prevailed on him to go for a drive. On impulse, too emotional to drive safely, they found their way to that picnic table and began to pray. As they prayed, they both began to have a sense of a presence. It was so powerful, so real, that the two of them were overwhelmed with awe. The young man so sensed the presence of the Holy Spirit that he accepted his calling, and the two of them departed. The young man attended a seminary, graduated, and accepted ordination.

One day, the newly ordained minister began to feel doubts about his calling. He began to question his decision. For several days, troubled by conflicting feelings about his work, he prayed without effect. One day his wife suggested they drive back to that Methodist church where it had all happened some years before. They did—the picnic table was still there, the two sat where they sat before, and again they prayed. Of course they had prayed regularly through the years. But now, as they sat there, once more that awesome presence overwhelmed them. Once more, they felt so affirmed in their earlier decision that from that time on, the young man remained confirmed in his ministry.

A year or two following this second experience, the young minister happened, by chance, to attend a conference in Denver, and there he told me his story. He concluded with this remark, "Please don't ever get rid of that table." Maybe there was nothing special about the picnic table. Perhaps those two were just especially open to a prayer response. Whatever the explanation, they will insist that God paid a special visit—both times.

◇

By the late 1970s, the women's movement was changing America. Gloria Steinem's observation that "a woman without a man is like a fish without a bicycle" symbolized the new independence of many women in American society. I won't try to dissect that phenomenon beyond observing that despite its many excesses and any number of downright silly declarations by this or that self-appointed spokesperson, the movement itself was inevitable and clearly brought about a healthy and liberating new element into the American spirit. One of its blessings was the fact that women in ministry became a reality in the Methodist Church. The nature of Methodism was about to undergo yet another revolutionary change. By the 1990s, total enrollment in Methodist seminaries nationwide would be about 50 percent women. Less than half as many men were entering the Methodist ministry as had been true in the fifties and sixties. Seminaries began searching for gifted women teachers, which inevitably affected the educational experience of all clergy. This was happening at the time that political correctness was becoming an American vogue among the intelligentsia.

One of the initial effects on the church was in worship. New versions of the *Holy Bible* and of the *Methodist Hymnal* were published, toning down the use of masculine pronouns. "Men" became "persons." Words like *Lord* (as used to describe God), *king*, *fellowship*, and many others became anathema to some people. There were excesses in the early going as some pastors tried to reword the Lord's Prayer and discovered the great majority of Methodists preferred it just the way it was, thank you very much. Some familiar hymns were slightly altered, not entirely pleasing to those who had memorized their favorites ("Time, like an ever-flowing stream bears all her sons away" became "Time, like an ever-flowing stream bears all who breathe away"). But mostly it was all done in good spirit, and currently, it is pretty well accepted as an appropriate correction to an earlier era's manner of speaking.

Male clergy belatedly supported the changes. In most cases, support was not enthusiastic at the beginning, but integrity won out. Also, the new generation of seminarians, exposed to the new view of things in their educations, supported the non-sexist view of ministry. In a few cases, imbued with more zeal than wisdom, student excesses were hurtful. One of Garrett Seminary's most distinguished professors, upon his retirement, was to be honored with a chapel service in testimony to his long and devoted tenure. Invited to prepare the worship portion of the service, he included his beloved Lord's Prayer—which the student committee promptly vetoed ("Father" was out). The last word received in Indiana was that the professor then opted not to participate. Such thoughtless bad manners on the part of the students were rare, one hopes. One assumes that students like those at Garrett have since matured and become more repentant. Or perhaps they are now serving some obscure appointment, wondering why they are not very well liked.

There were other stresses and strains as women clergy arrived on the scene. District superintendents began reporting that when a woman minister was proposed as pastor of a church, there was

R. Sheldon Dueker, senior pastor of Muncie High St. UMC at the time, was elected bishop in 1988.

almost always opposition, the most vocal opponents usually being women of the congregation. It became obvious that women could not expect to be received as equal to men as pastors without first undergoing a period of trial. Some women reacted with anger, intensifying their complaints about what they perceived to be a prejudiced and unjust system. But many other women smiled and began demonstrating their gifts for ministry. New dimensions of ministry surfaced in Methodism.

There was a period of arms-length relating as male clergy privately complained that some women were receiving desired appointments only because they were women and that the bishop was trying to show how egalitarian he was. Meanwhile, women were often left with the clear impression that the male-dominated system was offering patronizing platitudes while throwing the women the least attractive church appointments. There was some truth in both sentiments for a time. It was going to take years before true equality would be possible. Despite the fact that here and there a woman was appointed district super-intendent, or an occasional woman was elected to the episcopacy, the prime appointments to the large churches remained the prerogative of the male clergy. Only very recently has that glass ceiling been cracked. Since good preaching is the primary entree to the large church, and since some excellent preaching is being done by women clergy, one must feel assured the future will witness an eventual state of true equality. I recently listened to a fine sermon preached by Reverend Linda Craig in Culver, Indiana, at Wesley Church, and her sentiments probably express the feelings of most women clergy in the new millennium: doing good work and keeping the faith will send those career concerns fading into the past.

One important innovation in Methodist ministry which was initially viewed as a major problem was that of clergy couples— husband and wife both ordained and seeking appointment. One of the earliest of those couples was Susan and Richard Ruach. Dr. Susan Ruach, now director of the South Conference Council on Ministries, smiles when she recalls that Bishop Rueben Mueller breathed an audible sigh when he ordained her in 1969. The problems were obvious. If every Methodist minister must be amenable to the bishop and the cabinet for appointment where and when needed, the practical consequence would be divided families. Against this was (and is) the innate humanity of a system which is intended to be fair. While it may seem logical to appoint both spouses to a church desiring a senior pastor and an associate pastor, a bit of reflection will disclose the problems with that. While a couple may be ordained and may even be invincibly loving, it is doubtful that many could survive one being the "associate" to the other, although Reverends Harold and Andrea Leininger did just that for awhile at Brownsburg Church.

While some problems persisted, more and more superintendents began to look on the bright side. Some of the most talented clergy were members of an ordained couple. Somehow, probably not without some strains in a few households, quite a number of clergy couples are serving admirably in Indiana. Susan Ruach's role as director of the Council on Ministries is one example. Another is that of Reverend Mary Ann Moman, whose husband, Richard, is executive pastor of St. Luke's Church in Indianapolis. She was recently appointed as the associate general secretary of the Division

Mary Ann Moman touched off a wave of controversy when she presided over a union ceremony for two gay male members of her church, Indianapolis Broadway UMC, in 1992.

of Ordained Ministry. She took that post after having been senior pastor of St. Mark's Church in Bloomington. Reverend Andrea Leininger is now serving Bethel Church in Indianapolis, not far from her husband, Harold, at Brownsburg Church. Both are doing a great work. There are, of course, numerous other examples.

Retired Bishop Sheldon Dueker did point out the interesting fact that a fairly high number of women are leaving the ministry for a variety of reasons, not least of those being the demands of family. Also, many women seek appointments in church-related positions other than a preaching ministry in a local church. The matter of clergy couples also raises a thorny financial issue. At least one couple who both reside in the same parsonage still insist that each should be entitled to a full housing allowance. This would, of course, amount to extra income. On the other hand, they have a valid point. It is problems like these that explain why many clergy prefer never to become district superintendents.

∼

One sociological change which began to take place as the seventies drew to a close was a change in the work ethic in

America. David Frum in his book about the seventies put it this way: "The old work ethic was replaced by a new work ethic, in which one worked to fulfill oneself rather than to support others . . . if work failed to provide fulfillment and meaning, there was no discredit in quitting it." Only those of us who worked during the fifties, sixties, and seventies can appreciate the revolutionary changes in work in America. One article in the *New York Times* magazine in the spring of 2000 opened with this summary: "A decade ago, corporate America tore up the social contract that bound employees to their companies. Downsizing and re-engineering made it clear that employees were expendable commodities, not valued resources. Today many bright workers are getting their revenge by fleeing their fickle employers for better paying rivals—or dot com startups." The article goes on to point out that the average thirty-two-year-old in America has worked for nine different companies. The older generation was raised on the idea of two-way loyalty, and they were sorely suspicious of the undependable soul who had worked at two or three different places in a few years. To them, this seems a remarkable change. However, perhaps implying a sentiment for the future, the author of the article observed, "We are currently experiencing nostalgia for a golden age of company loyalty."

Writing in the *Sunday Times* magazine, another writer observed, "At some time in the mid-1980s, three things became apparent among most of the people I knew. None of them made anything, all of them were working unbelievably hard, and none of them could talk about anything but work." As regards the culture of the workplace, that author sees it this way: "Over a period of 20 years . . . company man—the organization man, the man in the gray flannel suit—went, to be replaced by anxious men in trainers, jogging pants and t-shirt." The whole concept of working has been transformed in modern America, a fact which must inevitably affect the way the working person in the pew hears a sermon.

Several effects of this evolving idea of work in the human psyche would affect the church. Educated women began to enter the workforce in large numbers. There would be endless debates about the "glass ceiling," about comparative incomes, and about sexual harassment. The incredible day would come in 2000, one which numbed the senses of all World War 2 veterans, when a lieutenant general (female) of the U.S. Army would charge a major general of the U.S. Army (male) with sexual misconduct. The terrified army promptly saw to it that the accused took early retirement. Shades of names like Patton and Bradley and McAuliffe awakened in an older generation's minds, which sharply pointed out the changing times.

Women in the police force, women airline pilots, women CEOs, women generals, even women boxers—the women's movement had begun to dramatically redefine vocation in America. In the early going, this produced some conflict between women who preferred to remain home to raise children and those who preferred to seek a career. Gail Sheehy's widely read book *Passages* proposed the popular thesis that women were facing a dilemma. According to Sheehy, at about age thirty, women who had opted for a career began yearning for home and family, and women who had opted for home and family began yearning for a career. Thus, many career-minded women began resigning and belatedly having families, and an increasing number of women with growing children began looking around for daycare facilities so they could enter the workforce. Along with other forces, this had a disabling effect on many families.

The 1979 movie *Kramer vs. Kramer* concerned a young mother who felt irresistibly drawn to a new career. She left her husband and explained it to her son in writing: "Being a mommy is one thing, but there are other things too." Studies showed that contrary to what one might expect, wives of men whose incomes were in the top 10 percent of the population were more likely to work than were women whose husbands were in the bottom 10 percent of the workforce.

Obviously, economic necessity was not the primary motivation for most women seeking careers. Self-fulfillment was surely one motivation. A more lavish lifestyle was clearly another. Middle-class families, those most likely to attend a Methodist church, were seeking larger homes, newer cars, better schools, up-to-date wardrobes, and exotic vacations. Clergy would begin to see increasing signs of family breakdowns as traditional homes began to give way to the two-income family with children often shunted aside. Studies began to emerge showing that the average father was spending only minutes a day with his children in close parental relationship. Divorce threatened many if not most homes. While most conservative churches remained steadfast in opposition to divorce, Methodist pastors began to take account of the fact that if nearly half of their congregational members were in second or later marriages that seemed to be happy, and if they wanted to hold their congregations together, they could not blister their people Sunday after Sunday about marital failures. So a permissive attitude toward divorce characterized most, though not all, Methodist pastors. This does not mean preachers began to condone family breakups. They did not. But the sentiment that the role of the church is not to be a judge but is, rather, to be a force for healing and renewal, moderated the frontline preacher's application of biblical teaching to the current situation.

The church rose to the occasion. In St. Luke's Church in Indianapolis, Reverends Lucinda Bates and Linda McCoy began a divorce recovery workshop which was immediately filled, requiring the opening of a second session which was also quickly filled. Nearly every divorce left someone emotionally, not to mention economically, damaged. Other churches followed suit. District workshops were begun. Pastors found their schedules increasingly devoted to counseling with people who were at some stage between an unhappy marriage and putting the pieces together again following divorce. Singles groups began to make a place for bereft former spouses. Thoughtful pastors began to preach sermons intended to help congregations be sensitive to the pain of those who had experienced divorce. The old attitude of rejecting anyone who had divorced gave way to sympathy and then—and only God can finally judge this—to general acceptance. Many discussions among ministers behind the scenes debated whether a stronger voice denouncing divorce from the beginning could have stemmed the tide, or whether it would only have kept people away from churches where they were now finding forgiveness and hope. Again, only God knows. It was the age-old issue of faith in culture versus faith above culture.

Values were under attack by the prevailing ethos. The self-fulfillment movement won that generation the sobriquet "the Me Generation." Taking care of me was the name of the game from the seventies through the eighties. Jogging, for instance, became extremely popular. David Frum reminds us of James Fixx's 1978 *Complete Book of Running* in which he insisted that if people run long enough and hard enough, they could experience a "trance-like state, a mental plateau where they feel miraculously purified and at peace with themselves. . . ." Another author observed, "Runners seek each other out. They regard other runners as good [and] trustworthy, particularly the marathon runner, and look down on other people, thinking of them as bad, lazy, indolent, immoral." An overstatement for most of us, granted. But fitness was definitely in and a large percentage of clergy were soon jogging. Then came cycling. Frum suggests that bicycle riders were the "most smug of all." While this outburst of exercise by millions of Americans had its beneficial values, it also utilized hours of time and units of energy therefore not available for work or other leisure—or volunteerism. A rather grim devotion to activities of various kinds typified young and middle aged people in the seventies and eighties. Exotic health foods were in. So was Perrier water. Never mind that tap water purification standards in America were higher than those for imported bottled water. People would pay for the water they might have had for free because it was, well, bottled water and therefore healthful.

Obviously, none of this applied to everyone. Millions of Americans got up, had breakfast, went off to work, came home, read or watched a little television, and then went off to bed. These were the values which characterized most members of the middle class, and that is who went to the typical Methodist Church. The movies depicted the new frantic lifestyles and an ongoing sense of resentment toward authority. Dolly Parton and Jane Fonda saw to the punishment of an overbearing boss in *9 to 5*.

In the 1981 movie *Take This Job and Shove It*, the hero reorganizes his hometown brewery and gets rid of hateful management. On the university front, *Animal House* appeared in 1978 to parody college life. Delta Fraternity at Faber College became a blueprint for many wild fraternity bashes throughout the country.

All restraints on obscene language in entertainment and on late-night television disappeared to the point that middle-aged people had one of two choices: get used to it or stay home. If one were to watch any of hundreds of current movies, and then watch an old Andy Hardy movie starring Mickey Rooney, or even a sophisticated movie such as *Charade* with Cary Grant and Audrey Hepburn, the revolution in entertainment would be clearly evident. Obviously, the use of profane and obscene language has now become part of everyday discourse in America. Preachers are no longer surprised to hear van-driving soccer moms report the salty language of their ten-year-old passengers on the way to the soccer game. And frankly, it seems very likely some of this is learned around the house from a generation of Baby Boomer parents who grew up in the sixties and are so used to off-color language that they often don't realize what they are saying. The 2000 movie *Dogma*, which outraged the Catholic Church, presents a twenty-first century view of religion on the part of many in the entertainment industry: profane and violent. Presented as a comedy, though only mildly amusing at times, it can very well serve as the nadir of American entertainment as of this moment.

~

In truth, there wasn't much that church people could do about this onslaught of societal upheavals. However, preachers could urge Methodists that if we can't change the ethos, we can remain faithful to our own beliefs. We can be true to our mates. We can spend time with our kids. We can see that our children attend church school. We can worship in our churches. We can practice our faith and try to emulate that most supreme of all Christian virtues: kindness. We can clean up our language. We can support worthy efforts to change things. We can go out among those who have less than we do, try to understand, and look for ways to help. We can encourage each other in all of this. These became the emphases of the preaching of the church.

And so a renewed search for spiritual formation began to move through the Methodist Church. Bible study groups were in. Programs like the Emmaus Walk drew a growing number of concerned Methodists who sought a way back to a time when values, family, integrity, and generosity were of paramount importance. Social activism, while not absent from church life, became more subdued. Methodist pastors observed that theologically conservative churches seemed to be the ones growing as many Methodist churches lost members. Biblical preaching characterized an increasing number of preachers. And, since we Methodists seem to delight in controversy, the focal point of such disagreements would now become the prevailing theology of the Methodist Church.

~

On July 20, 1975, a group of mainly southern Methodist pastors issued "An affirmation of Scriptural Christianity for United Methodists," which was adopted by the Board of Directors of Good News during a convocation of United Methodists for Evangelical Christianity meeting at Lake Junaluska, North Carolina. This became known as the Junaluska Affirmation. Pretty much ignored by northern Methodists for several years, the Good News movement began to awaken in many Indiana pastors a yearning for a more authoritative and more literal scriptural faith. Advocates of this persuasion began to join forces in an effort to influence the politics of the Annual Conferences. So long as the differences focused on biblical interpretations as such, most pastors were happy to live and let live. But one towering issue soon drove a giant wedge between the Good News pastors and a large number of those who were uncomfortable with what they saw to be the untenable Biblical literalism of the movement: homosexuality.

A theological upheaval loomed on the Methodist horizon by this time. The presiding generation of Methodist clergy had been trained in the era of New Reformation or, as its outcome was generally known, "neo-orthodox" theology. This began in Europe with the publication in the 1930s of a commentary on the book of Romans by Karl Barth. He was a Swiss-German theologian whose writings were much too guilty of "turgid German prose" for all but the most determined theologue to successfully read. Nonetheless, it triggered what might be called an entire new school of theology based on the thesis that traditional liberalism simply does not work, based as it is on the presumption that people can build a kingdom of God on earth, because even the best of us are flawed and selfish at heart. No, we must start with God. But Barth's emphasis was on the God "high and lifted up," with much less emphasis on the present God. God must act, man (and, of course, woman) must react. If the reader finds this a bit obscure, be assured this was all fuel for late-night debate between seminary students. It revived an interest in the theology of John Wesley and his doctrine of sin and salvation. It also had the tendency to intensify the focus on humanity's sin and, to some extent, undercut an individual's self-confidence in working toward a better world. Consistent with this was the approach to Bible study which emphasized critical interpretations, or the "what did the writer *really* mean?" method of interpretation. Advocates of the Good News and Confessing movements would counter that we know exactly what the writers meant because it is written there plain to see. At the time of this writing, the difference of belief persists.

CHAPTER ELEVEN

In all the relationships of the various members of the organized church they are to pursue the "more excellent way" of love. For only in this way can the outward church organization truly incarnate that other body, the body of Christ, the spiritual church. The first duty of the church is to be the church, the outward embodiment of the divine Word still living in the world "full of Grace and Truth." . . . Paul speaks to every church when he writes to Corinth, "Let all that you do be done in love."
—Harold DeWolf, theologian

A Time of Transition: The Eighties

In 1981 Bishop Alton retired and Bishop James Armstrong, former pastor of Broadway Church in Indianapolis and, for a time, bishop of the Dakotas, arrived back in Indianapolis as presiding bishop of the Indiana Area. Viewed as one of America's best preachers, Armstrong was featured in a widely read national magazine as America's most influential religious leader. As president of the National Council of Churches, Armstrong immediately established his priorities by declining a large episcopal parsonage, choosing instead to live in a modest home near the airport. It soon became apparent that one of America's most influential figures was our bishop and that his cabinets would be kept busy with the ordinary affairs of state. A man of exceptional personal qualities, Armstrong was very likely the most admired man to hold his office up to that time, possibly equaled by Bishop Raines. But the times were different. Already nationally known as a battler for human rights, Bishop Armstrong was gone much of the time to wherever the action was, nationally and internationally: Vietnam, Wounded Knee, Washington, D.C. Many clergy found themselves torn between admiration for their bishop and smoldering resentment that their leader was not very interested in the ordinary problems of the area. His credentials, in the minds of the Indiana clergy, were more those of his time at Broadway Church than those of his episcopacy. In time Bishop Armstrong, citing personal reasons, resigned both as bishop and as president of the National Council of Churches. Shortly after, he left the denomination and was said to have become the very well-regarded pastor of a non-Methodist church. He is still remembered fondly by many surviving members of great days past at Broadway Church when Armstrong and Broadway were the talk of the town.

～

Any hope that the problems faced by our country and by the United Methodist Church in the new decade might be less perplexing than had been true for the past several years were dashed by harsh reality. One entry in the 1981 South Conference journal contained this ominous warning: "The upsurge of violence, terrorism, and racism has cast a pall of fear over the whole world." Reverend Harold Criswell's report for the cabinet continued with this pessimistic outlook: "The strong emergence of the American Nazi party, the KKK, and the paramilitary training camps keep alive hate, brutality, and terrorism." Criswell continued: "Racism and hate is a problem of the spirit. This area of the spirit is where the church should have the most expertise and concern . . . the time has come to demonstrate it." That report laid before us the mandate for the years to follow.

There were other problems as well, financial ones. Inflation, while reducing the weight of mortgage indebtedness for many growing churches, was causing mounting budgets and pressure to build and otherwise make improvements as quickly as possible in order to avoid the cost increases which lay ahead. The pressure to cover local church costs began to erode support for the district and conference programs designed to address the problems noted. That same cabinet report in the 1981 journal again warned: "Finances are a recurring concern in the life of most churches. The inflationary spiral, particularly in energy and building costs, has put strains on church budgets. These stresses will likely continue in the foreseeable future." As examples, total support for the pastor of Meridian Street Church in Indianapolis rose from $18,100 in 1970 to $38,000 by 1980. By 1990, that support had risen to $71,000 plus expenses. A district superintendent received $29,600 in 1980 and $46,000 in 1990 in addition to parsonage plus expenses. By 1998 that amount was $65,520 plus expenses. Clearly inflation was raising church budgets. Most other expenses rose by similar amounts.

As the seventies faded and the eighties arrived, the heated feelings among many congregations had subsided as far as politics and racial issues were concerned. Multiculturalism had come to characterize most educational institutions. Middle-aged, middle-class white men began to see themselves as a minority group. They accepted this readjustment of cultural values, but decried the fact that nearly everyone was beginning to identify with one minority group or another. Women, Native Americans, Asians, Hispanics, the elderly, African Americans, poor people, millionaires, and gay people made it seem that there was no majority of anyone. It was a time when people speaking in public had to watch their language and many politicians got in serious trouble using wrong titles for anyone. Somewhere along the way, humor tended more to the off-color, and there was less willingness to poke fun at oneself. Apparently, the insecurities of the time made that difficult for most people.

Excesses of political correctness permeated the American culture. John Chasteen, president of the University of Connecticut and later president of the University of Virginia, published *Student's Handbook 1989–90* urging any black, Hispanic, or woman to immediately report any remarks made by others which felt like harassment. In the following years, many bright young people were expelled from colleges for reasons of political correctness. Writing of this, Paul Johnson in *A History of the American People* wrote: "Political correctness persecutions were in the long American tradition of the Salem Witch trials, the Hollywood black list, and other manifestations of religious and ideological fervor overriding the principle of natural justice." Over in England, a recent report told of a list of potentially offensive words released at Stockport College in

Manchester. The list includes *history* and *man-made* because of their gender implications. It was also suggested that the word *crazy* might offend someone with mental health problems, and *ladies and gentlemen* has class implications. The reporter who wrote the article couldn't resist observing that the school officials had not yet asked that the city of Manchester be known as "Person-chester." Of course the decision by the 2000 General Conference to urge the elimination of the Chief Wahoo figure by the Cleveland Indians made a lot of sense to many people, else the motion would not have passed. It is only fair to report, however, that I overheard a group of very loyal Methodists giving forth with loud, disbelieving guffaws when they heard what several hundred Methodists had spent their time doing at a General Conference. Still, sensitivity to the feelings of people of minority status must be seen as a sign of Christian kindness. James Finn Garner in his delightful book *Politically Incorrect Bedtime Stories,* included this tongue in cheek introduction:

> If, through omission or commission, I have inadvertently displayed any sexist, racist, culturalist, nationalist, regionalist, ageist, lookist, ableist, sizeist, speciesist, intellectualist, socioe-conomist, ethnocentrist phallocentrist, heteropatriarchalist, or other type of bias as yet unnamed, I apologize . . .

There were, of course, legitimate reasons for this concern for language. But like all new cultural developments, excesses inevitably occurred. Fortunately, one can only hope that most Methodists possess a sufficient sense of humor to poke a little fun at themselves and thus display mental health.

~

Looked upon by most easterners as a nineteenth-century city, by the 1980s Indianapolis began to take on some of the trappings of the new age. The Indianapolis Colts and the Indiana Pacers had arrived. The city also became the national headquarters for many amateur athletic organizations, like the Amateur Athletic Union (AAU). The day was not far when the National Collegiate Athletic

Association (NCAA) would choose Indianapolis for their national headquarters. The tennis tournament, the natatorium at IU Purdue, one of the country's few velodromes, world-class lobbying by movers and shakers of the city, and big-city quality mayors like Dick Lugar (a devout Methodist who introduced uni-gov), and Bill Hudnut (a Presbyterian minister and former congressman), and Indianapolis was no longer Indy-No Place. It was on the map. No one has ever quite understood why athletics defines a city, but such is the case. As Indiana's capital city changed, so did Indiana. While still very much a farm state, it has increasingly become an industrial state. When the Indiana Pacers play the New York Knicks in NBA basketball, the headlines routinely dub the contest "Hicks versus Knicks," but there is a difference now. It is the Indiana folks who use that phrase, because we know it isn't true. Not any more.

All of this bespoke the prosperous lifestyle. Cynics would grudgingly admit that Indianapolis had come bursting into the twentieth century—then on into the twenty-first. And Indianapolis was a strong church city. In the Methodist Church, congregations were experiencing prosperity, and many churches were expanding. In the small communities, progress was just as encouraging.

One of the unsung ministers of the South Indiana Conference was Reverend Loren Maxwell. His devotion was to smaller, rural congregations where funds were more limited, yet growth potential was real—churches which rarely got the headlines, yet which served God with unfailing energy. Maxwell was known to his admirers as a cattleman. Born and raised on a farm, he bought and sold cattle as a hobby—and as a way of making his contributions to other people. Many a minister bought a side of beef for half the normal price from Maxwell. He would purchase the cattle live, have them slaughtered, dressed, cut, packaged, and delivered. He didn't do it for profit. He would often sell part of the beef to cover his costs, then have the remainder ground and donated to the youth camps like Rivervale, thereby reducing the operating costs of those camps which he loved.

Reverend Maxwell was dedicated to enabling the expansion of small churches by remaining constantly alert for opportunities to purchase various building materials at bargain prices, which might be used as those churches built their new additions. Reverend Greg

McGarvey, Maxwell's district superintendent in 1985, recently observed that Maxwell would often call a farmer and ask if there was some spare barn space available to store this or that stack of building supplies, because someone would surely need it in a year or two. McGarvey opined that even today there are probably undiscovered caches of such materials.

One of Maxwell's projects was to assist the people of Lincoln Hills Church in English, Indiana, in building their new building. Maxwell's official title was conference mission secretary. His passion was helping to build new churches. His dedication was to help in any way he could. As construction proceeded on the Lincoln Hills Church, Maxwell worked behind the scenes to procure financing. Then he appeared on the work site in overalls and a tool belt to help volunteers in the common labor of building a church. Reverend McGarvey often found himself dragged to such duty, and being somewhat inept in construction matters, he nonetheless found such inspiration in this cattleman-minister's devotion to his mission and his willingness to do the dirty work which this entailed, that McGarvey too began to find satisfaction in doing the rolled-up-sleeves part of church building. When relating all of this, McGarvey became pensive for a moment and remembered, too, that Loren Maxwell cared. He cared about the people he served. He cared about those around him. One evening in 1985, borne down with the weight of his many responsibilities, fifty-five-year-old Reverend Loren Maxwell suddenly, quietly, and without warning passed away.

~

One of the defining truths of the Methodist Church continued to be her determined mission outreach. Whatever financial shortfalls may have marked other church activities, everyone seemed to possess a fiery determination to do something about problems worldwide. South Africa had become a source of prayerful concern as the African Development Fund was placed at the center of area awareness. Many clergy journeyed to Africa for firsthand knowledge of the crisis there, as did many laity. Doctors and other medical people under the program Operation Doctor, which began back in

the late sixties, continued to go with no reward other than the satisfaction of knowing they had saved and changed some lives. Many
people became alarmed at a report that Nestlé Corporation had sent
defective infant formula to third world nations, which resulted in a
motion at the 1981 South Indiana Annual Conference that the
Methodist Church boycott Nestlé. The motion passed, but with a
cautionary amendment by Nancy Couts that the Nestlé explanation
be included in conference mailings. A further amendment recommended that Nestlé send its own explanation. This was passed.

In 1982, a motion was made to call upon all governments
having nuclear capability to cease production. While this motion
may appear an empty gesture since it must have been obvious that
a group of Methodists in Indiana were not going to hold back that
surging tide, it did send a message to the membership of the conferences that we do have an official position against nuclear testing.
Nuclear testing and development was destined to continue for
many years. Still, the church was taking a stand.

In 1986 the council of bishops issued a pastoral letter entitled
"In Defense of Creation" to protest the dangers of nuclear war. At
the 1986 Annual Conference, Bishop Leroy Hodapp, who had
replaced Bishop Armstrong in 1984 after eight years as bishop in
Illinois, explained that this letter was not an attempt to state an official position of the Methodist Church but was, instead, a mutually
accepted position by the bishops, stating their personal beliefs. With
some insistence that opposing points of view be considered, the
conferences accepted the letter as a study document and took notice
that a more formal document would be made available in two years.

In 1988 a mission statement of the United Methodist Church
was issued, entitled "Grace upon Grace," and adopted by the
General Conference. Prepared by Dr. Thomas Langford of Duke
Divinity School, its essence was contained in the explanation:
"Missional vision is not created by the church, rather it is given to
the church by God's saving activity in and on behalf of the world."
The statement then set forth to "identify the sources of our faith
and life—Scripture and our tradition." Thus, the purpose of the
denomination's official statement was "to set forth as clearly as
possible the gospel of grace as it impels us to evangelize and serve

the world which God in Christ 'so loves.'" While statements like these seem to most laypersons to be glittering generalities, they do frequently issue in constructive, concrete actions.

~

Racism would continue to be a concern of Indiana Methodists. While it was generally believed that much progress had been made, and while the Methodist Church in general felt great satisfaction in the inclusion of black Methodists in the whole church family, its efforts would always continue to move toward total harmony. For example, in 1988 a Martin Luther King Jr. essay contest was held with 421 essays entered from seventy-five different high schools. The contest was won by Kris Kubick of Marquette High School in Michigan City and Karen Kidwell of Lincoln High School, Cambridge City. The two second place winners were Joe Emmick of Arlington High School, Indianapolis, and Ted Maple of Keystone Middle School, Indianapolis. It has been an annual competition.

On stage at the 1988 South Conference, the lights were dimmed, and a cardboard wall was displayed on which appeared the word *Racism*. Narration stressed how subtle the problem can be and how it is necessary to tear down that wall. Members of the Commission on Religion and Race then formed a circle of friendship and love. Programs like this typified the ongoing efforts by the church to highlight our progress toward equality through the 1980s.

There was a dark note during the 1988 South Conference. Bishop J. Clinton Hoggard of the Methodist Episcopal Zion Church had been invited to deliver the message at the evening service in the Indiana University auditorium. His address was interrupted by an embarrassed Bishop Hodapp, who had to announce that a bomb threat had been received and the congregation must immediately leave the building. Forty-five minutes later they returned, and Bishop Hoggard, apparently accustomed to roadblocks in his path, resumed his address.

Gambling troubled the leaders of the Methodist Church as Indiana prepared to institute a lottery and to legalize gambling vessels on the Ohio River. However, there was very little grassroots

John Wolf displays a bumper sticker used in the effort to stop riverboat casinos from being approved in various Indiana counties. Spearheading the anti-legalized gambling in the state, he forged a coalition of churches and social service agencies—a kind of "David" taking on the "Goliath" of big gambling interests determined to get a foothold in the area.

support for the opposition. Bishop Hodapp asked all pastors to request donations for a fund to be used in opposition to the Indiana gambling program. On two successive Sundays, I made such an appeal to an attendance of some nineteen hundred people at St. Luke's. I received a total of one contribution. Gambling became legal in Indiana under certain conditions. Still, diehard opponents of gambling continued to fight the good fight, always hopeful, standing as an exalted example of the tireless spirit of opposition to any social evil which threatens us. Reverend John Wolf, one of the early leaders of the Northwest Conference still serves as coordinator of the Indiana Coalition Against Legalized Gambling in Indiana (ICALG). Though long retired at the time of this writing, his unremitting efforts courageously oppose the gambling forces of the state.

For some reason, the abortion issue has never become inflammatory among Methodists. In the mid-eighties the General Conference added a phrase to its position opposing abortion under most conditions which read: "We cannot affirm abortion as an acceptable means of birth control, and we unconditionally reject it as a means of gender selection." A motion was made and passed at the 1988 South Indiana Annual Conference urging that counseling be made available to anyone facing a crisis situation in which abortion might be a consideration. This tepid position on the issue, generally opposing easy abortion, but understanding that there are unusual situations which make abortion acceptable, seems satisfactory to the church at large.

~

Sometimes a minister is called to stand up to threats. It can require courage. One such occasion took place in Elkhart's Trinity Methodist Church. Marcus Blaising, later to become assistant to the bishop, was pastor when something happened which could have split the congregation and could very well have seriously damaged other churches as well.

It is probably hard for younger people today to comprehend the strong feelings about the threat of Communism which kept so many people upset as the eighties arrived. As we watch the Russians flounder in their efforts to establish a stable society today, they don't seem so frightening. But in the sixties and seventies and into the eighties, they were an international threat, and many people believed there to be covert Communists in high places within the various institutions of our society, even the church. One organization which attracted many people of this suspicious persuasion was an extremist group known as the John Birch Society.

Several members of Trinity Church had a John Birch mentality and believed the church should take a strong anti-Communist stand in a public way. These people were, as Blaising recalls, "suspicious of our General Board of Church and Society, the General Board of Global Ministries, the Council of Bishops, the World and National Councils of Churches." He recalls that some twenty church members, determined to undermine these church organizations if they could, had made plans to attend a meeting of Trinity's administrative board with a motion to refuse payment of their assigned financial apportionments. Blaising got wind of this. As he headed for the meeting, he prayed a prayer he still recalls: "Regardless of my career, I will be faithful."

Sure enough, the motion was made, and it was obvious there was a lot of sympathy for this action among some members. When it was time to vote, Blaising got to his feet. It was time to put his career on the line. He looked out on the people he had come to know and love. "At the present time we have sixty thousand dollars in the current expense balance," he announced. "We will pay all apportionments," he continued, "until we have no money remaining. Then I will serve as pastor with no compensation until my family cannot be maintained. But as long as I am

Marcus J. Blaising, 1983.

pastor, we will pay apportionments." The motion was defeated. But it was still clear that there was a strong paranoid element who weren't done yet.

A group of like-minded people from several Methodist churches then gathered at another meeting. Still determined to drive the church into a strong anti-Communist commitment, they decided to invite a fiery right wing speaker from Wheaton, Illinois, to speak before a large assemblage of Methodists, hoping to reach as many as fifteen hundred people from the churches in the community. Blaising attended the meeting. First one, then another heated speaker decried what he believed to be the Communism permeating the highest levels of the Methodist Church. But one of the more reasonable participants asked Blaising what he thought about the plan. He knew his future with Elkhart Church was at stake, but Blaising also knew his own integrity was at stake. He stood his ground. "If you proceed with having this man come to Elkhart," he said, "you will injure the church for twenty-five years. People will be misjudged, families will be hurt, and anyone who disagrees with what will be

Carolyn Marshall, Veedersburg, has been one of the most influential laywomen of the Church in recent history. She was elected to the last six General Conference delegations and is now serving her fourth quadrennium as Secretary of the General Conference. She has also served as director of the UM-related Lucille Raines Residence in Indianapolis since 1996.

presented will be considered a suspect with Communist leanings." Then Blaising took a great risk. He announced, "Therefore, I object. If you invite him to come, I want you to know that beginning now, I will only serve you as your priest. I will baptize your young, marry your children, and bury your dead. Otherwise, I will have nothing to do with you." Blaising recalls that the air was electric as he stood before the group. The plan died there. This man, pledged to live the life of love, showed that love sometimes calls one to step up and risk oneself for one's convictions. Nearly everyone respected this stand and Reverend Dr. Marcus Blaising's pastorate, far from being damaged, was strengthened in the minds of a congregation who respected what he had done.

There was an interesting aftermath. One man challenged Blaising with the threat, "You have lost your credibility with the people of this group." To which Blaising responded, "But I have kept my credibility with God and with myself." Shortly after, a few families left the church, taking with them some eleven thousand dollars in pledges. That hurt, sure enough. But in the very next membership class, two new families each pledged one hundred dollars per week to the church. Blaising smiles now as he remembers. But at the time, with tears in his eyes, he bowed his head and prayed, "Lord, forgive me. I forgot that this was your church and that you do provide." Trinity Church, Elkhart, remained one of the fine, strong churches of the North Indiana Conference.

~

The heart of Africa, in the person of a little eight-year-old girl, sat at a school desk in Monrovia, Liberia, not long ago. She was alone. Her name was Deela. Each day she arrived at her school, which was torn apart by mortar fire, its windows broken, its faculty gone. There were no classes. Yet, hopefully, Deela took her place. The fighting had disrupted the schools as well as the lives of the people of Liberia. But little Deela somehow believed in the future. Lynne DeMichele saw her, but DeMichele had to hitch a ride on a relief flight from Sierra Leone to do so. There, in microcosm, she saw the plight of a people. Destruction. Privation. And yet a bright-eyed hope embodied in a child, a belief in the future, a deep assurance that something good was yet to happen. And so it has, partly because of Indiana Methodists, people from both conferences who support Operation Classroom. This splendid program was born of the creativity of the two Indiana Conference lay leaders, John Shettle in the North and Robert Bowman in the South, with the assistance of Bishop Hodapp. Since 1987, under the heroic leadership of Joe and Carolyn Wagner as coordinators for the project under the auspices of the General Board of Global Ministries, the United Methodist Church has sent hundreds of tons of supplies for schools in Liberia. They have made it possible for children like Deela to get an education, something which Bishop Arthur Kuhlah of Liberia believes is the one best hope for his country's future.

It doesn't stop there. Over in Sierra Leone, people are dying, not only from raging war and violence, but from disease and lack of medical care. It is a dangerous place to be. Outsiders aren't welcome. Supplies could not, as of recent reports, be brought in to help the people. By the year 2000, the United Nations issued a list

Operation Classroom's Buchanan Elementary School in Liberia. The children are carrying school bags made, filled with supplies, and sent by Indiana United Methodist Churches. Photo by Carolyn Wagner.

ranking 174 countries in a human development index based on income, education, life expectancy, and health care. The bottom 24 countries were in Africa. Sierra Leone ranked last. But somehow the Wagners found a way to bring in money for medical supplies. Indiana medical people, starting with one of the founders, Dr. Richard Nay of Meridian Street Church in Indianapolis, have gone there in Operation Doctor—dedicated men and women whose faith calls them out from their often comfortable and prosperous lives. They run the risks and suffer the inconveniences of serving a desperately needy people whose own suffering makes the hardships of most people seem small by comparison.

Early in the year 2000, William Nunery, an Indiana surgeon, stood ready to board his plane for South Africa for several weeks of medical service there. His wife, Vickie, and his mother, Grace Nunery, wife of Reverend Albert Nunery, were seeing him off at the airport. Mrs. Grace Nunery always loved to tell how she had prayed that her children would all find ways to serve Jesus Christ in one or another form of ministry. Now with a full heart, she was watching her son as he carried out his commitment to forego the professional profits of his work to spend his time—and his money—to serve a people whose needs are desperate. Warned that a foreigner in South Africa is in real physical danger, Nunery acknowledged this truth, but agreed to run that risk in order to follow the leading of God's Spirit. It was his second such trip.

Joe and Carolyn Wagner, Colfax, have been coordinators for Operation Classroom since its inception in 1987, making a total to date of approximately twenty trips to West Africa. They have built this mission program in cooperation with the West Africa Church, securing local-church support in Indiana and other states for each of the program's ten schools, along with its various clinics, refugee centers, and post-war health and counseling programs—all during a period of recurring and devastating civil conflict in the region. Loretta Gruver (center), a nurse missionary from Indiana, developed a nurses' training prgram and served the UM-related hospital in Ganta, Liberia for thirty-five years before her retirement in 1999. When she left Ganta for the last time the entire village turned out in a special parade in honor of this extraordinary woman whose life's work had blessed many thousands. Photo courtesy of Lynne DeMichele.

Nunery, who would probably refuse this recognition if asked, was one of many medical people who have sacrificed themselves in an effort to bring merciful care to a tragically troubled land. He was one of many Methodists willing to do what this faith asks of all of us: find a way to give part of what we have for others.

The mention of Grace Nunery brings to mind her own tireless efforts on behalf of hearing impaired people of all ages to provide worship and other religious services. Starting at Meridian Street Church in Indianapolis, she later moved the program to St. Luke's, where for many years the deaf ministry has offered worship and counseling for hundreds of deaf and hearing impaired people. Only when long past retirement age did she finally turn this ministry over to others. Reverend Gene Merrick still keeps that program alive. It is now called the Church of Grace.

This continuing sense of mission which dominates the Methodist psyche has its beginnings in the life of John Wesley. Reverend Robert Hunt's book *Bicentennial Moments* reminds us of the time Wesley, when eighty-one years old, was out walking through deep snow asking for donations for bread and coal to be given to the poor of the community. In his journal, Wesley observed of this day, ". . . my feet were steeped in snow-water nearly from morning till evening." He then came down with a serious infection which was then called flux. Wesley described his ailment as "violent," so a Dr. Whitehead was called at six in the morning. Wesley later wrote of his treatment: "His first draught made me quite easy; and three or four more perfected the cure. If he lives some years, I expect he will be one of the most eminent Physicians in Europe." Hunt, commenting on this, observed, "What compassion the eighty-one-year-old man had, to spend five days in January going to the homes of people through the snow to beg money for the poor! As the spiritual descendants of John Wesley, we are to have great compassion also." And so we are. And so we do.

∽

After several years of emphasis on social issues, the church began to look more closely at its theology. Spiritual Formation had become important. The appointment of Reverend Norm Shawchuk as area director of Spiritual Formation in 1981 turned our attentions forcefully, and blessedly, in that direction. In no time, Shawchuk was forced to complain that his schedule had become so filled with commitments to conduct spiritual workshops and retreats that an appeal was issued to the area to relent, to let others give leadership to those very important events so that Shawchuk could serve more in a directorial capacity.

Reverend Susan Ruach, South Conference council director, said that while immersed in the hard work of conference activities, she found it easy to lose sight of the comparative excellence of many area programs. But as she travels farther afield, she realizes how excellent some of them really are. She especially mentioned Spiritual Formation, and associates that with Reverend Charles "Chuck" Myers, as well as Reverends Phil Amerson, Charles Gipson, and Mrs. Marilyn Griffith, whose husband, Donald, is a pastor. Dr. Ruach believes this program is a leader in the church nationally.

Another program which has influenced many Methodist laypersons is the lay speakers' training which helps people develop skills in public speaking. Jerry Thomas, lay leader of the Logansport District, attributes his ability as a teacher as head of the mathematics department at Culver Academy in Culver, Indiana, to the inspiration and encouragement he received in this program. No doubt many Methodist leaders would share Thomas's enthusiasm for this program.

❧

Several Indiana ministers have been elected to the episcopacy. In the 1984 jurisdictional conference, David Lawson, then pastor of Carmel Church, had an interesting experience. He was, frankly, put off by the interrogation process which every candidate must endure. So much so that he made the decision to withdraw his name from consideration. He was literally walking to find a microphone for this purpose when a friend stopped him and asked that he step aside for a moment about a "very important matter." With some hesitation, Lawson did and in the process, missed his chance to withdraw. He then announced to friends his decision to withdraw the next day. However, the election process was well along, and by the time he was ready to withdraw, he discovered he had already been elected. He suspects the friend who interrupted him knew exactly what he was doing.

Incidentally, for all of us who have never been elected bishop, it might be interesting to hear Bishop Lawson's response to the question, "What did it feel like, suddenly becoming a bishop?" His reply was somewhat surprising. He said his first reaction was one of disconnection. When he walked forward to the front of the auditorium, he looked back and saw that the other members of his delegation had already moved over and occupied his seat. He realized then that after a professional lifetime of building friendships in the South Indiana Conference, he was no longer a part of it. For all the rewards of such a high office, there would be the price of building a new circle of friends in ministry.

Other Indiana men who have been elected include Ed Garrison, who was assistant to Bishop Raines; Leroy Hodapp and James Armstrong, both of whom returned as Indiana bishops; Sheldon Dueker and Michael Coyner, former superintendents; and John Hopkins, who most recently had pastored the campus church in Evansville, Methodist Temple.

~

The Good News movement began to make itself felt in Indiana. In the late 1980s, a group of Indiana Methodist clergy who identified themselves as Evangelicals approached Reverend Greg McGarvey, now senior pastor of Old Bethel Methodist Church in Indianapolis, to lead them in thinking through the role of those who were uncomfortable with the theological directions of the South Indiana Conference. McGarvey, then the conference's youngest district superintendent, agreed to help. It was decided they should form an organization whose purpose would be to urge a return to traditional Wesleyan teachings. They first examined the position of Good News which was already leading such a movement on the national scene. However, that group, in the opinions of McGarvey's friends, had become identified with a too strident and militant manner of presenting their views. Whether this was actually true, it was certainly the perception within the conference. So it was agreed that the wise move would be to innovate and create a new movement with the intention of placing greater emphasis on scriptural authority. In a year 2000 interview, McGarvey emphasized that the clergy and laity involved in this effort were doing so in good and friendly spirit, not in a spirit of judgmentalism. But they felt strongly about the truth of their beliefs.

Patricia Miller represented the South Indiana Conference at each of the past four General and Jurisdictional Conferences.

In 1988, a group of pastors from mainly southern churches in the United States issued what they called the Houston Declaration, urging an evangelical interpretation of scripture and the application of that conservative theology to contemporary social issues. In 1992, a similar document was proposed to be known as the Memphis Declaration. McGarvey was a signatory of that document. His associates, including Ms. Patricia L. Miller, an active member of Old Bethel Methodist Church in Indianapolis, decided an Indiana version of this movement should be formed. Accordingly, they created what they called Impact of South Indiana, Inc. This organization became a chapter of the Confessing Movement in 1999. Ms. Miller, a member of the Indiana State Legislature, became executive director of the national organization of the Confessing Movement within the Methodist Church, and the members of the organization established themselves as a political force within the area.

The Confessing Movement members identify themselves as possessing a "more moderate image than that of Good News" and are what McGarvey terms "neo-Evangelicals." They quite openly

Riley B. Case, 1996.

create their own slate of candidates for the various conference elections and have been successful in sending their chosen delegates to those gatherings. This was especially true of the General Conference of 2000 in Cleveland. McGarvey's leadership had recently been recognized as the conference chose McGarvey as their candidate for the episcopacy at the 2000 jurisdictional conference in Madison, Wisconsin. In the 1996 jurisdictional conference, Reverends John Hopkins from the South Conference and Mike Coyner from the North Conference were both elected to the episcopacy. That was a rare occurrence and pretty much precluded any Indiana candidate from election in 2000. Of course McGarvey lost.

In the North Conference, a strong desire for a more evangelical direction for Methodist theology led many pastors and laypersons to look to the Good News movement. Reverend Riley Case, former district superintendent, longtime pastor of St. Luke's Church in Kokomo, and a spokesman for Good News, refers to an article published in *Christian Advocate* by Charles Keysor in 1966, titled "Methodism's Silent Minority." In it Keysor took the denomination to task for the watering down of the Bible's demanding Word. Written at a time when most people's attention was focused on Communism and the general unrest which permeated American society, Keysor sought to bring attention back to the church's theology and the two ways in which most church people learn their theology: hymns and Sunday school literature. He believed that we were failing to retain the fundamental teachings by which Methodism had flourished through two centuries. Definitely a minority opinion, Keysor nonetheless won a growing number of adherents to his conviction that the church had drifted away from its roots in Christian holiness.

Dr. Case reminds us that there was no unanimous embrace of Good News since many North Conference pastors also felt some strong misgivings. Instead, the North Indiana Fellowship was organized in 1970. Case, Cecil Hendricks, and Carl Ricks were the organizers. Its appeal was to those who needed a safe place to be able to share faith experiences without the fear of being scorned or ridiculed. This organization met annually, always invited cabinet members, chose not to be a political organization, and had meetings attended by between forty and eighty people. Case credits Reverend Evan Bergwall, former president of Taylor University and one time superintendent of the Elkhart District, with wise leadership at a time when the Good News movement was being widely criticized.

In the years that followed, other organized evangelical occasions were provided, including a Labor Day weekend convocation patterned after the Good News convocation. Soon two hundred to four hundred people were attending this annual event. For twenty-three years it was held at Oakwood Park, until changed policies caused the program to be suspended in 1993. By then the needs it was designed to serve had changed, evangelicals felt more acceptance, and the hard feelings which had resulted from the merger of the two conferences had largely disappeared. Case also credits Dale Linehart and John Walls with the leadership which enabled the success of these programs.

Times do change. Riley Case observes that a growing number of people who were numbered among the early evangelical group have achieved leadership positions in the conference. In 1999, the Good News group in the North Conference disbanded in favor of the Confessing Movement. Steve Beutler is the current chair of the Confessing Movement. It is their hope that their numbers and, more importantly, their sentiments will be part of the mainstream of conference life.

CHAPTER TWELVE

God's way of salvation is not by enabling a number of individuals to grasp the truth— either by mystical union, or by intellectual inquiry, or by being given one universal and inerrant revelation in code or book; it is by calling a people to Himself, that they may be with Him and that He may send them forth.
—Lesslie Newbigin

The Nineties: We Methodists Find Our Way

In the summer of 1992, following the retirement of Bishop Leroy Hodapp, the new bishop of the Indiana Area, Woodie W. White, arrived. In a meeting of the pastors of his largest churches held shortly after his arrival, White was asked by one pastor, "What should we call you?" The bishop's answer was firm and quick: "Call me Bishop White." The initial reaction to this was puzzlement, as the two previous bishops, Armstrong and Hodapp, had been "Jim" and "Leroy," at least to the older clergy who had known both during their times as Indiana pastors. White, however, knew what he was doing. Perhaps he was speaking out of the black church culture. But it worked. First names subtly cultivate familiarity. When a man or woman must wield the power which is available to a United Methodist bishop, the power of economic and emotional life and death over nearly two thousand clergy and their families, there are times when the distance which Woodie White prefers adds strength to his authority.

If there were early fears that the new bishop planned to wield that power in any high-handed way, those fears were quickly stilled as White soon showed himself to be a spiritual man of sensitivity and kindness. Granted, every bishop must sometimes make decisions which are unpopular, and those decisions often produce the occasional displeased minister, but Bishop Woodie W. White has long since become highly respected and popular with the laity. A tireless leader of seminars and classes and a much sought after preacher, White is constantly busy. As I discovered, he is also hard to pin down. He is, to the nth degree, a man on the go.

Like all bishops, Woodie W. White has things he doesn't like to do. His reputation is that of a man who dislikes sitting through meetings and prefers to let others take care of the details of his role. Thus he is able to be with people, especially laypeople. He also loves leading tours of places like Africa and the Holy Land. Only recently he returned from a tour in Germany where he also visited the Methodist Church there. One detects affection from those who work close to White. Reverend Jim Jones, executive assistant, shared some inside information. The bishop likes chocolate, big band music, and—this is definitely inside information—Tina Turner. He even had a life-sized cutout of Turner until Mrs. Kim White insisted it be removed. Humor, pride in his role, and an evangelical spirit characterize this man who was recently assigned to the Indiana area for an additional four years. Reverend Jones also added, "Bishop White is a giant in combating racism in the church."

One insight into Bishop White's self-perception is revealed in his letter to the church contained in the June issue of *HUM*, which followed the 2000 General Conference. In it he depicted himself as being most comfortable sitting in the back row, observing the goings-on. "Actually, I enjoy anonymity," he wrote. "Strange, for one who chose so public a calling," he acknowledged. White's spirituality is evident in his quiet observation, "In spite of some low moments and disappointments at the conference, . . . I could see that God is ultimately in control." In truth, White is a genuinely unpretentious man who is quite comfortable out of the limelight.

An indication of White's character was supplied by Reverend Phil Amerson, now president of Clermont School of Theology in California, but formerly pastor of First Church, Bloomington. Amerson had become dissatisfied with the bishop's performance in an area which Amerson considered important. Before long, the two were at odds with each other in a public way. One day Bishop White invited Amerson to sit down over a meal to discuss their differences. Amerson later said that he was deeply impressed with White's openness and lack of defensiveness. White listened, understood, and even invited Amerson's counsel. Their differences were amicably settled, and the two parted with Amerson now most complimentary about his former bishop.

Perhaps the most remarkable report comes from Reverend William Schwein, former pastor of the South Conference's second largest church, Carmel, and now superintendent of the Indianapolis East District. He asked that the man not be named, but told of a pastor facing a very difficult time in his life. Struggling with personal and faith issues, the man received a visit from Bishop White. It proved to be one of the man's most memorable experiences. Schwein reported that the man said he couldn't remember ever receiving grace in his life—until that visit from White. He said it was so apparent that the bishop's only concern was for the welfare of the man. And when Bishop White was ready to depart, he looked at the man, who was torn by grief and inner struggle, and said, "I love you." It was a time of healing. Schwein, in reporting this encounter, said, "Bishop Raines cared about the church. Bishop White cares about people." This wasn't meant to disparage the towering figure of a bishop from another era. It was meant to say that now, when clergy are troubled, they will discover that they have a bishop who seems to be what bishops were envisioned to be long ago: fathers in the faith, emissaries of love.

⟆

In a recent book entitled *The Long March*, author Roger Kimball relates a story which appeared in the *New York Times* science section in 1994. It was about Phineas P. Gage, a respected and well-liked foreman on the New England railroad in 1848, whose primary duty was to set dynamite charges. He would light a fuse and then run for cover. But one day, a charge exploded

An ambitious evangelism campaign initiated by Bishop Woodie W. White was launched with parallel North and South Conference events in 1996. Here a crowd of approximately 10,500 from churches across northern Indiana have gathered for the "Vision 2000" event held at Notre Dame University's sports arena. The South Conference event, held in Indianapolis, drew a great crowd, as well. Both gatherings featured stirring worship, workshops, and evangelistic preaching. Photo by Lynne DeMichele.

prematurely, driving a metal rod through Gage's head. Amazingly, he made a complete recovery—physically. But from that time forward, Gage completely lost his moral sense. He began telling lies. He said hurtful things to people. He underwent a complete change of personality. Kimball submitted this true story as a parable for our time. He insists that something like this has happened to the American psyche in consequence of the many things we have discussed. Something fundamental has been changed in the moral realm, the author suggests, by the injuries thus received. If this seems a little harsh, one need only read the newspaper or watch television to see some merit in this judgment. Guns, drugs, crime, corruption in government, the failures of our courts, the endless arguments about education, and family disruptions all force one to honestly confront the many cases of malfeasance within the church. We have already discussed a number of examples of this unhappy decline.

Of course we can add to all of this the breakdown of the family in American life. If the church ever faced a time in its history when a renewed call to the biblically-based life so dear to John Wesley's heart held the only hope for a better tomorrow, a great many Methodists are convinced that time is now. If the present times are beset with theological disagreements, that seems to many to be a blessing. True, there are the usual harsh judgments by one person or another. It is hard, after all, to hold one's beliefs dear without speaking up for them in troubled times. A close look at our Methodist past quickly reveals that we have never all agreed on very much. But the give and take of earnest, praying people has consistently led the people of God to higher ground. It is not really bad when sincere Christians disagree about theology. That means we take our faith seriously and if, by being unique, each one of us arrives at firm beliefs different than those of other equally earnest believers, surely God will honor each person's faith conviction. And so the people of God in the nineties squabbled at times, but meanwhile tried to find the right way instead of giving in to the easy way, which moved them toward that higher ground.

The *Indianapolis Star* newspaper featured a major article on March 12, 1989, entitled "Baby boom went bust in mainline churches." The writer, Carol Elrod, pointed out that between 1970 and 1989, the United Methodist Church had lost 1.7 million members. The South Indiana Conference had lost approximately twelve thousand members in the preceding ten years. The writer had interviewed leaders of the Presbyterian, Episcopal, Christian, and Catholic, as well as Methodist churches, and learned that all had experienced more or less the same decline. She also pointed out that very conservative churches had held their membership, even increasing numbers in many congregations.

There was a bright note. The same newspaper included a companion article entitled "Baby boomers find their needs answered at St. Luke's." Elrod pointed out that St. Luke's Methodist Church in Indianapolis had doubled its membership in

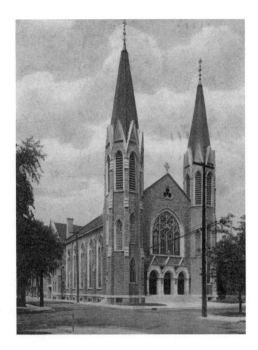

Meridian Street United Methodist Church, from a postcard circa 1900. Photo courtesy of DePauw University Archives and Special Collections.

that same ten-year period, and with a worship attendance of nearly 2,000 on a typical Sunday, had become the twelfth largest Methodist Church in America based on worship attendance. The singles program alone was attracting some 350 people each Wednesday evening. Elrod quoted one staff member as saying that St. Luke's "is a reentry church for baby boomers." The fact was that St. Luke's had a wide and varied program designed to supplement worship and Bible study with activities relevant to the daily lives of the people. Eleven years later, Robert Putnam's book *Bowling Alone* would point out that "Social Capital," the energy which enables people to live happy and successful lives, results from community participation. St. Luke's, by virtue of a large and splendid staff, had created a setting where people of diverse needs and interests could find that participatory sense of community.

In a book published by Discipleship Resources of the Methodist Church in 1990, authors Ralph W. and Nell W. Mohney reported on their visits to a few, what they called "churches of vision," in each jurisdiction. After detailing the growth which made St. Luke's the largest church in the jurisdiction, the authors wrote, "The big test for the stability of the church will come when McGriff [the pastor] retires. If the church can make the transition with a relative sense of ease, St. Luke's United Methodist Church will continue to grow."

Most experienced Methodists are aware that one of the most difficult undertakings which can face a minister is to replace another minister who has had a long and happy pastorate. It is almost a truism that the following pastor will have a short and not entirely pleasant tenure. Reverend Kent Millard promptly transferred to St. Luke's from a church in the Dakotas and proved this assumption completely wrong. His bright and energetic manner, coupled with an irresistible good spirit, soon caused the congregation to celebrate his arrival. The fact that he is a good preacher helped of course. So did the fact that I, as his predecessor, quickly became one of his most ardent admirers. After the usual period of staff changes which is always healthy, Dr. Millard quickly set forth to carry St. Luke's onward. He managed to raise several million dollars with which a splendid new sanctuary was built, along with expansive additional facilities. Seven years have passed and the congregation is currently looking to add even more space for the growth which they see to lie ahead. Millard, in addition to his leadership of this "flagship congregation," has become one of the leaders of the conference.

Incidentally, apropos of the observation that each congregation is unique, Dan Evans, one of Indianapolis's business leaders during the seventies, wrote a book detailing the history of Meridian Street Methodist Church in Indianapolis through the early nineties. That distinguished church was established in 1821. Evans referred to Meridian Street Church as "the mother church of Methodism in Indianapolis." It was once listed as the most prominent Methodist church in the city during Richard Lancaster's pastorate. In the book, Evans who watched as St. Luke's grew from a small suburban church to become the city's largest mainline Protestant Church, is quoted as having compared the two with the observation that "Meridian Street is a symphony, St. Luke's is a rock concert." Whatever Evans may have meant by that, it can be assumed both congregations considered the observation to be a high compliment. It is generally believed that Evans never attended St. Luke's, but his loyalty to his pastor, Dr. Lancaster, is to be commended.

Meridian Street Church was actually begun by a group of early settlers who met in the log cabin of Isaac Wilson. Its class leader was Robert Bruton. Here was born what would eventually be Meridian Street Methodist Church. After being located in several downtown locations, it suffered a disastrous fire in 1904. Rebuilt at Meridian and St. Clair Streets, the congregation finally moved to their present location at 5500 North Meridian Street in 1956.

Another Indianapolis congregation was featured in the Mohneys' book: Castleton Church. Once a small, rural congregation, it was displaced by an interstate highway and the members by majority vote chose to relocate in a strategically favorable location alongside that very highway. Soon Castleton Church grew to become one of the city's leading congregations. Much of that growth came under the leadership of Reverend Charles Armstrong, who became pastor in 1987. Describing him, the Mohneys wrote: "As in most growing churches, Castleton United Methodist Church reflects the leadership and spirit of its senior pastor, Charles (Chuck) Armstrong. A gregarious, warm person, Armstrong, according to church leaders, is extremely relational, a fine preacher and a good administrator." The Mohneys' added this: "Leaders say the senior pastor's wife is also a strength of the church. Her friendliness and hospitality in the life of the church are seen as assets." They predicted that under Armstrong's leadership, the formerly small, rural congregation, would exceed two thousand members and become one of the state's largest churches. By the time Armstrong had been there for ten years, that goal was nearly achieved. Sadly one of life's tragic ironies beset the Armstrong household. Both developed cancer. In early 1998, Chuck, so dearly loved by fellow pastors as well as by his congregation, followed his beloved wife Jean in untimely death.

The Mohneys' book also featured a third Indiana church in the North Central jurisdiction, one which had a much rockier history than the first two: Mount Auburn Church in Greenwood. At the time of the book's publication in 1990, Nelson Chamberlin was senior pastor and the inheritor of an unhappy congregational history. The authors wrote, "Just as the physical body experiences pain from trauma, the Body of Christ at Mount Auburn has suffered." Indeed it had. A very charismatic young senior pastor, who had taken the church to an attendance of about a thousand people on a typical Sunday, had left the denomination and moved to Florida. His associate pastor, also highly regarded in the congregation, had also left the denomination and started an independent congregation two miles away, taking with him several hundred Mount Auburn members and their financial support. The church was then hit by a tornado which nearly destroyed the sanctuary and damaged the education wing. It is hard to imagine a new pastor facing more difficulty than that. Naturally, by the time the Mohneys arrived, the formerly large and growing congregation had dwindled considerably. However, the Mahoneys wrote, "Under the able leadership of Nelson Chamberlin, his staff, and a corps of dedicated laypersons, the wounds seem to be healing and the church is courageously facing forward." While the church never returned to its brief state of exciting growth, it has remained a strong congregation and enters the new millennium with a healthy membership and attendance.

∾

Financial problems would continue to plague the Methodist Church. The 1991 cabinet report to the South Indiana Annual Conference by Lloyd Wright, chairman, reported that the fund raising program termed Gifts of the Spirit had not done well. In truth, the rank and file of pastors were not at all in favor of the program. They felt the goal was much too high and not realistic in the face of mounting costs in the local churches. Wright went on to observe, "This has been a disappointing year in conference finances. Our contingency reserve is depleted to approximately $1,100. This can be called nothing less than a crisis."

Another problem troubled the various cabinets as the nineties arrived. A growing number of pastors were resisting the traditional practice of bishops and cabinets moving them as needed without making allowances for their family wishes. Several factors had become dominant in church life since most of the members of the hierarchy had won their spurs. Younger pastors had acquired much more demanding attitudes toward their vocation than was true of earlier generations. Clergy spouses—many were now male—were not always willing to move on such short notice. Wives, formerly used to quickly finding teaching positions in new communities, now discovered that those positions were rarely available. Many clergy wives were entering other professions where longevity was necessary for advancement. Some pastors were buying homes as a hedge against inflation. "I trust the covenant and the system; send me where you will," wrote Reverend Wright in reference to the traditional point of view, one which he and other cabinet members hoped to reinforce throughout the area. It was destined to be an uphill battle. While the bishop retained the power to enforce moves as he deemed proper, he also needed to maintain high morale among the clergy, something which many bishops must find extremely discouraging at times. Since clergy are people too, with children and spouses and career aspirations—and given a different outlook by younger professionals in general—the practice of consulting pastors about their appointments was becoming common. Added to this was the fact that as young clergy aged and some became district superintendents, the cabinets were becoming less and less committed to the earlier way. In short, times had changed and the word was slow in getting to everyone. But of course, it finally did.

The church has continued its relentless effort to combat—better yet, were it possible—eliminate racism. The 1993 North Conference journal contains this affirmation by Reverend John Wolf, chair of the Committee on Ethnic Local Church Concerns: "It is the responsibility of our whole Annual Conference to incorporate into its agencies' budgets, programs, and agenda's goals and strategies for the continued development and strengthening of the local ethnic church. We are not alone in this effort. We are connected with our brothers and sisters throughout the entire conference." And then, in referring to this initiative which began in 1992 for all Annual Conferences, Wolf added this: "I am sure as the entire conference discovers its role in strengthening the ethnic local church that it will be accountable and we will get the job done."

~

Maybe the day will never come when racism, or at least the appearance of racism in the eyes of some beholders, will end. We're all sinners, and sinners have a devil of a time feeling completely at ease with people who are different from ourselves. On the other hand, if the Bible is to be believed and if love does, indeed, have the power to overcome all evils, then maybe down life's road lies harmony at last. The one certainty is that this can only happen with the power of love, exercised by individual Christians—Methodists—Methodists like the Reverend Lynette DeAtley, for instance. While a student at Christian Theological Seminary in Indianapolis and also serving a Methodist church, she heard one of her professors express the opinion that she, a white woman raised in a small town, could never understand life in the inner city.

Reverend DeAtley, accepting that challenge, went down to the Edna Martin Christian Center on the east side of Indianapolis and began to practice that Christian love. An article in the *Indianapolis Star* described the Martin Center as "an oasis of hope in a Near-Eastside neighborhood known for drugs, violence and wasted dreams." And into this world of wasted dreams, a young Methodist pastor went and began to practice that love which the Bible says can avail against all odds. Counseling, comforting, guiding, and praying with the needy people who came there, DeAtley soon became a part of the community.

One evening, while DeAtley was serving as a chaplain at Methodist Hospital, a young black woman was admitted in extremis with kidney disease. When the young woman died, the distraught family was very open and vocal in their mourning. DeAtley obtained some cool, wet towels and gave them to the aunt, the mother, and the sister, and then quietly remained with them as they grieved. The aunt asked her to pray with them. And then something wonderful happened—the aunt asked her for a hug. And so they hugged, and they wept together. "There was an openness that hadn't been there before," DeAtley said. Then, as the young woman's brother-in-law stood nearby watching the two women, something even more wonderful happened. The young man said he had never seen a white person hug a black person, especially one who cared enough to cry. He asked if she would give him a hug, too. Later, DeAtley put her finger on the solution to racism: "The fact that one young man who had never seen anything positive happen between an African American and a white person

Charles L. Hutchinson, 1990.

was moved to share a hug, shows there is a hope for humanity to look past the differences and come together."

Of course God also takes a hand when people sincerely seek to remove racism from their hearts. People who don't believe in miracles should talk to Charles Hutchinson. Some readers will recognize that name. Reverend "Hutch" Hutchinson has long been one of the leaders of the South Indiana Conference. But that is part of the miracle.

Go back in your mind a half century, to a little town in Alabama named Attalla. A young black tenth-grade boy walked with his dad to a nearby bus stop. His school, black children only, taught just to tenth grade, so Hutch and his dad were on their way to nearby Gaston, Alabama, a six-mile bus ride, where Hutch would go to school for his next grade. It so happened that this required them to walk past a neighborhood bar, and as they did so, a huge, white man barred their path. He began calling them names—names Hutch won't use, even when telling the story, though most of those names began with, "Hey, you black . . ."

As the bully directed his hateful attack toward the two of them, Hutch's dad asked the man to "please leave my boy alone." Instead, the man was joined by several more hate-filled men from the bar who took part in the attack. Soon it was apparent the two blacks were in serious trouble. Hutch hoped his dad would take care of those bums. But the mistreatment continued, and Hutch's dad finally, meekly bowed his head. Tiring of their abuse at last, the men drifted away amid a chorus of humiliating snickers.

Hutch and his father stood alone. Neither spoke. They boarded the bus when it arrived, and going to the back of the bus, they took their place in a seat designated for black people. Hutch, not understanding why his dad hadn't resisted, turned away to stare out the bus window. But windows can also serve as mirrors. He could see his dad's face, mirrored there. He saw tears coursing down that proud man's cheeks. His dad had had no choice but to swallow his humiliation. In the years that followed, this terrible experience was never discussed between the two.

But hatred was born that day—a mighty, furious anger. It spread through the boy's heart, possessed his very being. Most nights he tossed restlessly, beset by nightmares, reliving that day, fantasizing the punishment he would mete out to that inexcusable bully. The hatred spread through Hutch's very being. He hated all white people for what they had done to his father. For what they had done to all black people. A year passed, then another. The hatred smoldered in the boy's broken heart.

Then the miracle. One evening, the Hutchinson family attended a church service. As they sat there, Hutch heard the Word about a God of love, about a Lord who forgives, about the new life available to those who are in Christ. He realized he was being eaten up by his hatred, realized it could ruin his life. That night, young Charles Hutchinson prayed for God to take away his hatred. "I can't live like this any longer," he told God. Then he slept soundly. It was the first really good night's sleep he had known for a longtime. The next morning, Hutch awoke, and his world was suddenly beautifully bright. His heart was light. It was free of all his bitterness. God had answered his prayer. His hatred was gone. That wonderful morning, Hutch pledged to God that he would do everything he could from that day forward to help erase racism from every human heart. He went on to give his life to the service of that Lord. After serving in the South for several years, Dr. Charles Lesley Hutchinson moved to Indiana where he served twice as a district superintendent, first on the Bloomington District, then on the Terre Haute District, finally to go on staff at the University of Indianapolis.

Hutchinson plans to write his memoirs, stories about his time with Martin Luther King Jr. and about his tireless efforts to see that things like those which happened to him might one day pass from the human scene. "Hatred is a malignancy of the soul," he says. His quiet, loving manner does not completely obscure a fierce, determined character, however. Looking back, he remembers: "My body was in the back of the bus, but my heart was in the very front." I hope he writes those memoirs. I'd like to read them. We all should.

~

The issue of homosexuality became an explosive one throughout mainline Protestantism. The Methodist Church is not alone in struggling mightily over this issue. Many people are living in anguish, many in great pain, because of the inability of so many Christian people to arrive at even a workable agreement about the place of the homosexual person within the church. The General Conference ruling that an avowed homosexual may not be ordained is rigidly enforced in some places, not so carefully observed in others. The question of whether one is born homosexual without the option of choice, or whether a person who practices the gay lifestyle is really acting out a choice which could, if one really wanted to, be reversed, lies at the heart of the conflict. One wise Indiana delegate to the 2000 General Conference in Cleveland expressed despair over the fact that neither of the two extreme factions seems willing to give an inch, and the great majority of people in the middle seem unable to influence the issue at all. Five members of North Church in Indianapolis were among the many, including two bishops, who were arrested because of a gay rights demonstration which disrupted the conference in its

Issues related to the Church's stand on homosexuality have been divisive within the denomination for the past sixteen years. In this 1997 photo, Rev. Mary Hubbard shares the Communion blessing, a young parishioner at her side. Hubbard's church, Central UMC in South Bend, was the sole Indiana church—but one of several hundred nationally—to declare itself a "Reconciling Congregation," signifying openness to full participation of gays and lesbians in church life. A corresponding movement, "Transforming Congregations," emphasized the possibility of "healing" homosexuality. A subsequent Church Judicial Council ruling now prohibits churches and church agencies from using such labels. Photo courtesy of the South Bend Tribune.

closing hours. While nearly everyone viewed this as a matter of personal honor, and while the "arrests" were not very serious, it did raise other questions. Does disruption of orderly process have the effect of drawing attention to an issue in a constructive way? Or does it irritate the middle majority to the point that careful and prayerful consideration of the issue is subconsciously thwarted and replaced by disgusted amusement? Even this issue is the subject of widespread disagreement.

Those who declare homosexuality to be a sin point to the Old Testament and to the apostle Paul's strong condemnation of the offense. Those who declare homosexuality to be part of God's creation and acceptable in the faith point to the fact that Jesus made no mention of it at all, and that the sin to which Paul directed his disapproval was that of enforced homosexuality as practiced in Greek culture, involving slaves or young male prostitutes. It would appear, as of this writing, that no middle ground has yet been found and most of those who believe one way will never believe the other. This leaves the church with the necessity of finding some way for both points of view to exist in an otherwise harmonious environment. It also leaves many homosexual church members and potential church members feeling like pariahs in the eyes of their fellow members.

Some congregations have designated themselves "reconciling congregations," meaning the pastors and leaders accept homosexuality as a God-created condition and welcome gay people as worthy members. Many other congregations simply try to make it clear that such people are welcome in the congregation. But some congregations, through stern denunciations by their preachers, make it clear that in that house, homosexuality is a sin and anyone who is homosexual is called to change to a heterosexual lifestyle. Of course there are many congregations which simply ignore the issue and, like the United States armed forces, follow a "don't ask, don't tell" policy. A few congregations call themselves "transforming congregations," featuring people who, formerly gay, have turned straight. Since there is no final authority to which the church can turn, and since even the bishops—who are supposed to be the wise parents of the church—cannot agree, it seems clear at this time in our history that unless some new information of a medical or scientific sort is discovered, the members of the Methodist Church will simply have to learn to live together with this very volatile unresolved issue.

There is another overarching issue which always more or less confronts the church. How do we interpret the Bible? Words like *conservative* and *liberal* are of limited value in the twenty-first century as they are sometimes claimed as a badge of honor, and sometimes used as an epithet. However, behind the words in regard to theology lies the issue of how literally one should interpret the Bible's words. The Confessing Movement members are urging a more literal use of the Bible than is generally common among Methodist pastors. The critical approach to biblical interpretation as taught in Methodist seminaries has admittedly left a rather broad range of choice in interpretation. The question, of course, remains as to which is correct. This has always been an issue in every mainline Protestant denomination. One argument is that the current state of disarray in American society in regard to family life, marriage, addictions, and ethics in general, reflects the failure of the church to clearly and loudly declare God's unequivocal call to a holy and righteous life. In the opinions of some observers, the current urgency to return to the fundamental precepts of Methodism reflects a sense of theological weakness in today's church. While not all church leaders agree by any means, there does seem to be a growing desire on the part of many Methodists to hear more about the Bible's commands. Churches which are growing seem to be those which heed this call.

The danger, of course, is an excess of zeal which, contrary to the accepting and loving message of Jesus, assumes a harsh and unbending tone—one which is judgmental, humorless, and which fails to make allowance for the humanity of humans. Author Ian C. Bradley, writing on the effect of an evangelical revival in nineteenth-century England, told of the fifth earl of Darnley after his 1827 marriage to Emma Parnell. A hard-nosed revivalist, Lady Darnley, upon her arrival at Cobham Hall in Kent, began the process of converting her new husband and his family. When the earl arranged a pleasant reception for the celebrated actress Sarah Siddons on her seventy-second birthday, Lady Darnley marched him out of the room when some scenes from Shakespeare were being performed, and refused to allow him back until he called off the entertainment.

Lady Darnley put a stop to all parties and all entertainment and made her husband get rid of certain expensive paintings which offended her. Her son, who succeeded to the title in 1835, became so neurotic in his fundamentalism that he destroyed several precious works of art which showed pictures of too much flesh. He was said to fear divine judgment so intensely that he read his Bible even while shaving. As Lord Melbourne said to Queen Victoria upon her accession to the throne of England, speaking at a time when the word had a different meaning than it does today, "Nobody is gay now; they are so religious." So seems to be the fate of those who become too grimly serious about their theology.

Perhaps we all need to be reminded of something Bishop Woodie W. White said when addressing a group of his pastors shortly after his arrival in Indiana. He said, "I'm not nearly as interested in your theology as I am in how you treat me." I don't think he really meant he was uninterested in theology. His point was an important one. He meant that the final measure of my theology is what kind of person it causes me to become. How do I treat other people? How do I treat people who are different from me and who believe differently? The nineteenth-century Scottish evangelical writer Henry Drummond once said that the true measure of a person's Christianity is in how he or she discharges the common charities of life. Catholic Bishop Fulton Sheen said there are three characteristics of true Christianity: kindness, kindness, and kindness. Perhaps there is a direction here for those of each persuasion. Quite possibly it is in that direction that some workable mutuality is possible for all of us well-meaning, if not always entirely wise, Methodists.

Author Robert Putnam recently wrote a sobering word in referring to those studies by Finke and Stark. He observed, "The revitalization of evangelical religion is perhaps the most notable feature of American religious life in the last half of the twentieth century." After pointing out that this phenomenon is a familiar one through the years of our history, he reports that "one insurgent, more disciplined, more sect-like, less 'secularized' religious movement overtakes more worldly, establishmentarian denominations." Then this sobering observation: "The Methodists did this to the Episcopalians in the mid-nineteenth century, and now the fundamentalists have done it to the Methodists."

One must think twice before questioning the value of education. On the other hand, we recall that, as Finke and Stark pointed out, the enthusiastic vigor of the early Methodist Church began to wane as clergy became educated. Most clergy of today will probably be amused at those early attitudes toward education. Clearly, men and women who are subjected to the discipline of study and scholastic performance are better prepared in many areas, including counseling, administration, teaching, and certainly preaching. The question becomes: is there such a thing as too much education? Several very experienced and highly effective pastors believe there is. In a conversation with retired Bishop Dueker, Virgil Bjork and Donald LaSuer (who both served as district superintendents), and Steve Burris (who is the director of the North Conference Council on Ministries), I found general agreement that the current custom of going beyond one's basic theological studies to win the popular Doctor of Ministry degree is contributing to the growing professionalism of many clergy. Those men suggest that this may be replacing the spirit of believing oneself called by God to preach. That must probably be evaluated case by case. Perhaps the point is at least worth thinking about. This is not, however, to detract in any way from the fine people who have those degrees and who are serving admirably. But this may point to a need for the church at large to begin placing some good old-fashioned emphasis on the belief that God calls people into ministry and equips them for the work.

∾

Many good things happened in the nineties. The Berlin Wall came down, and Communism, if not dead, at least proved to be much more nearly moribund than some early-day doomsayers had predicted. While the United States was involved in a number of relatively minor military actions in places like Iraq, Kosovo, and Africa, there has been nothing at all like the wars of the past. The national economy tended generally upward, and the general welfare could be said to have continued to improve. As Jesus predicted, the poor will always be with us, and the church has taken commendable leadership in trying to care for those in need, by one-on-one ministries, by organized programs, and by

In the foreground from left, John Hopkins (Evansville) and Mike Coyner (Indianapolis) kneel for their consecration as bishops, following their election at the 1996 Jurisdictional Conference, held in Fort Wayne. They now serve the Minnesota and Dakotas episcopal areas, respectively. Photo by Dave Hyde.

constantly pressuring elected leaders on all levels to make provisions for those in need. Still, to those who have prospered, and this probably describes a large majority of Methodists, the decade of the nineties seems a welcome relief from the divisive issues of the three preceding decades.

Strange, then, how unhappy so many people seem to be. The prevalence of child abuse has been astounding. Spousal abuse as well. The anger levels of many families have been sky-high. Suicides among teenagers have mounted steadily. University campuses are struggling to do something about the widespread prevalence of binge drinking. Illicit drugs are easily available. One recent estimate reported by columnist Linda Chavez predicts that 60 percent of all new marriages will fail, "with even higher divorce rates for second marriages." She reports that one-third of all children born in America are born out of wedlock. *USA Today* recently surveyed teachers born between 1946 and 1964. They asked them about the relative importance of several life characteristics during their school years, as compared with how they see those same characteristics to weigh in importance to their students today. Fifty-nine percent of the teachers responded that religious faith was "very important" to them in their student days, but saw it as important to only 19 percent of students today. Doing well in school was important to 83 percent of the teachers but, they say, it is important to only 37 percent of students today.

That is all well and good, but just recently *USA Today* also printed an article with the heading: "Teachers Fail Ethical Test." It went on to report widespread abuses by teachers who give their students answers to the tests which those students are required to pass, thereby making the teachers appear successful. Numerous instances were reported. To be fair, an opposing article was printed defending the practice on the grounds that the tests themselves are unreasonable. But either way, we have teachers—some teachers—breaking the rules, and we have an education system adrift on a sea of confusion about the best way to educate young people.

Guns have been front-page news for years as crimes committed by children have increased, and schools have adopted strict zero-tolerance rules which prohibit kids from having anything remotely resembling a weapon. Unfortunately, zealous administrators have sometimes been unwise in their methods. One high school honor student recently won a contest in the Boy Scouts, and his dad rewarded him with a scout axe, something every boy had when I was a kid. The boy left it in his car trunk, a friend reported him, and the kid was expelled for the rest of the semester. The great number of good kids are suffering because of a few bad apples.

Columnist David Frum recently said in the *American Spectator*: "Pollsters find that when you prod voters to talk about what's really bothering them, sooner or later you come up against a deep and widespread feeling that the country's troubles can be attributed to moral decline." William Bennett put it this way: "We are a nation that has experienced so much decadence, in so short a period of time, that we have become the kind of nation to which civilized countries used to send missionaries." Something seems to be wrong. We are a nation which enjoys unparalleled prosperity in a time as peaceful as a nation can hope for, with a people who enjoy technological miracles—yet somehow we seem to have trouble finding the peaceful coexistence and the peace of mind which the Christian gospel offers. Sad to say, the gospel Word almost seems not to have sufficient currency in America to correct the evils of our time.

Is that a discouraging word? There is nothing to gain by pretending these problems aren't before us. They are. And they are the responsibility of the church if anything is to change. There is no other known source of redeeming power which can turn the present state of things around. Only God can cause a revival, and for that the church must pray. But God can't cause a revival among a people who choose to turn from the hard demands of that gospel. Clearly, the church needs to intensify its search for preachers— good, talented preachers—dedicated preachers and lay leaders who stand tall above the fray, what Peter Marshall called "sun-crowned" men and women, who can cease squabbling about inconsequential matters, who can make the sacrifices necessary to spread the saving word of Jesus Christ among the people of the nation, and who do this not only with words but with deeds. It can be done. The Methodist Church grew out of revival. The Methodist Church is premised on the call to the righteous life, to Christian perfection. But it is also premised on the conviction that God's empowering Spirit will lead us safely through dark days. In John Wesley's words:

Through waves and clouds and storms,
God gently clears the way;
Wait thou God's time, so shall this night
Soon end in joyous day.

CHAPTER THIRTEEN

The past is not meant to be a source of traditions and events that the church embalms. The past contains a history that is most revered when it is recalled and interpreted to energize the church to meet its new challenges. The God of history is not time bound. The vitality of God expresses itself in every age. Disciples therefore must be responsive to a God not only of the past, but also of the present and the future.
—*Luther E. Smith Jr.,*
Intimacy and Mission

And Now for Our Bright Tomorrows

everend Richard Lancaster, former pastor of Indianapolis's Meridian Street Church used to tell of his vacation home on the coast of Maine. He had a speedboat and could take friends and family out to an island a couple miles offshore. The island was unoccupied, with a high hill that offered a lovely view for a delightful afternoon visit. But to make his way safely through a narrow channel to open water, Lancaster said he used to line up his boat by looking forward to the island, his destination, then looking behind him, to a pile of colorful lobster traps on the beach. He said it was by focusing on what was ahead, but also by referring to what lay behind, that he made his way in safety. His analogy serves us here as well, since it is that which lies ahead for us, which claims our many resources, and yet it is in a long look backward that we can finally see where we must go.

Incidentally, Dr. Lancaster served Meridian Street Church for twenty-six years, retiring in 1988. He was well established as one of the denomination's finest preachers, a fact which he would probably deny. Years ago he was chosen from among the nation's clergy to be the preacher on the "Protestant Hour," a national radio pulpit. When his stint was completed, he was asked to put several of his sermons in written form so that they might be published as a book. Lancaster, in a most memorable quote, refused on the grounds that "my critical faculties are more highly developed than are my creative faculties," meaning he wasn't impressed with his own work. Others disagreed, however. One Sunday, a member of the staff of *Together* magazine, at that time the national publication of the Methodist Church, was visiting Indianapolis and happened to attend Meridian Street for

Richard L. Lancaster, 1988.

worship. He was so impressed with Lancaster's sermon that he obtained a copy, and it was printed in the following issue of *Together*.

∾

Looking back, there was humor, of course. In one very small southern Indiana Church (which should probably remain nameless), a very elderly, kindly shut-in lady, wanting to make some contribution to her church, had a relative obtain a paint-by-number picture of Jesus. With devoted but unsteady hand, she filled in the various colors and then prevailed upon that family member to visit the church on Saturday evening to hang her surprise gift in a location where the pastor could see and appreciate. It was hung in the center of the chancel above the altar where everyone could see. Gift of love though it was, the pastor at last report was trying to find some diplomatic way to remove that well-intended but distinctly unappealing picture of Jesus to a more discreet location. (In reflecting on this, I think maybe I would have left the picture in view as a statement that if we do our very best, God will accept that as good enough).

Then there was the evening the pastor of Hillsboro Church arrived at midnight to visit a fellow pastor for advice. It seems a then-famous personage who resided in the town was a popular Sunday school teacher. Being a seminary student, the pastor had quickly learned who ran things when he saw that Sunday School attendance was just about double his worship attendance. That evening, he had gone to his church to make last minute preparations for Christmas morning worship and discovered a large Santa Claus on the altar. Now if a seminary student was taught anything back in the early sixties, it was that nothing must ever be on the altar save the table and the cross. But—Santa Claus? This would not do. Neither would it do for the new student-minister to interfere with the preparations made by the town's most famous and most revered citizen. Especially since student-pastors tended to come and go about every two years, while revered citizens remained a lifetime. The two young pastors debated this crisis for an hour or so and arrived at what they decided was a prudent decision: the young man left the Santa Claus and prayed for forgiveness.

Ben Garrison told of the young student-minister in a farm community who, distressed that attendance always fell when it was Communion Sunday, asked his superintendent for advice. It seemed that when people arrived and realized what Sunday it was, many of them quietly departed. The busy superintendent, assuming a tongue-in- cheek view of the matter, said, "Well, all I can think of for you to do is lock the doors when the service starts." But it wasn't many weeks later that the superintendent had a visit from some discontented worshipers who protested that when Communion was served in their church, the pastor kept the elements hidden until everyone was present, then locked the doors before revealing the elements and setting the table.

In the very early days of Asbury Church in Indianapolis, services were held in an incompleted house chapel. On the Sunday of a very large baptism service in this new church, I as pastor realized there was no water in the chalice. This was our first big baptismal service. The church was full of families and friends present for this special and reverent moment. But I was already in the middle of the ritual. My part-time associate Ken Harrison, who was later ordained and moved to Texas, was with me. I whispered to him to take the chalice, go back to the restroom which was in the immediate rear of the makeshift chapel, fill it with water, then return. Meanwhile, I would give a little speech on the meaning of baptism. Accordingly, Harrison solemnly headed for the bathroom with the chalice, and I began what I hoped would be a one minute sermonette. But the speech became five minutes, then eight. I could feel myself repeating my words, and the people in attendance were beginning to become restless. Then we heard a loud crash, and then Ken Harrison, with grand aplomb, returned down the aisle with the chalice, now filled with water, held elegantly before him. With equal majesty (and great relief) I accepted the chalice and whispered, "Where in the world were you?" Ken replied without changing expression: "The door was locked, and I couldn't get out." That service was long remembered at Asbury Church.

∾

Worship has undergone some dramatic changes throughout the church. In Indianapolis, Reverend Linda McCoy, a staff minister at St. Luke's Church conceived the idea of a contemporary service performed at the venue of a dinner theater. Her story is at once inspiring and, in some ways, indicative of the future of Indiana Methodism. As McCoy tells the story, she was completing her doctoral studies at United Theological Seminary after having served many years at St. Luke's. That church was undergoing a leadership change, and McCoy was struggling with her sense of calling. Then one day, on an airplane flight to Denver where she was to conduct some television interviews, she read a book by Tom Peters in which he related the story of a Japanese gentleman who had asked his boss what he was to do next. The boss had replied, "Make something great." So the man had invented Nintendo. McCoy describes what followed this way: "After reading that story, I fell asleep and when I awakened, I knew exactly what I was to be doing in ministry.

Language is always limiting, and the only way I could describe it
was that I was going to be doing something very different, very
creative. I didn't know where, or when, or how, but the sense of
peace and assurance that I felt in that moment has never left me. I
knew this was a 'God thing.'" The result was an offshoot from her
primary congregation, a new concept in worship so far as Indiana
Methodism is concerned. It was to be called the Garden.

The Garden is located at Beef and Boards, an equity dinner
theater on the far north side of Indianapolis, which is owned by
two gifted thespians, Doug and Suzanne Stark. The Garden service
features two to three minute video clips on two large screens,
supplemented by strategically located small screens. Music is
performed by the Good Earth Band, a group of musicians using
guitars, drums, and other instruments familiar to the younger
generation. The music is sometimes Christian, but often secular
with a Christian theme on the theory that God is in everything,
including secular music. "In purely demographic terms," McCoy
writes, "we were attempting to reach unchurched Boomers."

Participants wear casual dress, and McCoy preaches an excellent ten-minute sermon. The service is carefully focused on a
unifying theme. The response was so immediate that it was necessary to go to two morning services. Attendance was soon
approaching six hundred people per Sunday, at which point a third
service was added for Easter in 2000. There continues to be an
increase in attendance. Children are welcome and elements in the
service are designed to appeal to them. A surprising variety of
people attend, including an eighty-eight-year-old gentleman who
had never before attended church, who is now a regular attender.
There is an ethnic mix, and gay people are welcome. Some attenders are longtime active members of the Methodist Church who
feel the need for something different. Many are people who, as
McCoy puts the matter, "have never been part of a church, or have
been 'turned off or turned out' by their past church experiences.
We are, indeed," she writes, "a very diverse gathering of people,
but we share one thing in common—we are seeking to have our
spiritual lives enriched." One interesting encounter took place
recently. Several women from Zimbabwe attended the Garden.

When the service concluded, one of the women embraced McCoy and said, "You know me." McCoy returned the embrace but admitted that no, she really didn't know her. The woman explained that she meant that the service, and especially the sermon, spoke so directly to her present life situation that it was as though McCoy had known her personally.

This new style has its detractors. Some point to a lack of participation in the service as most of the music is performed rather than congregational, although the leaders occasionally try to encourage some participation. Since the Garden is an outpoint of a larger congregation, it is not totally dependent on its own income, so it places little emphasis on sacrificing financially for the church in the way other churches must do. The style also requires a new type of church musician, quite different from the traditional church musician. The style of worship is also labor intensive, as each week involves the search for video material and, since the Scripture for the day is often dramatized, it requires lengthy preparation. Most churches may be hard-pressed to find the qualified personnel as well as the technological equipment for this to work. Time will tell what elements of this innovative form of church will find their way into the general life of the Methodist Church. Some factors must be kept in mind as we wonder to what extent the Garden's form of worship is reproducible. The music is good, and Reverend McCoy is especially gifted in motivating creative people. Her associate, Suzanne Stark, is a professional singer and actress with extraordinary musical talent. This may be a word to the wise in our seminaries that professional-level training in these skills is soon to be in much greater demand than ever before.

There is no denying the reality that such variant forms of worship are sweeping through the Methodist Church, and in all likelihood, as a younger generation of clergy arrives with more open attitudes toward what is generally referred to as contemporary worship, the new form will become commonplace. Dr. McCoy is kept busy leading workshops on contemporary worship. Many pastors are looking hard at current worship styles, asking themselves whether a radically changing world calls for a revamping of worship for a generation of computer-literate, Walkman-wearing, media-savvy young people. The question clergy struggle with is the decision as to what elements of worship must not be tampered with, and what elements have outgrown their effectiveness. Once that young generation ages to positions of leadership and decision making in their churches, it is almost foregone that presently traditional worship forms will be dramatically altered.

Someone once asked the bridge expert Charles H. Goren how he would bid a particular set hand. He is said to have responded: "First, tell me who is my partner and who are my opponents." His point was that his decisions would hinge on knowing exactly what he was up against and what resources were available to him. So it is for preachers. When deciding what to preach and how to compose the sermon, one must first consider to whom one is speaking. A fellow preacher and friend of mine recently used an experience from a long vacation cruise he had recently taken with his family as an illustration. That illustration worked well in his suburban congregation of high income people who know all about cruises. It might not work so well in an inner-city church or a small rural church where people work too hard for their money to spend it on cruises. So, too, with the entire worship experience. If the children who will become the church in the years ahead are growing up in a milieu completely different and more technologically oriented than my generation, it almost certainly follows that some rather definite evolution in worship is already taking place.

Music is changing. Music currently called praise music, not all of it very good, is becoming popular. It is not in the *Methodist Hymnal*, and is frequently either printed in the morning bulletin or shown on a video screen which, more and more, are commonplace in Methodist churches. The lyrics are usually simple, repetitive, pietistic in sentiment, and easy to memorize. Larger churches with growing budgets are installing high tech facilities which allow the use of PowerPoint® presentations. Not everyone of the older generation approves of this. When Zionsville Church installed a screen, the majority liked it, but a small minority saw it as a threat to the way things were and—thank you very much—the way things ought to remain. Reverend Allen Rumble, like pastors all across Indiana, is having to use his skills of diplomacy to mediate these changes. But two things must be kept in mind. One, the older generation won't be around all that long. Two, the rapid advances in technology having to do with audio and video equipment make it almost certain that worship services will be dramatically different from those of yesterday in most churches.

Some recent studies suggest that the very youngest generation is beginning to yearn for the old style, the traditional, or what some are now calling classic worship. There is no way to know at this point in time what the future will finally hold. But as of the present moment, experimentation in worship with many forms of innovation is the order of the day. Not all forms are effective. Preachers coming out from behind their pulpits and striding across the chancel can be more irritating than inspiring. Various new colors and styles of clergy garb appear to some to defeat the purpose of the traditional robe, that purpose being to take attention off the messenger and place it on the message. As of now, as the second century of Indiana Methodism ends and a third begins, there is no consensus about the future of worship in the Methodist Church.

Certain very large independent congregations in America are impacting this process in important ways. Willow Creek Church, for example, a non-denominational congregation in Barrington, Illinois, has an average worship attendance of about twenty thousand people per week. As of the present moment, that enormous building complex, many times the size of even the largest Methodist church, has announced a seventy-million-dollar building addition. This is relevant to Indiana Methodists because large numbers of clergy, staff, and laity are visiting Willow Creek to worship, but also to attend classes on worship and church growth. That church has a twenty-five-piece orchestra of professional musicians, uses dramatic enactments of biblical themes, shows video facial close-ups of various performers because of the very large auditorium, features individual testimonies of faith, and concludes each service with a lengthy sermon of excellent quality and effectiveness. While the church on Main Street cannot mimic something like that, it is being influenced by the style. As the old World War 1 song put the matter: "How You Gonna Keep 'em Down on the Farm after They've Seen Paree?" Once the growing number of church leaders has been exposed to exciting new departures in worship, it is not very likely that traditional forms will remain unchanged for long. It is true, however, that there are those people who prefer a very liturgical form of worship. There will always be a place for that, but at present, that seems likely to remain a small percentage of worship services in Indiana.

Preachers and laypeople debate, sometimes heatedly, as to what changes are appropriate. Just one point of agreement binds all together: Jesus Christ must be the heart of worship. Whatever is done must be done to honor him, to honor God, and to foster in the worshiping congregation a sense of divine presence and a determination to do this honoring by living a Christian life. One thing is certain: the entertainment element must not outweigh the elements of reflection, prayer, and the personal involvement of each worshiper. John Wesley said it must prompt "a desire to flee the wrath to come." Maybe if he could address a new generation with a new understanding of the Holy Bible, he would urge us to place our lives in the hands of the God of Love, the only truly safe place to be. And, I suspect, one thing all worshipers will agree on is this: the better the preaching, the more effective the worship.

∾

Had it been possible by some bending of time for a typical Methodist church member of the 1940s to view the world as it is today in the early twenty-first century, it is likely that person would have been flabbergasted by the morality of today's culture. A rap singer named Eminem (real name Marshall Bruce Mathers III), was recently mentioned in two articles in the *Indianapolis Star*. In one, the singer was reported to be under indictment for assault and possession of a weapon. In the other, his music was discussed this way: "Eminem's current recording isn't the first time he's threatened his wife, Kim, with violence real or imagined. On his first album, he described pulling her body from a car trunk and dumping it off a pier. He takes their daughter along for the ride in the lyrics of the song." The columnist added this commentary: "It's a charming little ditty in which Eminem describes murdering his mother and other women." Now lest the reader think this is an exception to the current rule in music, it is enlightening to note that his current album sold 1.7 million copies in its first week on the market.

This is the era in which two singers at the top of the charts have been murdered and a third is under indictment for the illegal use of a firearm. The primary market for such music is young kids, mainly boys. Violence and obscenity are the attraction, not only in music but in video games and television.

Two popular movies vied for best picture in recent years. One was *American Beauty*, which depicted America in microcosm—America without firm moral foundations, without religious faith. It told of a rebellious teenage girl who eventually left her totally dysfunctional home and ran off with the drug-dealing teenage boy next door. The father sought an affair with his daughter's blonde sixteen-year-old friend. Meanwhile, the father of the boy next door made a homosexual pass at the girl's father, who rebuffed him. Shortly thereafter, the father next door sneaked over and shot the girl's father in the head. And finally, the mother who had been having an affair with a business competitor came home and, as the picture ends, is seen screaming on her closet floor. Replete with obscenity, nudity, and violence, that's it. Another movie was *Saving Private Ryan*, which featured the theme of heroism, loyalty, and patriotism starring two-time Academy Award winner Tom Hanks. *American Beauty* won.

A 1996 survey of certified fraud examiners recently estimated that as much as six cents on the dollar is lost by American businesses because of insider dishonesty. According to the Securities and Exchange Commission, scammers pitching phony securities are costing Americans at least a million dollars an hour. Meanwhile, we learn that the Bank of New York has laundered millions of dollars for Russian mobsters, and one of America's largest insurance companies is paying millions of dollars to investors for having misrepresented their insurance coverage. A major manufacturer of automobile tires was recently revealed to have sold defective tires which have cost what at present is estimated to be nearly a hundred deaths from accidents. In July of 2000, it was announced that the chief justice of the Supreme Court of New Hampshire has been impeached for ethics violations, while the Los Angeles district attorney is proceeding with prosecutions of a large number of police officers who have admitted breaking the law. A columnist for the *Indianapolis Star*, Tim Swarens, recalled the role models for young boys a few generations ago as The Lone Ranger, Superman, and Tarzan. Lost is the concept of the high-minded hero and heroine, standing strong against oppression, always defending the weak, the poor, and the lost. Those days seem gone.

Where are young people supposed to find the countervailing forces by which they can learn those values which will resist these market forces? The Methodist answer is twofold: the church and the family. But what of the family? A recent *Newsweek* magazine article, discussing one successful executive's rise to power, described the ethos of the success culture this way: "In the macho arena where [the executive] thrived, he knew that talking about family values could brand him as at best a wimp, and at worst, a liar. 'In the power alleys of Wall Street and the East Coast, it's not manly to admit that work/family is an issue.'" The executive, shrugging, went on to observe, "'In fact the manly thing to say is I don't have a life and I'm proud of it.'" Now granted, that's extreme, and not everyone works on the East Coast. But that same attitude in a more subdued form is part of the corporate cultures of many organizations. It is a value shared, in modified form, by too many fathers in the beginning of a new millennium.

These are not bizarre exceptions—they characterize the day in which we live. The Sunday morning preacher in a Methodist church in Indiana today is faced with a culture in which many worshipers accept compromise of values, trade-offs of family life, and the redefining of love as mere sexual attraction and fulfillment. Referring to our preoccupation with appearance, David Brooks in his insightful book *Bobos In Paradise*, assessed the age this way:

> If you live in a society like ours, in which people seldom object if they hear someone taking the Lord's name in vain but are outraged if they see a pregnant woman smoking, then you are living in a world that values the worldly more than the divine. . . . You can't really know God if you ignore His laws, especially the ones that regulate the most intimate spheres of life. You may be responsible and healthy, but you will also be shallow and inconsequential.

It all helps explain why a generation of young people are finding it difficult to harmonize their popular culture with the gospel Word. And it makes clear the profound necessity for a strong and unambiguous declaration of Jesus' call to a different, higher set of values. When preachers gather, they may be overheard to express their unwavering confidence in the young generation to respond to that declaration, provided it is heard. In the face of this prevalence of violence and lost values, churches are realizing an almost hungering response from many young people to the words of Jesus and the teachings of the faith.

Church leaders are discovering an interesting and encouraging phenomenon. Young people are responding enthusiastically to leaders who are firm and outspoken in their values. As churches have realized the need for strong youth leadership, the call for more talented young men and women to enter that field is ringing through the Methodist Church.

~

A visitor to Broadway Christian Parish in South Bend, Indiana, will notice a beautiful mosaic on the front wall. It is made of colorful broken glass. Though it is attractive, its beauty lies in the story behind it.

The story began with tragedy. A little boy named Columbus Coleman was playing in the yard of his grandmother's home. In most neighborhoods, that would be a very safe place for a little boy. But not where Columbus's grandmother lived. Someone shot him to death. The next night, a large, angry crowd gathered in the church which was only a block and a half from the scene of the little boy's death. They were determined that something good must come from that tragedy. The violence must not go on.

One family approached the pastor Mike Mather and told of another boy named Aaron. He was on the verge of ruining his life because of his involvement in things which deeply troubled his parents. Mather had an idea. He was going to do something to prevent the kinds of crimes which had cost that other little boy his life. Find a college boy, Mather suggested to the concerned family. The right kind of college boy. Let him move in with Aaron's family. Pay the family for the student's board, and let him try to bond with Aaron.

They found Joe. He was the right kind. Before long, Joe and Aaron had become friends. Joe noticed that the nearby Boys and Girls Club had several computers which were not in use. He got Aaron interested in working on those computers and in showing younger kids how to use them. Aaron was hooked. Pretty soon the kids of the neighborhood began to follow Aaron and Joe, so those two came up with the idea of starting a neighborhood cleanup. Fifty kids pitched in. Neighborhoods like that one are filled with broken glass. They began sweeping up the glass, until they had gathered more than 140 pounds of glass.

It was quickly evident that there wasn't much of a market for broken glass. But then God took a hand—or so those folks believe. They got the idea of separating the glass, green, clear, and brown. Needing some additional colors, they spray painted some of the pieces. Then the kids divided into three groups and went to work. For eight weeks they worked, fixing the glass on a piece of plywood four by eight feet, "until they had created a dazzling mosaic, made up from broken glass swept up from the streets," wrote Reverend Mather. Above it, they created this motto: "You are the light of the world."

Other signs of creative new life emerged. The kids, with their new sense of the beauty of the world around them, began drawing pictures of that world as they had come to see it. The newspapers had described the world as a terrible place after the death of little Columbus Coleman. But the pictures drawn by the children told a different story. Mather described them: "They drew pictures of a boat on the St. Joseph River, of a car driving through the neighborhood, of a house. They drew pictures of Broadway Church, and of the sun, and flowers, and birds. They drew a picture of the downtown Valley American Bank Building . . . a neighbor's backyard who sold candy and pop to the kids after school." In other words, the kids drew pictures of a world at peace. And then, "they drew a picture of people singing at the Gospel Fest that was held in the neighborhood park that summer."

New life. That's what Jesus promised. Out of the death of a little boy, a community of faith turned to Jesus Christ. Through the faith of people like Joe, Aaron, Mike, and a bunch of kids, new life has been happening up there in South Bend, Indiana, where children have made something beautiful.

~

Ministers sometimes struggle with the question: how relevant is my ministry to the problems facing my people and my society today? No better example of such relevance comes to mind than that of the work being done at Barnes United Methodist Church, an all-black congregation on Indianapolis's west side. Shortly after his arrival at Barnes in 1993, Reverend Charles Harrison, working with his United Methodist men's group, led some half donzen other churches in the formation of what is called the Ten Point Coalition. Their objective is to reach kids on the crime ridden streets of the surrounding neighborhood. Kids growing up there are almost certain to affiliate with a gang, which usually leads to crime, sale and use of drugs, and all too often, prostitution. Somehow, Harrison believed, the church must reach these people. Three programs resulted.

First, volunteers took to the streets. In areas where many people would fear to walk, members of Barnes Church along with those from a growing number of other churches, began to walk the neighborhood on Friday nights, meeting kids, telling them about a better way of life, offering them hope, inviting them to walk a new and different way. And offering to help. Today some twenty-five nearby churches are assisting in the program. Reverend Harrison reports that many of the young people they meet are grateful for a chance to get away from gang activity and to do something useful with their lives.

Second, a mentoring program was begun in which young people whose job outlook is bleak receive training in preparation for employment. Today the first thing to catch the eye of a visitor to Barnes Church is a row of computers where young people can begin to learn computer skills which are increasingly indispensible to meaningful employment. And along with training comes that essential commodity which can help a young man or woman turn in a creative new life direction: encouragement. Christian men and women of Barnes Church are putting their faith to work in helping to save lives by offering that encouragement.

Rev. Charles Harrison (far left), pastor of Barnes UMC in Indianapolis, along with two other area pastors talk with an ex-gang member in this 1999 photo. "The Ten-Point Coalition" was formed by Harrison to address burgeoning teen crime and other community troubles from a faith base. Photo by Shon Casey.

Third, through an arrangement with a local judge, teenagers who seem to have potential for change but who have come before the judge for a variety of crimes are welcomed to the church and are mentored there. In association with members of St. Luke's Church, Barnes members are also going into the schools, reaching out to vulnerable children, and making such a difference in young lives that Harrison is able to report that as a result of these programs, the homicide rate in that part of the city has been cut nearly in half.

In recent years, newly empowered by dedicated laypeople and by Harrison's ministry, Barnes Church, once down to some hundred or so members, has now grown to the point that two worship services are full every Sunday. Granted, there are growing pains as a mainly middle class congregation begins to reach out to the low income members of the community. But Harrison's faith is secure that the power of God's love will lead him and his people onward in their mission of saving love. Encouraged by the mayor of Indianapolis as well as the chief of police, that church's work is what is meant by being relevant.

It is easy to note the achievements of Indiana's large congregations and to overlook the many acts of dedicated faithfulness in our smallest churches. Superintendent Kate Lehman Walker reminds us of little Mount Gilboa Church up in Benton County. It is a congregation of thirty-six members with a typical Sunday morning attendance of fourteen. Until recently, they didn't even have a minister. That little church has not only survived, but in many ways understood by the members, thrived since 1851. It is smaller than most Sunday school classes in larger churches. But the people there, with a variety of visiting preachers, held Holy Week services, Christmas services, and have even managed to make recent improvements in their sanctuary. When Jesus once assured that where two or three are gathered together in his name he is there, he gave the assurance as well that churches like Mount Gilboa, every bit as much as the large congregations of the major cities, are the objects of his presence and love.

And some, like Battle Ground Church, are growing. It is another church that has been around for a longtime, since 1857. There are only 153 members there. But remarkably, their average attendance, under the pastoral leadership of Reverend Tamara Mills, is 154. Clearly, not all the

Katharine Lehman Walker has served as Lafayette District superintendent since 1995 and was the sole woman nominated for the episcopacy by the Indiana Conferences in 2000.

action is in the cities and the big churches. It is everywhere that Methodist people seek to worship and live out the life of faith.

~

It is also important to note that though Broadway Church in Indianapolis has been mentioned as having once been the celebrated premiere church in the city, only to decline to a point where mere survival seemed at times in doubt, it has in very recent times begun to once more become a strong congregation. Under the leadership of Reverend Franklin Sablan, Broadway has made something of a comeback. Located in one of the city's most economically depressed areas, the Broadway congregation is reported to present an optimistic and heartfelt welcome to those who visit. With a membership back up to more than five hundred and better than half that number in morning worship, the often troubled church has become one of the city's growing congregations.

~

As one looks back across the years, several truths are apparent. The history of the Methodist Church is the history of God's unfailing loyalty to those who try to keep the faith, and who, through courage and unwavering determination, face and ultimately transcend the difficulties which seem to endlessly buffet the American people. The apostle Peter once warned, "Christ suffered for you, leaving an example that you should follow." Certainly, suffering has repeatedly marked the pathway down which the people called Methodist have walked. From those early days of circuit riding young men who gave themselves in selfless service; through the courage of the women who supported and encouraged the church's leaders and in later years have become those leaders; and through the sacrifices of the depression years, the privations of our nations' wars, the leadership of the Civil Rights movement by white and black alike, the protesting of the sadness of Vietnam, and those who today oppose the evil and destructive forces of an American society beset by moral erosion

The future of our Church is in the hands of bright young souls like these. The young acolytes are readying for the grand liturgical procession that begins the Service of Ordination—1996 South Indiana Annual Conference session at Indiana University auditorium. Celia Campbell peeks out from behind the bishop's processional banner, Katie Macklin, and Jillian Richards carry the Bible and Cross, 1996. Photo by Lynne DeMichele.

and compromise—it has been demonstrated again and again that Saint Paul was right: "I can do all things through Christ who strengthens me." If all that has been said here implies a certain pessimism, while there is every evidence that such an attitude makes sense, one need only be reminded that a Higher Power, one which transcends all our troubles, accompanies our every step when faithful people walk with him.

∼

Sacrifice and courage have been hallmarks of the Methodist Church, demonstrated by so many people, lay and clergy alike. People like Reverend Jim Morin who, having been pastor of a large church in Lafayette and then a district superintendent, chose to be appointed to Broadway Church in Indianapolis at a time when that church was down to a couple hundred members in a depressed part of the city, instead of moving on to some choice appointment. There was David G. Owen working with Father James Groppi at the height of the Civil Rights disturbances in Milwaukee, who drove down to Montgomery, Alabama, to take part in a Civil Rights march in the early sixties when danger stalked those who went. And John Adams, who risked his life in a dozen racial confrontations, and Harold Leininger's organized defiance of the Klan. There was John Mote, a St. Luke's layman and officer at Methodist Hospital, who risked his career to introduce an employ-ment program for "unemployable blacks," and Reverend Richard Hamilton, who took part in a Civil Rights demonstration in Washington, D.C. long before doing so had become fashionable. There was Reverend Kevin Armstrong, who refused appointment to a prestigious church to carry out his dedication to the needful people of downtown Indianapolis, and James Armstrong whose courageous and risky preaching on controversial issues at Broadway Church in the sixties could very well have sent him packing back to Florida.

There were so many others: Reverend Lynette DeAtley going into the crime-ridden areas of Indianapolis; John Stone, a dentist from Meridian Street Church, who opened a free dental clinic for the poor; Anita Stone of Broadway Church in Indianapolis who founded Training, Incorporated to help young black women prepare for new vocations; and Grace Nunery's steadfast ministry to the hearing impaired. There was Bob Gingery facing down an armed bandit, Ray Sells standing in a cold night to peti-tion the governor on behalf of the poor, and Ralph Karstedt who, though blind, pastored a church and led bicycle tours, his wife riding the front seat of the tandem bike. There was Marc Blaising, refusing to give in to a threatening group of rabid John Birchers in Elkhart; Edna Wilson, quietly helping to integrate the swimming pool in Greendale; and the Mississippi ministers who came here only after risking their lives on behalf of Civil Rights in the South. There was Luther Hicks walking the streets at night to head off a riot, and John Wolf, long after many retirees would have been sitting on some Florida beach, taking on the gambling forces. Mike Mather refusing to give in to the forces of violence in South Bend, Dr. William Nunery heading for Africa in time of revolution. The list of unsung acts of faithfulness to Jesus' call to the service of others goes on and on. This has been the Methodist Church in Indiana, and elsewhere, for two hundred years. It will go on.

As for those who have fallen short? There is forgiveness. There is God's Grace. Not all

Bishop David J. Lawson, 1992.

have kept the faith—some through weakness, a few through infidelity. Yet this, as I write, is the year of Jubilee, a year of setting free, of newness for all who are genuinely sorry for their sins, a time of forgiveness. For all who have a repentant heart, there is this sentiment from one old song, sung in the early camp meetings by long ago Methodists:

> Ye labouring souls of Adam's race,
> With Satan's fetters bound,
> Throw off your chains, your hands upraise,
> And hail the joyful sound.
> Ye slaves of Satan, toil no more,
> The gospel cries "be free;"
> And raise the shout from shore to shore,
> "The year of Jubilee."

What does the future hold? On April 23, 1971, Alvin Toffler, author of a best seller, *Future Shock*, gave an address at North

Methodist Church in Indianapolis, in which he predicted, among other things, that by the year 2000, technology would have so changed our society that there would be very few employment opportunities. He predicted the demise of unskilled labor and held that those who would be happy must cultivate leisure activities: gardening, golf, painting, and woodworking. Only the technologically gifted would have jobs. Robotics would operate the production workplace. Incomes would be such that everyone could live comfortably. Toffler urged us all to prepare for this revolutionized new world. It all seemed so logical. Now the times of which he spoke are here. And he was wrong. Employment is so high that restaurants and other service businesses are begging for workers. Young people, far from sitting home doing woodworking, are running at double time in their efforts to succeed in a highly competitive society. We still have the poor with us. Projections of the sort Toffler made are almost certain to be wrong. Only God knows what lies ahead for us. We only have one certainty: God loves us and will oversee the futures of those who welcome the Holy Spirit into their lives and who make their best efforts to live as the Christian faith calls us to live. That is the one sure message for the Methodist Church to deliver for tomorrow's world.

∽

A long conversation with Bishop David Lawson, now retired, though still extremely active, brought up some interesting speculations about the future. Bishop Lawson served as a district superintendent and as director of the South Conference Council on Ministries. He then served for two years as pastor of one of the South Conference's largest churches, Carmel, before his election to the episcopacy in 1984. He knows Indiana Methodism, though he also served as bishop of the Wisconsin Area for eight years, and bishop of the Illinois area for four years. Now an Indiana resident once more, he has also served, since his retirement, as liaison for the Council of Bishops to all Methodist seminaries, each of which he has visited. In many of them, he took time to attend classes. In addition, he has been the official

A particularly bright light in the worldwide Church connection is Africa University, founded in 1994 in Zimbabwe. Indiana United Methodists, with the encouragement of their bishop have supported this Church-related pan-African university since its inception. In recent years both Indiana Conferences have each funded construction of two three-story dormitories on the campus. In this photo, a work team from South Indiana churches pose, while workers, background, take a break from construction work on the buildings Indiana churches have funded. Photo by Lynne DeMichele.

representative of the council in Africa, including Liberia, Burundi, and Kenya. He spends some three months a year in Africa, close to some of the heaviest fighting by rebel and government troops. These wide experiences qualify Bishop Lawson to make some observations worth noting.

Bishop Lawson sees America as no longer subject to a Christian worldview. If there was a time when most people in America looked upon their Christian churches as guides for moral direction, those days are, he believes, gone. The Christian point of view is a minority point of view. And if the churches are to reestablish themselves as a major force in American culture, it will be through involvement in the gut level issues of the day. He believes the effective Christian will be the person who, acting out of a deep personal faith, addresses the issues of government, education, international affairs, commerce, finance, law, and medicine. Christianity cannot survive as a sentiment. It must make itself felt in positive and redemptive ways in the crucial issues and institutions of American life. On the other hand, Lawson is deeply moved by the evidence of the power of the Christian faith as he sees it displayed in Africa. In one African nation, at the very time when church people are suffering terrible abuse, the Methodist Church has grown in recent years by thirty percent. Lawson is not at all pessimistic about the future. But he insists that Christian people may not rest on any laurels, but must immerse themselves in this changing world in ways that make the teachings of Jesus Christ relevant. Pious sentiments will not be enough. Sacrificial action for the good of others may be. The French mystic Father Terilhard De Chardin said it well: "It is in free and loving service to his fellow men that the individual finds himself, finds the world, and finds God."

Lawson also made another point worth noting. He is encouraged by what he sees in Methodist seminaries across the country. They are not all the same, some liberal, some conservative. But collectively, he stated that he sees some exciting things happening, citing in particular a new generation of young professors and women scholars joining seminary faculties. Any pessimism about theological education felt by some is not shared by Bishop Lawson, and he is in a better position than most observers to make such judgments.

∼

This we believe: God continues to raise up the leaders needed for the day. I will never forget the time St. Luke's in Indianapolis needed someone to teach the Bible to a waiting class of searchers. It so happened that David G. Owen had changed vocations from clergy to become an executive with the Indianapolis Art League and a counselor at the Gallahue mental health clinic. We knew Owen to be one of the most gifted teachers in Methodism, and we knew him to be a very knowledgeable student of the Bible. So we

Each spring since 1992, following the annual Service of Ordination, Bishop Woodie W. White invites all those "who feel they may have heard a call from God to some form of ministry" to come forward and declare it. Here a North Conference pastor prays with two young women as they begin the process of discerning God's will for them in service. Photo by Lynne DeMichele.

asked him to consider teaching at St. Luke's, and for that we offered a stipend of nine hundred dollars for the year. After thinking over this offer, Owen declined, being already immersed in a very busy life. A few days later, I received a call from Owen who said he was trying to purchase a home in the city and had just learned that his income was slightly below that required to be granted a mortgage. He said the bankers had told him he was short—by nine hundred dollars. Yes, he would take the teaching job after all. So David G. Owen was back in the ministry, at least a little bit. Coincidence? We thought not. That was in 1981. In the years that followed, Owen returned to full-time ministry for several years at St. Luke's, and then as senior pastor of St. Mark's Church in Bloomington. At the time of this writing, he is the highly regarded senior pastor of North Church in Indianapolis. When I related this to Lynne DeMichele, she smiled and said, "Yes, ours is a sneaky God." And so he is (or so she is, if one prefers). God surely finds ways to call into service those who can lead this church into the future.

Looking back over the two hundred years of Indiana Methodism, it is so clear that despite the almost continuous difficulties which have beset our nation and our times, the Methodist Church has been led by men and women with just the courage, faith, and resourcefulness necessary to lead us through these often dark days. Limited, flawed, often failing and falling, yet getting back up, going on, doing what must be done, sometimes rising to exalted heights of service and moral excellence—the men and women whom God has sought, whom God has prepared from their very beginnings, have kept this church great. And so our faith informs us it shall continue to be. A writer of the last century, Gerald White Johnson observed that "faith and loyalty are still able to lift common men to greatness." Those who serve today and those who will be called out to serve in our tomorrows will surely rise to that kind of greatness.

~

What should the church's message be in the twenty-first century? What are ministers saying? What about the members of the church, the rank and file, those of us who worship most Sundays in our church of choice? Is the message any different, really, from that of John Wesley? Perhaps it's too early to make broad assumptions, but clearly, the time has never been more demanding of a clarion call to moral recovery—what Wesley's era called Scriptural holiness. Maybe we'll need to use other words, as each generation must hear the gospel in its own language. Call it what you will. But the heart of the church's message must be an earnest summons to a personal relationship with the man who died so this renewal might take place, coupled with some serious intention to live the life that he commends.

Reverend James Gentry, a highly regarded South Conference leader who twice served as a district superintendent, is what might be called guardedly optimistic about the future. At present, he sees a shortage of talented clergy in the Indiana area. But he also expresses the confidence that God will call out those men and women into ministry who can and will lead the church onward, who will join with the presently dedicated Methodists, lay and clergy alike, in facing and transcending the current problems of America. Because of this conviction, Gentry joins many of us in prayerful anticipation of a bright tomorrow.

Recently, a young high school senior stood before his classmates and their families at Zionsville High School and told of his unhappy years. He spoke of the defiance he had felt toward all authority, the troubles he had caused his parents, his alienation from former friends, and the wrongs he had committed. Then, as

Spirited, joyous camaraderie is in high supply with this North Indiana youth group. They are the newly elected Conference Board of Youth Ministries officers, and friends, at the 1997 Annual Conference session at Elliott Hall, Purdue University. Photo courtesy of Hoosier UM News.

The Rev. Heather Olson Bunnell coaches her young charges, children from the daycare ministry of Indianapolis East Tenth Street UMC, as they prepare for a special Rally for Children and Poverty at the Indiana statehouse in January 2000. The event drew United Methodist clergy and laity from across the state to the capitol rotunda to advocate on behalf of the state's children and the poor. Photo by Lynne DeMichele.

this young man began to fight back strong emotions, he told of the evening some of his friends talked him into attending a meeting of the youth group at their Methodist church. At first he felt strange and unwelcome. But he began to realize this was not true, it was only something in his own mind. As first one, then another young person showed him welcome, and he began to wonder how such spirited, joyous camaraderie was possible. It was something he had been searching for in all the wrong places. And then, standing before an audience of parents and classmates, he did something which surely required great courage. He said that in that setting he had met Jesus Christ. And when it took place, he said that all the things for which he had searched began to happen. A great burden fell from his heart, and he discovered a happiness in Christ which could never, ever be found in his world in any other way.

The respectful, appreciative quiet which followed his admission was a memorable time for several hundred people. I think it was in that quiet moment that we all realized that there is the answer for us all. All the searching, the envy, the competition, the dissipation, the clamoring for more and more of worldly goods—all of those things are feeble in their rewards as compared to the new life to be found in Jesus Christ. That message, phrased as we will, spoken in the language of a changing world to be sure, is the message of the United Methodist Church for tomorrow. It must be laced with joy. We must remember Jesus' words when he said to his people, speaking of the command to remain in his love: "I have told you this so that my joy may be in you and that your joy may be complete" (John 15:11). But that message will also lay a firm demand on each of us to live out divine love in the many opportunities which life will place before us. With those with whom we live. With friends, and with those whom we encounter in the marketplace. But also with the people who are different, the suffering people of foreign lands, and those who come from far away seeking shelter and hope. Perhaps the gospel Word for tomorrow's world is in those words which Jesus spoke to his followers: "Happy are those whose greatest desire is to do what God requires; God will satisfy them fully."

~

In Bunyan's classic *Pilgrim's Progress*, a lost soul approaches Evangelist for directions to the Holy Celestial City. "Why standeth thou still?" asks Evangelist. "Because I know not whither to go," replies the man. He is handed a parchment scroll on which is written: "Fly from the wrath to come." "Whither must I fly?" asks the worried man. "Do you see yonder wicket gate?" asks Evangelist, pointing in the darkness. "No!" replies the man. "Do you see yonder shining light?" Evangelist then asks. Squinting, the man replies, "I think I do." "Keep that light in your eye," says Evangelist, "and go up directly thereto, so thou shalt see the Gate. . . ."

So with us. Most of us do not see so clearly as we might wish. But we can see yonder shining light. We can go up thereto, follow where the darkness is not so dark as all the rest, until, like Christian in Bunyan's story, "Your walk and talk shall be every day with the King, even all the days of eternity."

Index

296

About the Author

One of America's premiere preachers, E. Carver McGriff has had a distinguished life and career. As a teenager, he was wounded and captured by a German SS battalion during World War II. After receiving a Bronze Star and two Purple Hearts, he returned home to earn a degree in business administration from Butler University. Following a career as a salesman and business owner, McGriff entered Garrett Theological Seminary, where he was voted Best Preacher by the faculty and graduated with distinction. He was then appointed by the bishop of Indiana to start a new congregation on the northeast side of Indianapolis. He built the membership of the congregation from 900 to over 4,400, with Sunday attendance increasing from 300 to over 1,850.

During his Indianapolis ministry, McGriff received an honorary degree from the University of Indianapolis and the Outstanding Alumnus award from Butler University, and was voted the Distinguished Alumnus of the Year by Christian Theological Seminary. McGriff was also honored with the Sagamore of the Wabash by Governor Evan Bayh. His sermons have been distributed nationwide by the Methodist Publishing Company.